BEHIND
THE URALS

An American Worker in
Russia's City of Steel

BY
JOHN SCOTT

ENLARGED EDITION PREPARED BY
STEPHEN KOTKIN

INDIANA UNIVERSITY PRESS
Bloomington & Indianapolis

This edition was prepared with the assistance of
Maria Scott, Elka Schumann, and Elena Whiteside.

This book is a publication of

Indiana University Press
601 North Morton Street
Bloomington, IN 47404-3797 USA

http://www.indiana.edu/~iupress

Telephone orders   800-842-6796
Fax orders   812-855-7931
Orders by e-mail   iuporder@indiana.edu

The paper used in this publication meets the minimum
requirements of American National Standard for Information
Sciences—Permanence of Paper for Printed Library
Materials, ANSI Z39.48-1984.

Manufactured in the United States of America

Library of Congress Cataloging-in-Publication Data

Scott, John, 1912–1976
Behind the Urals : an American worker in Russia's city of steel /
by John Scott. — Enl. ed. / prepared by Stephen Kotkin.
        p.   cm.
Reprint, with new introd. and addendum. Originally published:
Boston : Houghton Mifflin, 1942.
ISBN 978-0-253-35125-8. — ISBN 978-0-253-20536-0 (pbk.)
1. Magnitogorsk (R.S.F.S.R.)—Description. 2. Scott, John, 1912–1976—
Journeys—Russian S.F.S.R.—Magnitogorsk. 3. Soviet Union—Politics and
government—1917–1936. 4. Steel industry and trade—Russian
S.F.S.R.—Magnitogorsk.   I. Kotkin, Stephen.   II. Title.
                DK781.M3S35   1989
        947'.87—dc19   88-46214

14 15 16 17 18 13 12 11 10 09 08

To Masha

Contents

Illustrations follow p. 134

Introduction

Stephen Kotkin

In *Behind the Urals* John Scott takes a slow-motion camera to show us what it was like to live in the USSR during the formative period of the 1930s. Without losing sight of larger issues of interpretation and significance, Scott brings into sharp focus the often startling details of his life and the lives of those he came to know in the new industrial city of Magnitogorsk. This absorbing depiction of the story of Magnitogorsk is justifiably regarded as the classic firsthand account of the daily life of Stalinism.[1]

Several decades after Stalin's death we are still debating the nature and causes of Stalinism, its relation to the October Revolution, and its bearing on our understanding of the current Soviet regime and society. These controversies impinge not only on the way in which we write history, but also on the proportion of the state budget that we allocate to the military and on the assumptions on which we base our foreign policy.

A full appreciation not only of Stalinism as a political system but of the experiences of working people during the reign of Stalin and of the relations between the political system and the people has proved elusive. One of the most intriguing and perplexing aspects of the debate on Stalinism continues to be the fact that

[1]The author gratefully acknowledges the helpful suggestions of Martin Malia and Reginald Zelnik. Research for this essay was supported by grants from the Social Science Research Council and the International Research and Exchanges Board.

while many Soviet citizens who lived through the Stalin era look back on it with horror, many others remember it as the most fulfilling time of their lives. Scott's book offers many insights into this double-sided perception of Stalinist reality. Moreover, through the portrayal of living examples, Scott enables us to see that direct experience of hardship and repression coexisted in the hearts and minds of many people with a deeply felt satisfaction about the course of events and optimism about the future.

John Scott was born in Philadelphia on March 26, 1912. He came from an unusual background. His father, Scott Nearing, was a professor of economics at the prestigious Wharton School of Business of the University of Pennsylvania and a noted radical. In 1915 Professor Nearing was dismissed in an academic freedom case for his outspoken opposition to capitalism, and in 1918, as a result of his anti-war activities, he was indicted for sedition (though later acquitted). Scott Nearing joined the Socialist Party and the Communist Party, from which he was expelled in 1929 for refusing to alter a book manuscript to conform to the party line. Yet he remained a radical until his death in 1983 at the age of 100. He published scores of books, all from a leftist point of view, including some favorable to the USSR based on visits there in 1925 and after.[2] Nearing's wife, Nellie Seeds, whom he had married in 1908, was also highly educated and active in politics. They had two sons, the older of whom was John Scott Nearing.

It should come as no surprise, given his family background, that as a young man John Scott Nearing readily absorbed radical ideas and political activism. At the same time, he seems to have resented the enormous pressure to conform to the example of his parents, particularly his father, in whose shadow the whole family lived. At the age of seventeen or eighteen, to secure his own

---

[2] For example: *Glimpses of the Soviet Republic* (New York, 1926). A bibliography of Nearing's works is given in his autobiography, *The Making of a Radical* (New York, 1972).

identity and independence, he changed his name, dropping the Nearing and becoming simply John Scott. Nevertheless, the critical perspective on his own society which his parents had transmitted to him was not abandoned; indeed, it was reinforced by his education outside the home at a series of exclusive schools, including one in Switzerland, where he learned French and German before beginning college.

In 1929 John Scott entered the University of Wisconsin's Experimental College, founded in 1927 by Alexander Meiklejohn (1872–1964), an innovator in education who in 1920 had been a founding member of the ACLU. The Experimental College offered what was then a radical educational program: there were neither exams nor grades, professors and instructors lived together with students, and the curriculum, focused on ancient Greek culture, took up the moral and political values of Western Civilization. While it lasted, the Experimental College attracted much favorable attention and was generally held in high regard.

As a student of the Experimental College John Scott dreamed of becoming a writer. During his student years he wrote a novel and some essays on the cultural elite in ancient Athens and the role of the thinker and writer in modern America. Located among his personal papers on deposit at the State Historical Society in Madison is an essay composed towards the end of his first semester in which, under the pseudonym of Smithers, he contemplates his program of study and his future:

> Now the important thing is the class struggle. . . . Smithers, your place is in the struggle now.
>
> But an interesting question comes up. Could Smithers serve the class struggle better if he stayed in school in his little white room [with maid service] and looked at the whole thing objectively and then went out as a leader? The answer is no. . . . The place where there is work to be done now is among the workers themselves. . . .
>
> What Smithers should do is to leave off studying Plato and Aristophanes and get a good foundation in Marxism and the more modern interpreters like Lenin. . . . Smithers is still young and has a

great deal to learn, but he is learning and he is beginning to see where he is to fit into the scheme of things. He may stay in his white room a while longer, but it is Marx and not Plato that he will concentrate on, and he realizes that his place is with the workers helping to set up a new world.

Scott would stay at the Experimental College for two more semesters. Then, in the winter of 1931, he decided to head off for the real-life experiment everyone was talking about, the Soviet Union, where the workers were said to be building a new world.

In 1931, when John Scott made the decision to travel to the Soviet Union, America was in a deep depression. Plants were closing. Millions of people were out of work. By contrast, in the USSR hundreds of new plants were under construction, unemployment had disappeared, and there was even an acute labor shortage. Many people felt that something was deeply wrong with the USA, that something extremely important was taking place in the USSR. As Arthur Koestler has written, "if History herself were a fellow-traveller, she could not have arranged a more clever timing of events than this coincidence of the gravest crisis of the Western World with the initial phase of Russia's Industrial Revolution. . . . The contrast . . . was so striking and so obvious that it led to the equally obvious conclusion: They are the future—we, the past."[3]

Just as American technology and civilization exerted considerable influence on the Bolsheviks, construction projects in the USSR were making a deep impression on Americans. Scholars, educators, industrialists, and poets were lining up to visit the "vast laboratory" of the new Russia. An advertisement that appeared in *The Nation* on 16 January 1929 exhorted the periodical's readers to "go to Russia":

> Intellectuals, social workers, professional men and women are welcome most cordially in Russia. . . . where the world's most gigan-

[3] Arthur Koestler, *Arrow in the Blue* (New York, 1952), pp. 277–78.

tic social experiment is being made—amidst a galaxy of pictur-
esque nationalities, wondrous scenery, splendid architecture, and
exotic civilizations.

Another magazine editor, Ray Long, lauded a trip to the Soviet
Union as "the most interesting journey one may make today," and
christened the Soviet experiment "the most important human step
since the birth of Christianity." The American intoxication with
the USSR, which gave birth to countless frivolous books in the
new genre "The Country With a Plan," did not fail to overtake the
imaginations of American political reformers. Edmund Wilson
appealed to progressives to "take Communism away from the
Communists" and Charles Beard called for a "five-year plan for
America." In the most memorable phrase of all those uttered
about the new Soviet Russia, Lincoln Steffens exclaimed: "I have
been to the future, and it works."[4]

Thousands of Americans were departing for that strange, far-
off, and mysterious land of Soviet socialism, some out of political
conviction, others desperate for work, and not a few in search of
adventure. In addition to the prominent and not-so-prominent
"personalities" who traveled to the Soviet Union there was a sizable number of American engineers and skilled workers who went
to direct or take part in the great projects of the Five-Year Plan.
Not only did these American specialists make an indispensable
and not generally appreciated contribution to the Soviet industrialization effort, some of them also left behind a valuable record
of their experiences, a record that, with the exception of a few
published books, remains buried in obscure journals or scattered
in archives across the United States. None of the many interesting
or important accounts of the Soviet Union under Stalin by foreigners, however, can match the one by John Scott.

After leaving the Experimental College, Scott, on the advice of
his father, undertook to learn a useful trade before embarking for

[4]Peter Filene, *Americans and the Soviet Experiment, 1917–33* (Cambridge,
1967), pp. 141, 196–97, 199, 242–43.

the USSR. He therefore went to the General Electric Plant in Schenectady, New York, where he completed a several-month training course and received a welder's certificate. He was now ready, but there were some obstacles to overcome, such as arranging his transit to Europe. In August 1932 he attended the Anti-War Congress in Amsterdam as a member of the American delegation, accompanied by his father, who paid for Scott's passage to Europe. Once in Europe, Scott still had to obtain permission to travel to the USSR. Since the Soviet Union did not have diplomatic representation in the United States until after November 1933, Scott followed the path of all but those few Americans recruited in New York by the Soviet trade agency, Amtorg, and applied for entrance to the USSR at the Soviet embassy in Berlin. Then, in the fall of 1932, with visa in hand, Scott boarded the train for Moscow. This American college student, not quite twenty years old, disgusted by life in Depression America, enthusiastic about Soviet Russia, equipped with a sharp mind and a three-decker Corona typewriter, set off on the adventure of his life.

When he arrived in Magnitogorsk, John Scott must have been taken aback. The "city" was little more than a disorganized construction site, without roads or sewage pipes, littered with trash and debris. The only housing consisted of endless rows of indistinguishable hastily built barracks and unsightly makeshift huts of sod and thatch. With famine raging in several areas of the country, food was extremely scarce. Compared with American expectations, the workers of Magnitogorsk were shoddily clothed. Accidents were frequent. Sanitary conditions were abominable, disease widespread. Thousands came and left the site daily, as if it were a chaotic train station rather than a new model city. Paradoxically, the nascent world of socialism looked more like a sordid scene out of the old world of nineteenth-century capitalism, such as Marx or Engels might have described it.

John Scott was no doubt startled by the deprivation and the primitive living conditions, but he was no less struck by the energy and sense of purpose everywhere in evidence. In Magnitogorsk he saw illiterates learning to read and the unskilled learning to operate machines. He saw workers who stayed on the job for sixteen hours straight, with little food and in freezing temperatures without adequate clothing. The enthusiasm! People were working to create a new world, a world without exploitation and misery; they were working not for some master but for themselves, with a radiant future extending before them. Scott too was caught up in the excitement, fired by the vision and the promise.

Like virtually everyone in Magnitogorsk, Scott lived in a barrack, although as a foreigner, he was assigned segregated living quarters. There were three recognized foreign settlements in Magnitogorsk: Berezka, originally Amerikanka, where foreign engineers had been housed, but which was soon to become an enclave for the local Soviet elite; block No. 7 of the "socialist city," in which a few hundred skilled foreign workers and technicians lived; and barrack No. 17, on a hill behind the socialist city, made up of fifty rooms housing about one hundred people, all Germans except for two Americans, one of whom was John Scott.

As barracks went, No. 17 was by far one of the best in the city. It had a seven-acre vegetable garden cultivated by the residents, a sizable and well-equipped "red corner" for recreation, and an *insnab*, or special foreigners' store, that offered better quality food at reasonable prices. Still, a barrack was a barrack, with no running water, toilets, or washrooms, and often without enough light, or fuel for heat.

Although his description of life in barrack No. 17 generally rings true, Scott used poetic license when he described his roommate as a Russian named Kolya. We should not, however, take this to mean that Scott did not know Russians such as Kolya. Scott moved unencumbered in the city, attended school in the

Russian language with Russians, and had many Russian friends. One eyewitness, after pointing out that Scott spoke Russian and even taught it to the other foreigners, reported that he was "very popular among the Russians."[5]

In Magnitogorsk Scott was known as a young enthusiast. One eyewitness who singled Scott out for his exemplary conduct boasted that "Jack came to the Soviet Union to build socialism."[6] Another contemporary noted that Scott "organized a wall paper in English, in addition to his many other tasks."[7] Scott himself reveals that he attended the Communist University, something which only a select few were able to do. Even before the Party purges [*chistki*] that began in the city in 1933 had drastically reduced the number of members, no more than two or three per cent of the local population belonged to the Communist Party. Of that small number, even fewer were really active. John Scott was among the active.

It was while at night school that Scott met and was "bowled over," as he put it, by one of the teachers, Maria Ivanovna Dikareva, better known as Masha. The daughter of a poor peasant from a village in Tver Guberniia (now Kalinin Oblast) near Moscow, Masha had come to Magnitogorsk in 1933 after having attended school in Moscow. Her older sister was already living in Magnitogorsk with her husband, a minor official, and a stream of letters from her sister describing life in the new city enticed an already eager Masha to make the trip in 1933. "I just wanted to see the new cities," Masha recalled. "I didn't know if I would stay. But then I wanted to stay. There was something so light and bright and interesting about Magnitogorsk."[8]

Masha worked as a teacher and also went to school, later becoming one of the first twenty graduates of the city's fledgling

[5] *Moscow News*, 30 June and 4 July 1934.
[6] Ibid.
[7] *Moscow News*, 26 May, 30 September, and 2 October 1933.
[8] Pearl S. Buck, *Talk About Russia (with Masha Scott)* (New York, 1945), p. 94.

pedagogical institute. Seven months after arriving in the city she met John Scott at school. They began playing chess, went to the movies and on picnics. In 1934 they were married. In 1935 they had their first child, and in 1938 their second. Their marriage endured until John's death in 1976.

Masha took her new husband to visit her native village, where Masha's father had become the chairman of the new collective farm. The arrival of the American no doubt caused a stir. Indeed, such an improbable event must have further confirmed the impression that momentous changes were taking place in the country. "Certainly we knew [about America in our village]," Masha later told Pearl Buck. "I remember after the Revolution we had a magazine at our house, and in it were pictures, very beautiful machines and very beautiful horses, and my father told us, 'This is an American magazine and the pictures are American.' And he told me, 'You know, Masha, in our country someday it will be also this way. We will have machines, too, and we will have such beautiful things, because now we are already beginning.'"[9] The young couple embodied that new beginning.

In Magnitogorsk the Scotts worked and studied long hours. John Scott was also busy writing. "He wrote all the time," Masha recalled. "Everyday he was writing something, notes, stories, I don't know. He was always hitting away at the typewriter."[10] Scott, who spent long hours toiling in the local archives, interviewing officials, and mostly just observing, took pains from the very start to record his impressions of life in the Soviet Union. The reader is liable to be startled at the fullness of Scott's descriptions and the sense of duty he displays when describing something. So keen was his devotion to detail that, when revealing a

[9] Ibid., p. 13.
[10] From an interview conducted on 17 February 1986 at Masha Scott's home in Connecticut.

wealth of normally inaccessible information about an aviation factory in Sverdlovsk, he apologizes for not being enough of an aviation specialist to explain the technology of the planes themselves!

Scott scrupulously chronicles the deprivations and hardships of the time. He presents the cold and lack of fuel, the grumbling in the workers' canteens and the struggle to fill one's stomach, the hazardous working conditions and frequent accidents—in short, everything, just as he and other inhabitants of the emerging steeltown experienced it. Similarly, he carefully notes the use of prison labor, the activity of the security police, and the role of political violence. But if, unlike the authors of many foreigners' accounts of the period, Scott refuses to whitewash what he and the others had seen, he also refuses to engage in sensationalism. He confronts the deprivation and terror squarely, but without making them the focus of his book.

If the poignancy of Scott's book lies not simply in his descriptions of daily existence but in the way he tells the story, it also lies in the story itself—the almost magical creation of an enormous factory-city, in an uninhabited area remote from other urban centers, in a few short years.

Founded in 1929, Magnitogorsk instantly became the symbol of the revolutionary transformation of society that the October Revolution had promised. At the site of an iron-ore deposit just beyond the southern tip of the Urals, as far to the east of Moscow as Berlin is to the west, the Soviet government decided to build not just a steel plant, but one that rivaled (indeed that was modeled after) what was then the largest and technologically most advanced steel plant in the world, the Gary (Indiana) Works of the U.S. Steel Company. When completely finished, the "Soviet Gary" was to produce as much steel annually as the entire Soviet Union had produced in the year before the beginning of the first Five-Year Plan!

Though well behind schedule and producing far short of the plan targets, by 1932 Magnitogorsk Works was producing pig iron, and by 1933 steel. A gigantic steel plant equipped with the latest word in technology, in the empty steppe, in so short a time—how was it possible! It was *not* possible, but there it was. "In speaking of our achievements it is not at all necessary to resort to statistics and percentages," People's Commissar for Heavy Industry Grigory "Sergo" Ordzhonikidze told an already convinced audience in Magnitogorsk in 1933. "It is sufficient simply to recall that as late as 1930, there was nothing here."[11]

By the end of the 1930s the Magnitogorsk Works was producing ten per cent of the country's steel output. Only the stubbornest apologists refused to acknowledge the horrible inefficiency and waste, but those, like John Scott, who participated in the great effort at Magnitogorsk, knew that much more than errors were being made. For all the absurd mistakes and blunders, it was clear that the country was industrializing, and doing so very rapidly.

Everyday the people of Magnitogorsk were inundated with vivid impressions not only of the hardships of daily existence but of the telescoping of time. Time, as Valentin Kataev had written in his 1933 novel based on Magnitogorsk, was swiftly moving forward.[12] Horse-drawn carts, makeshift shovels, hand-operated cement mixers, winches and pulleys, on the one hand; and, on the other hand, gigantic blowing stations, several-ton ladles for handling molten steel, mechanized internal freight movement, automated rolling mills—there could have been no greater contrast between the technology employed in construction and the technology that was being installed, between the country's past and its future.

[11] G. K. Ordzhonikidze, "Dognat' i peregnat'" ["Catch and Overtake"], in *Stat'i i rechi* [Articles and Speeches] (Moscow, 1957), vol. 2, p. 477.
[12] Valentin Kataev, *Time, Forward!* translated by Charles Malamuth (Bloomington, 1976).

Technology and revolution; iron, steel, and Bolshevism. "The Magnitogorsk steel plant," gloated the propagandists, "is living proof of what Bolsheviks are able to achieve."[13]

Along with the colossal steel plant, the Soviet government intended to build a new city, a planned "socialist" city of the future. Magnitogorsk was to be a city in which all the problems of cities known up to that time—congestion, poor sanitation, disease, poverty, and crime—would be eliminated. The socialist city was a dream for a better way of life, for literacy, health, justice, abundance, happiness. But unlike the factory, the city of the future was never built.

Notwithstanding the two superblocks of apartment buildings with attractive public squares and decorative fountains, in appearance the city that emerged more closely resembled the cities of Bolshevik reprobation than those of utopian fantasy. Even after the steel plant had pumped out over a million tons of steel, in the pages of the local newspaper writers were still debating whether Magnitogorsk, with a population of 200,000 people but with no sewage system, permanent hospital, or clean water supply, with only a handful of paved roads, and with a housing stock comprised of one-half wooden barracks and another one-quarter huts made of sod, could be considered a "city" at all.[14]

In his chapter "Socialist City," Scott sometimes uses the term to refer to the specific part of Magnitogorsk in which he and Masha—along with no more than fifteen per cent of the population—lived, while at other times he uses it to mean the entire urban agglomeration, without ever making clear in what way either all or part of the city was "socialist." Was Magnitogorsk a "socialist" city, and if so, what made it "socialist"?

The planned city of the future fell victim to inexperience, incompetence, impatience, but, above all, to an inherent contradiction in its conception, for despite the plan to construct a utopian

[13] *Buksir* [Tugboat], Magnitogorsk, June 1932, No. 4, p. 2.
[14] *Magnitogorskii rabochii* [the Magnitogorsk Worker], 1 January 1937.

city, Magnitogorsk was always destined to be a settlement attached to a huge and important industrial center. That center was also a dream, a dream entailing a technological leap from wooden ploughs to automated steel-making shops, and that dream was somehow more urgent and perhaps more fundamental than the dream for a better way of life. Indeed, paradoxical as it might seem, the better life was supposed to result from the building of the automated steel-making shops.

The story of Magnitogorsk became—as the story of the Five-Year Plans had always been—a tale of pig iron and steel, of blast furnaces and open hearth ovens. All else could wait. For now the country needed metal, for which the whole country was mobilized.

Victory, victory at all costs! Steel, steel, and more steel! Parades, campaigns, speeches; endless production statistics, world records, and plan fulfillment—the epic process of socialist construction was perhaps best evident in Magnitogorsk, but it was happening all over the Soviet Union. The 1930s were, in addition to a time of ration tickets, barracks, and barbed wire, a time of construction, heroism, and tangible progress. Of the many thousands of eyewitnesses, it was John Scott who best captured the revolutionary mood and the hopeful spirit of those hectic and paradoxical times.

Like Scott himself, the reader may puzzle over the relation between the events of 1933, as told in the section "A Day in Magnitogorsk," and those of 1937–38, as told in the section "Administration and Purge." It should come as no surprise that, of all the book's chapters, the one on the purges underwent the most revisions.

The events of 1937–38 clearly shook Scott's faith in the Soviet system. Many of his friends and associates, whom he knew to be innocent of any wrongdoing, were arrested. Scott himself was forced from the factory simply because he was a foreigner, Masha was subjected to severe recriminations at Komsomol meetings, their friends were summoned and interrogated, even the three-decker Corona was eventually confiscated.

In an outline for a book on the Soviet Union never written, Scott headed one chapter: "The Purge sours technical success into inhumanity and degradation. Initial hopes of the 1936 constitution become monsters in the hands of the GPU."[15] It was precisely this dichotomy—economic and social progress versus senseless political repression—that Scott and many others who had been so impressed with the undeniable energy and purposefulness they had witnessed found most difficult to comprehend. When examining Scott's explanation of the purges, the reader should keep in mind that although his valiant effort cannot be considered satisfactory, even with the benefit of several decades of reflection specialists are not in a position to offer a convincing explanation for what remains one of the great mysteries of the Soviet experience.

Despite the role the purges played in bringing his time in Magnitogorsk to an end, it is significant that Scott did not end his account of life in Magnitogorsk with them. To be sure, he was appalled by the number of people who suffered unjustly, but he recognized that for most people life went on. The purges did not eclipse what for Scott remained the ultimate defining experience of Magnitogorsk, the heroic struggle to build a steel plant and a new way of life. It was Scott's controversial opinion that such a view was shared by most Soviet citizens. "This was the Magnitogorsk in which I passed five years of my life," Scott concluded in an earlier version of the book. "I look back on it with profound respect for those who built it in such a short time under such difficult circumstances. It was a city full of vitality and life. The people were studying, looking forward, striving to build something, [something] in which at least many of them believed."[16]

---

[15] State Historical Society, Madison, Wisconsin. The John Scott Papers, outline for "The Soviet Commonwealth," undated.

[16] Ibid., manuscript "Behind the Urals," yellow-sheet draft.

The reader would do well to bear in mind that Scott wrote his book during the Second World War, just when the Wehrmacht's initial lightning advances into Soviet territory had been halted. By the time he was preparing his manuscript what had looked like a total Soviet defeat had come to look like a miraculous Soviet victory. What could help to explain this remarkable turn of events? Whence the Soviet ability to resist the Nazi onslaught? These were the questions which occupied Scott as he was composing his memoir. As the final section of his book makes clear, he had no doubt about "what makes Russia click."

The very title of the book, *Behind the Urals*, hints at Scott's ultimate purpose. Among the alternative titles he considered for the book were the following: "Swords for the Soviets," "Russia's Ten Years of War," "Russia's Ural Stronghold," and "Stalin's Ural Stronghold." In those discarded titles as well as in the one finally chosen, Scott was trying to point to what he felt was the secret of the Soviet war effort. As he saw it the secret had two parts: (1) the strategic location of industry in the Ural Mountain region, beyond the reach of an invading army, which Scott attributed to the genius of Stalin; and (2) the fact that the Five-Year Plans involved not simply the construction of new factories but the training of millions of "new" people who could operate machines and who, even if they had come to have certain expectations of the regime based on the unwritten "social contract," more or less accepted the "political realities" of Communist Party rule.

There can be little doubt that Scott showed remarkable insight into the period of "socialist construction" and its contribution to the country's ability to fight the war. His use of his own experiences in a far-off steel city to make sense of what was then the baffling Soviet capacity to match the Germans blow for blow must have profoundly impressed his contemporaries. Indeed, it impresses us today, even though we would also want to emphasize the importance of Hitler's mistakes and geography. The Soviet

Union could lose territory equivalent to the size of two or three "Frances" and still carry on the war.

At the same time, Scott rendered certain judgments that we may wish to question. He tended to exaggerate the relative weight of the admittedly striking development of heavy industry east of the Urals. While whole new industries were built in eastern regions, there was proportionally more investment in the older, established centers of industry in the European part of the country, around Leningrad and Moscow, and in the Ukraine. Something of which Scott was aware but was not able to witness was the extent to which the industry in the East that played a vital role in the war effort had been evacuated from the West. And while the presence in the East of a modern industrial infrastructure to which the evacuated factories could be attached certainly enhanced the impact of those mobile factories, it is not at all clear that Stalin alone should be credited with the decision to locate the newly constructed plants in the East. Moreover, as great an accomplishment as the evacuation of industry was, it had become necessary only because of the shocking vulnerability shown by the country's critical western border regions in the early phase of the war. The eastward movement of industry was carried out amidst the chaos that followed the long-predicted German invasion, and this chaos was clearly the result of Stalin's own failure to prepare properly for a war whose necessity he still did not recognize even after it broke out.

While applauding Stalin for what he, Scott, considered to be the Soviet leader's foresight to build up an eastern industrial base, Scott was also convinced that Stalin's industrialization policy, with its uncompromising emphasis on heavy industry at the expense of consumer goods and its ruthless disregard for human life, was vindicated by Russia's performance in the war against the Nazis. However, we may well express astonishment that the Nazis' capture of roughly half of all Soviet industry nevertheless did not prevent the Soviet Union from winning the war. Does not this fact, even leaving aside questions of morality, vitiate Scott's belief that Stalin's policy of breakneck industrialization was necessary for the very survival of the country? What if we also take into account the fact that the frantic speed and some of the irrational aspects of Stalinist industrialization contributed significantly to the poor operation of many of the new and rebuilt factories well beyond the 1930s? Does not this consideration further enhance our skepticism toward the view that the war conclusively proved that Stalin's policy was the only "correct" one? Given the international environment and the situation internal to the USSR, might there have been other less hasty and less violent ways to industrialize Soviet Russia? If alternatives existed at the time, what were they and—most important of all—why were they not followed?

These questions, which are provoked by a reading of Scott's memoir, are central indeed. How we answer them shapes our view of the possibilities of change within the USSR. The reader will find much of relevance for understanding today's Soviet Union in John Scott's vivid exploration of daily life in the formative days of Stalinism.

BEHIND THE URALS

PART ONE

PART ONE Blood, Sweat, and Tears

I

I LEFT the University of Wisconsin in 1931 to find myself in an America sadly dislocated, an America offering few opportunities for young energy and enthusiasm.

I was smitten with the usual wanderlust. The United States did not seem adequate. I decided to go somewhere else. I had already been in Europe three times. Now I projected more far-flung excursions. Plans for a motor-cycle trip to Alaska, thence by home-made sailboat to Siberia and China came to naught. Where would I get the money to finance the project, and what would I do in China? I looked around New York for a job instead. There were no jobs to be had.

Something seemed to be wrong with America. I began to read extensively about the Soviet Union, and gradually came to the conclusion that the Bolsheviks had found answers to at least some of the questions Americans were asking each other. I decided to go to Russia to work, study, and to lend a hand in the construction of a society which seemed to be at least one step ahead of the American.

Following wise parental counsel I learned a trade before going to Russia. I went to work as welder's apprentice in the General Electric plant in Schenectady, and several months later received a welder's certificate. Armed with this, with credentials from the Metal Workers' Union of which I was an active member, and with letters from several personal friends, I set off for Berlin, where I applied for a Soviet visa.

For some five weeks I lived with friends in Wedding, went to Communist demonstrations, and attended numerous turbulent political meetings organized by several parties. Things were bad in Germany. It was shocking to see thousands of able-bodied men living with their families in the Laubenkolonien, the German Hoovervilles, while block after block of apartment houses in Berlin where they had previously lived stood empty. Such things, I felt sure, did not happen in the Soviet Union.

In due course of time Soviet consular wheels ground out my visa and I entrained for Moscow. For ten days I bounced back and forth between several Soviet organizations, trying to make arrangements for a job. The welding trust was glad to give me work. They needed welders in many places. They were not able to sign me up, however, until the visa department had given me permission to remain in the Soviet Union as a worker. The latter organization could grant such permission only to people with jobs. Neither would put anything in writing.

Finally arrangements were completed, and I started out on the four-day train trip to a place called Magnitogorsk on the eastern slopes of the Ural Mountains.

I was very happy. There was no unemployment in the Soviet Union. The Bolsheviks planned their economy and gave opportunities to young men and women. Furthermore, they had got away from the fetishization of material possessions, which, my good parents had taught me, was one of the basic ills of our American civilization. I saw that most Russians ate only black bread, wore one suit until it disintegrated, and used old newspapers for writing letters and office memoranda, rolling cigarettes, making envelopes, and for various personal functions.

I was about to participate in the construction of this society. I was going to be one of many who cared not to own a second pair of shoes, but who built blast furnaces which were their own. It was September, 1932, and I was twenty years old.

II

IN 1940, Winston Churchill told the British people that they could expect nothing but blood, sweat, and tears. The country was at war. The British people did not like it, but most of them accepted it.

Ever since 1931 or thereabouts the Soviet Union has been at war, and the people have been sweating, shedding blood and tears. People were wounded and killed, women and children froze to death, millions starved, thousands were court-martialed and shot in the campaigns of collectivization and industrialization. I would wager that Russia's battle of ferrous metallurgy alone involved more casualties than the battle of the Marne. All during the thirties the Russian people were at war.

It did not take me long to realize that they ate black bread principally because there was no other to be had, wore rags because they could not be replaced.

In Magnitogorsk I was precipitated into a battle. I was deployed on the iron and steel front. Tens of thousands of people were enduring the most intense hardships in order to build blast furnaces, and many of them did it willingly, with boundless enthusiasm, which infected me from the day of my arrival.

I plunged into the life of the town with the energy of youth. I literally wore out my Russian grammar, and in three months I was making myself understood. I gave away many of the clothes I had brought with me, and dressed more or less like the other workers on the job. I worked as hard and as well as my comparatively limited experience and training permitted.

I was liberally rewarded. My fellow workers accepted me as one of themselves. The local authorities urged me to study, and arranged for me to be accepted into the 'Komvuz,' or Communist University, to which only Communist Party members were usually admitted. They helped me to make arrangements to go on trips around the country.

While political leaders in Moscow were scheming and intriguing, planning and organizing, I worked in Magnitogorsk with the common soldiers, the steel workers, the simple people who sweated and shed tears and blood.

For five years I worked in Magnitogorsk. I saw a magnificent plant built. I saw much sweat and blood, many tears.

PART TWO

A Day in
Magnitogorsk

I

THE big whistle on
the power house sounded a long, deep, hollow six o'clock. All
over the scattered city-camp of Magnitogorsk, workers rolled
out of their beds or bunks and dressed in preparation for their
day's work.

I climbed out of bed and turned on the light. I could see my
breath across the room as I woke my roommate, Kolya.
Kolya never heard the whistle. Every morning I had to pound
his shoulder for several seconds to arouse him.

We pushed our coarse brown army blankets over the beds
and dressed as quickly as we could — I had good American
long woolen underwear, fortunately; Kolya wore only cotton
shorts and a jersey. We both donned army shirts, padded and
quilted cotton pants, similar jackets, heavy scarves, and then
ragged sheepskin coats. We thrust our feet into good Russian
'valinkis' — felt boots coming up to the knee. We did not eat
anything. We had nothing on hand except tea and a few potatoes, and there was no time to light a fire in our little home-
made iron stove. We locked up and set out for the mill.

It was January, 1933. The temperature was in the neighbor-

hood of thirty-five below. A light powdery snow covered the
low spots on the ground. The high spots were bare and hard as
iron. A few stars crackled in the sky and some electric lights
twinkled on the blast furnaces. Otherwise the world was bleak
and cold and almost pitch-dark.

It was two miles to the blast furnaces, over rough ground.
There was no wind, so our noses did not freeze. I was always
glad when there was no wind in the morning. It was my first
winter in Russia and I was not used to the cold.

Down beside the foundation of Blast Furnace No. 4 there was
a wooden shanty. It was a simple clapboard structure with a
corrugated-iron roof nailed on at random. Its one big room was
dominated by an enormous welded iron stove placed equidistant
from all the walls, on a plate of half-inch steel. It was not more
than half-past six when Kolya and I walked briskly up to the
door and pushed it open. The room was cold and dark. Kolya
fumbled around for a moment for the switch and then turned
on the light. It was a big five-hundred-watt bulb hanging from
the ceiling and it illuminated every corner of the bare room.
There were makeshift wooden benches around the walls, a
battered table, and two three-legged stools stood in a corner.
A half-open door opposite the entrance showed a tremendous
closet whose walls were decorated with acetylene torches, hose,
wrenches, and other equipment. The floor of the closet was
littered with electrodes, carbide generators, and dirt. The walls
were bare except for two cock-eyed windows and a wall telephone. Kolya, the welders' foreman, was twenty-two, big-
boned, and broad. There was not much meat on him, and his
face had a cadaverous look which was rather common in Magnitogorsk in 1933. His unkempt, sawdust-colored hair was
very long, and showed under his fur hat. The sheepskin coat
which he wore was ragged from crawling through narrow pipes
and worming his way into various odd corners. At every tear

the wool came through on the outside and looked like a Polish customs officer's mustache. His hands were calloused and dirty; the soles of the valinkis on his feet were none too good. His face and his demeanor were extremely energetic.

The telephone rang. Kolya picked up the receiver and growled in a husky voice, 'Who do you want?... Yeah, speaking.... No, I don't know. Nobody's here yet. Call up in half an hour.' He hung up, unbuttoned his coat, blew his nose on the floor. I went into the closet and got our emergency stove. It was an iron frame, wound haphazardly with asbestos tape and eighth-inch steel wire. I put it down near the desk and Kolya took two wires and connected them to a couple of terminals on the wall. The light dimmed and a low hum told of the low resistance of the coil, which was red-hot within half a minute. Kolya grunted, took the inverted electric light socket, which served as an inkwell, and put it on the floor under the stove. While he was waiting for the ink to thaw out, he opened the drawer of the table and pulled out some threadbare dirty papers.

The door opened and two besheepskinned figures entered the room. 'All right, you guys, how about a fire?' said Kolya, without looking up. 'We can't heat this whole room by electricity.' The two riggers pulled their scarves down from around their noses, took off their gloves, and rubbed the frost from their eyelashes. 'Cold,' said one to the other. 'Nada zakurit!' [1] They approached the electric stove, produced rolls of dirty newspaper and a sack of 'Makhorka,' a very cheap grade of tobacco, and rolled themselves newspaper cigarettes as big as Havana cigars. I rolled one too and we lit them from the stove. The riggers were youngish and had not shaved for several days. Their blue peasant eyes were clear and simple, but their foreheads and cheeks were scarred with frostbite, their hands

---

[1] 'It is necessary to smoke.'

dirty and gnarled. The door opened again admitting a bearded man of fifty-odd, so tall that he had to stoop to enter. 'Good morning, comrades,' he boomed good-naturedly.

'Hey, Kusmin,' said Kolya, looking up, 'make a fire, will you? If the super comes and finds the place warm and nothing but the electric stove going, he'll raise hell!'

'Whoever heard of the super getting here at six-thirty?' said one of the riggers, rolling his enormous cigarette to the corner of his mouth.

Kusmin smiled good-naturedly. 'O.K.,' he said, without paying any attention to the rigger's remark. He opened the door of the big iron stove. Seeing that he actually intended to make a fire, the two riggers joined him, and within five minutes the stove was full of scraps of wood, most of which had been taken from a pile of railroad ties outside the shanty. Kolya looked the other way while Kusmin poured a pint or so of gasoline from a burner's apparatus into the stove. One of the riggers tossed a match into the ashpan; a dull explosion made the windows rattle and then there was a roaring fire.

Workers came, one after the other now, and gathered around to warm their cold hands, faces, and feet. At about six-forty, Ivanov, the riggers' foreman, came in, shook hands with Kolya, and picked up the telephone receiver. He was a broad-shouldered, middle-aged man with a deeply lined face and a quizzical expression around the corners of his mouth. He was a Pole and a party member who had fought three years in the Red Army and worked on bridge construction jobs from Warsaw to Irkutsk. After an unsuccessful attempt to call the storehouse and try to get some bolts he needed, Ivanov hung up and took Kolya by the arm. 'Come on, let's look the job over,' he said. The two foremen left the shanty together, Ivanov tucking a roll of blueprints into his pocket and swearing good-naturedly at the cold, the storehouse manager, the foreigners who projected structural steel with inch-and-a-half bolts, and the telephone operator.

In the meantime, the iron stove was nearly red-hot, and the men gathered round in an ever-widening circle, smoking and talking.

'I don't know what we're going to do with our cow,' said a young fellow with a cutting torch stuck in the piece of ragged rope that served him as a belt. He rubbed his chin sorrowfully with the back of his rough hand. His blue peasant eyes were looking through the shanty walls, through the blast-furnace foundation, through the stack of unerected trusses, across two hundred miles of snow-swept steppe back to the little village he had left six months before. 'It took us two weeks to get here,' he said earnestly to a bewhiskered welder sitting next to him, 'walking over the steppe with our bags on our backs and driving that goddam cow — and now she's not giving any milk.'

'What the hell do you feed her?' asked the welder thoughtfully.

'That's just the trouble,' said the young cutter's helper, slapping his knee. 'Here we came all the way to Magnitogorsk because there was bread and work on the new construction, and we find we can't even feed the cow, let alone ourselves. Did you eat in the dining-room this morning?'

'Yeah, I tried to,' said a clean-cut-looking fellow; 'only fifty grams of bread and that devilish soup that tastes like it was made of matchsticks.' He shrugged his shoulder and spat on the floor between his knees. 'But then — if we are going to build blast furnaces I suppose we have to eat less for a while.'

'Sure,' said a welder, in broken Russian. 'And do you think it's any better anywhere else? Back in Poland we hadn't had a good meal in years. That's why our whole village walked across the Soviet frontier. It's funny, though, we thought there would be more to eat here than there is.'

Vladek, the Polish welder, was one of many who, dissatisfied with their lives in Pilsudski's Poland and afire with enthusiasm for the Socialist construction, word of which came across the White Russian countryside through the Polish border guards and censors, had left, taking only what they could carry, to throw in their lot with the Soviet workers. When Vladek spoke, all the workers around him turned and listened with interest.

'Tell me,' said a young worker, 'why don't you make a revolution in Poland?'

'Don't you think they're trying?' said a burly rigger. 'Why, the Komsomol in Poland is a wonderful organization.'

Vladek wrinkled up his nose. 'Yeah, but it's not as easy as it sounds,' he said quietly. 'They put you in jail, they beat you up, and vot, tebye na; [1] try and make a revolution.'

'Don't tell me,' said Kusmin. 'Our regiment revolted on the Galician front, we killed our officers, got our comrades out of jail, and went home and took the land.'

At this point a young, boisterous, athletic-looking burner burst into the room and pushed his way up to the stove. 'Boy, is it cold!' he said, addressing everybody in the room. 'I don't think we should work up on top today. One of the riveters froze to death up there last night. It seems he was off in a bleeder pipe and they didn't find him till this morning.'

'Yeah?' said everybody at once. 'Who was it?'

But nobody knew who it was. It was just one of the thousands of peasants and young workers who had come to Magnitogorsk for a bread card, or because things were tough in the newly collectivized villages, or fired with enthusiasm for Socialist construction.

[1] 'There you are.'

II

I WAS more or less warmed up by this time, so I pulled my scarf up around my face and went out after the two foremen. They had ascended a rickety wooden ladder and were walking along the blast-furnace foundation, looking at the tons and tons of structural steel in process of erection on all sides. Over their heads was a ten-foot diameter gas pipe, one section of which was not yet in place. To their left was the enormous conical bosch of the fourth blast furnace. They walked past this, and down through the cast house toward No. 3. A few dim bulbs cast a gray dawn around the job. Several scurrying figures could be seen — bricklayers, laborers, mechanics, electricians — getting things lined up for the day's work. I caught up with them and the three of us climbed up to the top of No. 3. We found a little group of riveters standing silently around a shapeless form lying on the wooden scaffold. We discovered that it was the frozen riveter, and having ascertained that a stretcher had already been sent for to take the body down, we went on to the very top to look over the coming day's work.

'How's school going?' asked Ivanov. 'You'll be a technician pretty soon, won't you, Kolya?'

'It's pretty tough studying when it's as cold as this,' said Kolya. 'We have to take our gloves to the classroom with us. Not enough coal.'

'Yeah, I know,' said Ivanov sympathetically. 'It's tough studying; but then, what the hell! If you want to learn, you've got to work.'

By the time the seven o'clock whistle blew, the shanty was

jammed full of riggers, welders, cutters, and their helpers. It was a varied gang, Russians, Ukrainians, Tartars, Mongols, Jews, mostly young and almost all peasants of yesterday, though a few, like Ivanov, had long industrial experience. There was Popov, for instance. He had been a welder for ten years and had worked in half a dozen cities. On the other hand, Khaibulin, the Tartar, had never seen a staircase, a locomotive, or an electric light until he had come to Magnitogorsk a year before. His ancestors for centuries had raised stock on the flat plains of Kazakhstan. They had been dimly conscious of the Czarist government; they had had to pay taxes. Reports of the Kirghiz insurrection in 1916 had reached them. They had heard stories of the October Revolution; they even saw the Red Army come and drive out a few rich landlords. They had attended meetings of the Soviet, without understanding very clearly what it was all about, but through all this their lives had gone on more or less as before. Now Shaimat Khaibulin was building a blast furnace bigger than any in Europe. He had learned to read and was attending an evening school, learning the trade of electrician. He had learned to speak Russian, he read newspapers. His life had changed more in a year than that of his antecedents since the time of Tamerlane.

Ivanov, Kolya, and I entered the shanty just as the whistle started to blow. The cutters' brigadier [1] was already in the center of the room assigning his men to their various places for the day. Welders were getting electrodes and buttoning up their coats. The burners were working over their hoses, swearing graphically as they found frozen spots or as disputes arose about torches, generators, or wrenches. By the time the whistle had finished blowing, most of the men had left the room, whistling cheerfully, kidding each other and swearing at the cold.

---

[1] Brigadier: a sort of straw-boss in charge of a gang of eight or ten men and subordinate to the foreman.

The foremen gathered around the table. The telephone rang incessantly — a welder was wanted at the blowing station, two of the riggers in the gang working on the open-hearth gas line had not come to work. The gang could not hoist the next section of pipe short-handed. Ivanov swore at the absentees, their mothers, and grandmothers. Then he went out to borrow two men from another gang. Kolya wrote out a list of the welders and what they were doing. He wrote it on newspaper. The ink was a semi-frozen slush. This list formed the basis on which the workers would get paid for the day's work. He thrust it into his pocket and went to the clean gas line to see how things were going. I took my mask and electrodes and started out for No. 3. On the way I met Shabkov, the ex-kulak; a great husky youth with a red face, a jovial voice, and two fingers missing from his left hand.

'Well, Jack, how goes it?' he said, slapping me on the back. My Russian was still pretty bad, but I could carry on a simple conversation and understood almost everything that was said.

'Badly,' I said. 'All our equipment freezes. The boys spend half their time warming their hands.'

'Nichevo, that doesn't matter,' said the disfranchised rigger's brigadier. 'If you lived where I do, in a tent, you wouldn't think it so cold here.'

'I know you guys have it tough,' said Popov, who had joined us. 'That's what you get for being kulaks.'

Shabkov smiled broadly. 'Listen, I don't want to go into a political discussion, but a lot of the people living down in the "special" section of town are no more kulaks than you.'

Popov laughed. 'I wouldn't be surprised. Tell me, though How did they decide who was to be dekulakized?'

'Ah,' said Shabkov, 'that's a hell of a question to ask a guy that's trying to expiate his crimes in honest labor. Just between the three of us, though, the poor peasants of the village

get together in a meeting and decide: 'So-and-so has six horses;
we couldn't very well get along without those in the collective
farm; besides he hired a man last year to help on the harvest.'
They notify the GPU, and there you are. So-and-so gets five
years. They confiscate his property and give it to the new
collective farm. Sometimes they ship the whole family out.
When they came to ship us out, my brother got a rifle and fired
several shots at the GPU officers. They fired back. My brother
was killed. All of which, naturally, didn't make it any better
for us. We all got five years, and in different places. I heard my
father died in December, but I'm not sure.'

Shabkov got out his canvas tobacco pouch and a roll of
newspaper, and thrust both toward Popov. 'Kulak smoke?'
He smiled grimly.

Popov availed himself of the opportunity and rolled a cigarette.

'Da. A lot of things happen that we don't hear much about.
But then, after all, look at what we're doing. In a few years
now we'll be ahead of everybody industrially. We'll all have
automobiles and there won't be any differentiation between
kulaks and anybody else.' Popov swept his arm dramatically
in the direction of the towering blast furnace. Then he turned
to Shabkov. 'Are you literate?'

'Yes,' said Shabkov, 'I studied three years. I even learned a
little algebra. But now, what the hell! Even if I were really
well-educated, they wouldn't let me do any other work but this.
What's the use of me studying? Anyhow, they won't even let
me in to any but an elementary school. When I get home from
work I want to raise my elbow and have a good time.' Shabkov
touched his throat with his index finger, to any Russian a
symbol of getting drunk. We arrived at No. 3. Shabkov swung
onto a ladder and disappeared up into the steel. Popov looked
after him with wrinkled forehead. Shabkov was one of the

best brigadiers in the whole outfit. He spared neither himself nor those under him, and he used his head. And yet he was a kulak, serving a sentence, living in a section of town under the surveillance of the GPU, a class enemy. Funny business, that. Popov didn't thoroughly understand it.

Popov and I set about welding up a section of the bleeder pipe on the blast furnace. He gave me a break and took the outside for the first hour. Then we changed around. From the high scaffolding, nearly a hundred feet above the ground, I could see Kolya making the rounds of his thirty-odd welders, helping them when they were in trouble, swearing at them when they spent too much time warming their hands. People swore at Kolya a good deal too, because the scaffolds were unsafe or the wages bad.

III

It was just about nine-fifteen when I finished one side of the pipe and went around to start the other. The scaffold was coated with about an inch of ice, like everything else around the furnaces. The vapor rising from the large hot-water cooling basin condensed on everything and formed a layer of ice. But besides being slippery, it was very insecure, swung down on wires, without any guys to steady it. It swayed and shook as I walked on it. I always made a point of hanging on to something when I could. I was just going to start welding when I heard someone sing out, and something swished down past me. It was a rigger who had been working up on the very top.

He bounced off the bleeder pipe, which probably saved his life. Instead of falling all the way to the ground, he landed on the main platform about fifteen feet below me. By the time I got down to him, blood was coming out of his mouth in gushes. He tried to yell, but could not. There were no foremen around, and the half-dozen riggers that had run up did not know what to do. By virtue of being a foreigner I had a certain amount of authority, so I stepped in and said he might bleed to death if we waited for a stretcher, and three of us took him and carried him down to the first-aid station. About halfway there the bleeding let up and he began to yell every step we took.

I was badly shaken when we got there, but the two young riggers were trembling like leaves. We took him into the little wooden building, and a nurse with a heavy shawl over her white gown showed us where to put him. 'I expect the doctor any minute,' she said; 'good thing, too, I wouldn't know what the hell to do with him.'

The rigger was gurgling and groaning. His eyes were wide open and he seemed conscious, but he did not say anything. 'We should undress him, but it is so cold in here that I am afraid to,' said the nurse. Just then the doctor came in. I knew him. He had dressed my foot once when a piece of pig iron fell on it. He took his immense sheepskin off and washed his hands. 'Fall?' he asked, nodding at the rigger.

'Yes,' I said.

'How long ago?'

'About ten minutes.'

'What's that?' asked the doctor, looking at the nurse and indicating the corner of the room with his foot. I looked and for the first time noticed a pair of ragged valinkis sticking out from under a very dirty blanket on the floor.

'Girder fell on his head,' said the nurse.

'Well,' said the doctor, rolling up his sleeves, 'let's see what we can do for this fellow.' He moved over toward the rigger, who was lying quietly now and looking at the old bearded doctor with watery blue eyes. I turned to go, but the doctor stopped me.

'On your way out, please telephone the factory board of health and tell them I simply must have more heat in this place,' he said.

I did the best I could over the telephone in my bad Russian, but all I could get was, 'Comrade, we are sorry, but there is no coal.'

I was making my way unsteadily back to the bleeder pipe on No. 3 when Kolya hailed me. 'Don't bother to go up for a while, the brushes burnt out on the machine you were working on. They won't be fixed for half an hour or so.' I went toward the office with Kolya and told him about the rigger. I was incensed and talked about some thorough checkup on scaffoldings. Kolya could not get interested. He pointed out there was not enough planking for good scaffolds, that the riggers were mostly plowboys who had no idea of being careful, and that at thirty-five below without any breakfast in you, you did not pay as much attention as you should.

'Sure, people will fall. But we're building blast furnaces all the same, aren't we?' and he waved his hand toward No. 2 from which the red glow of flowing pig iron was emanating. He saw I was not satisfied. 'This somewhat sissified foreigner will have to be eased along a little,' he probably said to himself. He slapped me on the back. 'Come on in the office. We are going to have a technical conference. You'll be interested.'

IV

At about ten o'clock a group assembled in the wooden shanty, far different from that which had been there three hours before. First Syemichkin, the superintendent, arrived. Then came Mr. Harris, the American specialist consultant, with his interpreter; then Tishenko, the burly, sinister prisoner specialist.[1] They came into the shanty one by one, unbuttoned their coats, warmed their hands, then set to talking over their blueprints. Mr. Harris produced a package of fat 'Kuzbas' cigarettes from the special foreigners' store. He passed them around with a smile. No one refused. Kolya, who had just come in, got in on it too.

'Well,' said Mr. Harris, through his taciturn interpreter, 'when do you expect to get the rest of the riveting done up on top of No. 3? They were telling me about this new time limit. The whole top is to be finished by the twenty-fifth. That's ten days.'

Tishenko, the chief engineer, convicted of sabotage in the Ramzin trial in 1929, sentenced to be shot, sentence commuted, now serving ten years in Magnitogorsk, shrugged his shoulders. He did not speak immediately. He was not a wordy man. He had been responsible engineer for a Belgian company in the Ukraine before the Revolution. He had had a house of his own, played tennis with the British consul, sent his son to Paris to study music. Now he was old. His hair was white. He had

---

[1] Prisoner specialists: a group of several thousand eminent engineers and scientists convicted of various anti-Soviet activities in the late twenties and exiled to outlying industrial and construction towns where they held responsible technical and administrative posts.

heard a great deal of talk since 1917, and had decided that most of it was worthless. He did his job, systematically, without enthusiasm. He liked to think that he was helping to build a strong Russia where life would one day be better than it was for his son in Paris or his sister in London. It certainly wasn't yet, though.

Mr. Harris looked at Tishenko. He understood the older man's position and respected his silence. Still, he was a consulting engineer being paid good American dollars, being supplied with caviar in a country where there was little bread and no sugar, to push Magnitostroi through to completion on time. He pressed the point. And Tishenko finally answered slowly: 'A riveter froze to death last night. Cold and malnutrition. This morning four of the girls we have heating rivets didn't show up. Two of them are pregnant, I think, and it's cold up there. The compressor is working badly.' He stopped, realizing it was all beside the point. If he said that the job would be finished by the twenty-fifth he was a liar and a hypocrite and Mr. Harris would be perfectly aware of it. If he said that it would take longer, he was sabotaging the decision of the Commissar of Heavy Industry. He was already under sentence for sabotage. He looked out of the dusty window. 'It'll take at least a month,' he said.

'That is just about my opinion,' said Mr. Harris, 'but certain things will have to be done and done immediately, or it will take much longer.' They got out their blueprints and their pencils and discussed in low, serious voices the steps necessary to ensure the completion of the top of No. 3 in triple the allotted time.

Syemichkin looked on. His attitude was partly one of respect, partly disdain. These 'bourzhies' didn't understand Bolshevik tempo. They didn't understand the working class. They did understand blast furnaces, though, much better than he. They had had years of experience building steel mills in several different countries, whereas he, Syemichkin, had graduated only a year ago, after a rather superficial course in engineering. When it came to questions like the construction of the tuyer zone, or the situation of the water jackets, both of these men knew by heart how every large blast furnace in the world was put together. He, Syemichkin, knew vaguely where Berlin was, knew that Paris was somewhere beyond.

The door opened and Shevchenko came in. Shevchenko was the great activist among the technical personnel. He was called engineer by his subordinates. Actually he was a graduate of the Institute of Red Directors, had been in the party since 1923, had been trade-union organizer, party functionary, director of a large Donbas construction job. His technical knowledge was limited, and his written Russian contained many mistakes. His present job was sectional assistant director of construction. He was responsible to the director and to the party for the fulfillment of construction plans.

But Shevchenko had learned years before that from his standpoint it was much more important to make it seem that his own job was being well done, his own house in order, than that the work in general should go on as fast as possible. It was all very well to talk of construction of Socialism and the Ural–Kuznetsk Combinat at meetings; for him these things were truisms, axioms which it was necessary to understand, but which were insufficient basis for a sound career as a Bolshevik administrator. In any race only one person can be first. It was essential that he be first even if it meant hindering the progress of his competitors by any means that presented themselves. Stalin would get credit from history for the successful construction of Socialism in one country. Shevchenko would get the Order of Lenin if he succeeded in persuading Moscow that, because of objective reasons, Blast Furnace No. 3 could not possibly be finished until June, by which time, if things went well, they could have it in operation. Shevchenko's main energies, therefore, were directed toward finding 'objective' or political excuses for the failure of his organization to adhere to the super-ambitious Moscow construction schedule which everybody knew was impossible of fulfillment.

In addition to this, however, Shevchenko was a good administrator and an enthusiastic speaker whose words carried weight with the workers. He worked hard, particularly when his superiors were likely to be watching, he demanded strict discipline from his subordinates. As he came into the room, Tishenko looked around and nodded his head; Mr. Harris smiled and extended his hand. Kolya and I were not important enough to exchange an individual greeting with the assistant director.

'Have you seen the new order?' said Shevchenko belligerently, advancing toward the table and shaking hands casually with Harris and Tishenko.

'Da,' said Mr. Harris, who had understood the Russian without the aid of his interpreter.

'Well?' Shevchenko looked from one to the other.

Syemichkin, Kolya, and I listened with great interest. We all realized that Shevchenko was a boor and a careerist. But it seemed to take people like that to push the job forward, to overcome the numerous difficulties, to get the workers to work in spite of cold, bad tools, lack of materials, and undernourishment. It took all types to make Magnitogorsk. That was clear. And Syemichkin, realizing full well his limitations, was content for the moment to draw his five hundred roubles a month, fulfill his more or less mechanical functions as superintendent, and watch how those above and below him worked. Kolya was a tough foreman, trying to become an engineer, trying to build Socialist blast furnaces quickly. I was a stray American, dropped in Magnitogorsk as an electric welder through a series of accidents.

Mr. Harris was jotting down figures on a piece of paper. He beckoned to Shevchenko and began reading a list of materials necessary for the completion of the top of No. 3, none of which were available.

'Now, Mr. Shevchenko,' said the American, 'orders are orders, but you can't rivet steel with them and you can't heat rivets with them. We must have these things or the job won't be finished by next Christmas. You're an influential man in the party and with the construction administration. It's up to you to get these materials.'

Shevchenko knew that this was sound. However, Harris's remark created a situation in which it appeared that he, Shevchenko, was the one who was not doing his job as he should. This would not do. The assistant director launched into a long tirade. He quoted Marx and Stalin, referred to the records of the Ramzin group, to foreign agents and to opportunism. 'Surrounded as we are by hostile capitalist nations, we are forced to industrialize our great country in the shortest possible time, leaving no stone unturned, sparing no one. Magnitogorsk is the most important single heavy industry center in the Soviet Union. Millions of roubles have been invested, thousands of workers have come from far and wide. The country is waiting for our iron and steel. Here we have assembled all the materials and equipment for two new blast furnaces. They must be erected and blown in at the earliest possible date, and yet if I were to believe you I would be forced to think that the whole job must be held up for lack of a few rivets. You, Tishenko, you have thirty years of industrial experience, and you sit there and do nothing. Haven't you got ingenuity enough to think up some way to keep the job going, some way to surmount these obstacles? Or perhaps you're not interested. Perhaps you remain unconvinced by the last fifteen years.'

Shevchenko's rhetoric carried him away. His face was

flushed, his arm extended. Then, having asserted himself, having placed the party line before the old wrecker and the foreign specialist, thus acquitting himself of his obvious political obligation under the circumstances, he took one of Mr. Harris's cigarettes, drew a stool up to the table, and proceeded to look over the list of materials that the American had made out. There was no question about it, of course; no amount of proletarian enthusiasm, no speeches, could take the place of the inch-and-a-half rivets. Shevchenko picked up the telephone. He called the storehouse director, the director of supplies of the whole combinat, finally he called a personal friend of his who worked in the rolling mill. He talked in a low, friendly voice. There was mention of a couple of drinks the next night. Then a casual allusion to inch-and-a-half rivets. When he hung up, Shevchenko grunted, 'I think we'll get the rivets.'

The four men, as heterogeneous a group as one could find — a Cleveland engineer, a prisoner specialist, a Red director, and a young, inexperienced Soviet engineer — sat down around the table to discuss the rest of the points on Mr. Harris's list.

V

At eleven o'clock a whistle blew and the workers descended from truss and girder, roof and pipe, to go to lunch. I looked enviously at the overhead bead Popov had been laying in the bleeder pipe. It was as nearly perfect as I ever saw. Popov was a crackerjack structural steel welder, as good as or better than any of the men I had learned from in the General Electric plant in Schenectady.

Popov knocked his hands against the rungs of the steel ladder to restore the circulation, then we climbed down. We were ruddy-faced from the cold wind. When we got to the ground we joined Shabkov and a couple of riggers who had been hoisting up an expansion joint for the dirty gas line with a hand-hoist, and set off together in the direction of the dining-room.

Both Shabkov and Popov were comparatively well-dressed. Their leather gloves, while they had some holes burned in them, were still sound. They wore valinkis coming up to their knees, long sheepskin coats with the wool inside, leather fur-trimmed hats, and woolen scarves. The two riggers who had been working on the ground, however, were not so well off. One wore ragged leather shoes instead of felt boots, and anyone who has been in a cold climate knows of the torture of leather shoes. The other wore felt boots, the soles of which were coming off. He had tied them on with a piece of wire, but the 'portyankis' or rags which he had wrapped around his feet in place of stockings showed through in two places. Their sheepskins were ragged and burned, their gloves were almost palmless. They were young recruits from the village who had not yet learned to be real steel workers and therefore got the left-overs in clothes. Shabkov clapped one of them on the back.

'Well, Grishka, want to come up this afternoon and try working high? If you get dizzy you can go down again. Misha here needs somebody to line up the flange of that expansion joint while he's tacking it.'

Grisha's chest swelled. He had been waiting for this opportunity for some time. 'What do you mean get dizzy? Of course I'll go up. Only, listen, how about some felt boots? It's cold up there.'

'I know,' said Shabkov, 'I told the foreman about you and I'll tell him again. But if there aren't any boots in the storehouse, what can I do?'

'But we have to get them,' said the young rigger, with an oath. 'It's in the collective agreement. I read it myself.'

Nobody answered. Everyone had either read the collective agreement himself or heard others read it aloud, but, as Shabkov said, if there were no boots, what could one do? The other rigger said nothing. He was a little afraid that the brigadier would suggest that he work high. At the moment he was interested in staying on the ground. He had become accustomed to stairs and short ladders, but climbing a sixty-foot steel column to work on a pipe set up on top of it, walking on these suspended wooden scaffoldings that swayed and shook — no, no. It was much better on the ground turning the crank of the hand-hoist, even if he had only third category and made one hundred and twenty roubles a month, while the riggers that worked high generally got fourth and made up to two hundred.

We crossed numerous railroad lines, passed in front of Blast Furnace No. 2, which was already in operation, and after climbing over piles of structural steel, unfinished foundations, and mounds of earth, approached a long low wooden building toward which workers were streaming from every direction. Over the door there was a sign: 'Dining-Room No. 30.'

'How many cards have you got?' Popov asked Shabkov in a low voice. 'Oh, that's right, you're a "special"' (by which he meant a disfranchised kulak), 'you have only one.'

Shabkov grinned. He had two. Ivanov, the foreman, had given him an extra one for the simple reason that in his opinion an extra dinner invested in Shabkov produced a maximum of return in units of labor.

They entered the dining-room together. There was very little distinction made by the workers themselves between the 'specials' and everybody else. They or their fathers had been kulaks, but now they were all doing the same work, living similar lives, while very frequently the 'specials' worked better than the average, since they usually were the most energetic elements of the village, who had become prosperous during the NEP.[1] Shabkov was universally respected. He pushed a brigade of eighteen, only two of whom were 'specials,' and yet he had no trouble maintaining discipline.

The dining-room was jammed full. The long bare wooden tables were surrounded by workers, and behind almost every seated client somebody was waiting. There was much noise and confusion. Young waitresses ran around the room carrying large wooden trays with plates of soup and large chunks of bread on them. It was cold in the dining-room; one could see one's breath before one's face; but it was so much warmer than outside that everybody unbuttoned his sheepskin and rolled his hat up from around his ears. At the doorway a burly Tartar examined the cards of those who entered and gave a wooden spoon to each.

The cards themselves were simple affairs, printed on very poor quality brown paper. 'Dining-Room No. 30' was stamped on each and there were numbers from 1 to 31 around the edge of the card. These numbers were torn off by the waitresses before they served the meal. One card entitled the owner to one meal per day for the month. Shabkov and I shouldered our way to a far corner, found a table where the meal had already been served and took up our stations behind two bricklayers who were eating.

'Doesn't look bad,' said Popov, sniffing, 'if they'd only give us more bread. Two hundred grams [2] isn't enough.'

'I understand they get three hundred grams in the engineers' dining-room next door,' said Shabkov, wiping his spoon on the inside of his sheepskin. 'Were you ever in there?'

[1] NEP: New Economic Policy, 1923–28, providing a temporary restoration of individual initiative and small capitalism in industry, trade, and agriculture.

[2] Half pound.

'Yeah, once,' answered Popov. 'Kolya lent me his card. The meals aren't much different from ours, only you don't have to wait so long and there isn't so much of a crowd. The soup is just the same, I think.'

We were joined by other workers waiting for a free space, and before we sat down there were others waiting behind us for our places when we should have finished.

'I understand a bricklayer fell down on the inside of the swirlers yesterday,' said a rigger to Popov.

'Yes, so they say,' he answered. 'It's time the safety-first trust got to work and enforced some of these fancy regulations.'

There was talk like this every day, but the safety-first organization was not in a position to take effective steps in the direction of cutting down accidents. There were three main factors: in the first place, the inexperience of the workers and their childish lack of understanding of danger; in the second place, lack of sufficient lumber to make the necessary scaffoldings, ladders with railings, etc.; and in the third place, a shortage of electric light bulbs, which meant that workers working high on the inside of pipes or stacks, and on the outside in the early morning and late afternoon, had to work in the dark. In all of these three cases the safety-first organization was powerless. There was not enough lumber and when some did arrive it went to more essential things than to scaffolding, or else disappeared into the stoves of workers' rooms. As for the electric light bulbs, in December something had happened at the big substation and three hundred and eighty volts had gone into all the lighting lines instead of two hundred and twenty. Every bulb turned on at the time was burned out, and there was no reserve supply.

About half an hour after entering the building, we seated ourselves on newly vacated stools, put our cards on the table, and waited for the waitress to come. She was halfway down the room serving another table, swearing good-naturedly at the workers for trying to get two meals on one card and occasionally getting her behind pinched. It was ten minutes before she arrived at the end table and began tearing off our cards. Shabkov and Popov, each having two cards, were hard put to it distracting her attention so that she would not realize there were more cards than people at the table. It did not work, however. After having torn off twelve numbers she counted and saw that there were only ten at the table. Popov saved the situation. 'Oh, yeah,' he said, 'that's Petya and Grisha left their cards and went down to wash their hands.' Popov grinned. The waitress grinned too. No one ever washed his hands in the winter in Dining-Room No. 30. However, she had witnesses, so that if the director checked up, which was highly improbable, she had an excuse. She dashed off smiling and returned shortly with twelve large lumps of black bread. On the next trip she brought twelve plates of hot soup. It wasn't bad soup. There was some cabbage in it, traces of potatoes and buckwheat, and an occasional bone. It was hot, that was the main thing. The workers ate with relish, some of them having put mustard in it for flavor. Most of them had eaten all their bread before the soup was gone. Shabkov and Popov, however, had two pieces each (two pieces of two hundred grams each make just one pound of black bread), so that theirs lasted through till the end of their soup and they even had some left to eat with their second course. The latter consisted of a soup-plate filled with potatoes covered with thin gravy and a small piece of meat on top. Having brought these, the waitress went on to the next table.

Popov and Shabkov ate ravenously.

'Good dinner,' said Shabkov. 'Wish it was like this every day.'

Popov didn't answer. He just grunted. He was hard at work on his two plates of meat and potatoes.

'I understand that Lominadze, the new head of the party, is raising hell about the dining-rooms and insisting that we should have the right to order as much bread as we want and the choice of at least three second courses,' said the worker next to Popov to a burly, fat-cheeked, beshawled rivet-heater girl who was swilling potatoes just opposite him.

'I'll believe that when I see it,' said the girl, with a Ukrainian accent. She sat at the table with the men, though there were only some twenty or thirty women in the room. Most of them wore the same felt boots and sheepskins as the men and were only distinguishable by the heavy shawls they wore over their heads.

As soon as we had finished, the waiting workers crowded their way to the stools. Popov and Shabkov stood up, loosening their belts and belching. 'Da,' said Popov. 'Good dinner.'

When we got back to the job, it was twelve-thirty according to the wooden clock in the compressor house. We had spent only fifteen or twenty minutes in actual eating, but had lost an hour and a half of working time. Bad organization again. The director knew it, the trade union and party functionaries knew it. But it was another story to remedy the situation. Thousands of workers had to be fed. There were not enough dining-rooms, or tables, or stools, or spoons, or food itself. Three years later increasing food supply made possible the liquidation of the card system, much better meals, and less lost time; but in 1932 and 1933 the situation was bad and no one seemed able to do anything to improve it.

VI

T HE   trade-union
organizer pasted a piece of newspaper on the shanty door.
An announcement was painted on it in misspelled Russian:
'Meeting — election of new shop committee chairman — five
o'clock in the Red Corner. Attendance obligatory.' Most of
the gang had seen this, but there was little interest. The shop
committee had little significance to most of the workers. It
organized poorly attended meetings, addressed by trade-union
functionaries who talked on the building program of Magnitogorsk, the second Five-Year-Plan, the international situation. Also when the workers had been sick or hurt they took
their clinic slips to the chairman to be O.K.'d. That was all.
The administration meant a good deal to the workers. It hired
and fired, gave them their orders, paid their wages. The party
meant a good deal too. You could get a room through the
party, get a new job, lodge complaints, or make suggestions
with some assurance that they would get attention. The shop
committee, however, did none of these things, and the election
of a new chairman aroused no interest for most of the riggers,
cutters, and welders who saw the announcement. Thus it was
that at five o'clock in the Red Corner the old chairman, who
was being transferred to different work, and two members of
the shop committee stood around smoking and watching the
door. One worker came, two, five — but no more.

'This is a hell of a note,' said the old chairman, a nervous,
slick-looking, middle-aged fellow, with an expensive black seal-
skin hat. 'I put up the announcements all over the place. I
don't know why more people didn't come.' A tall, youngish

fellow with a scar on his mouth, standing near by, shrugged his shoulders. He was the one who had been sent by the district trade-union committee to be the new chairman of the blast furnace construction workers' shop committee. It did not look promising, this; when only five workers came to the elections. He made a remark to this effect to the colleague whom he was replacing. 'You seem to have done a hell of a lot of social work here. What are we going to do? I can't be elected by a meeting of five in an organization of eighteen hundred workers. And you have to leave tomorrow for your new job.' The new chairman was distressed by this formal dilemma. The others were not, however.

'Nuts,' said one of the members of the shop committee. 'Don't get upset. It's just a formality, after all, this election. We'll put you through at the next meeting, and in the meantime you can begin functioning normally. It is not so good that we couldn't get more out to the meeting than this, though.'

The reasons why the workers did not come to the meeting were pretty obvious to anyone who was looking for them. In the first place, the shop committee was almost dead. It did nothing to help defend workers against bureaucratic and over-enthusiastic administrators, and to assure the enforcement of the labor laws. For instance, most of the skilled welders on the job were working two shifts a day regularly, because there were not enough of them, and the work had to be done. This was distinctly against the law, but the shop committee did nothing at all. How could they buck Shevchenko and hinder the work by taking the welders off the job? Everywhere it was the same. Then in the matter of the elections themselves, things were bad too. The chairman of the shop committee theoretically was supposed to be one of the workers in the shop, elected by his shopmates as the one in the outfit most able and competent to represent the interests of the workers. Actually it had become

the custom for the district committee to send a man, a professional trade-union functionary, trained in the representation
of the interests of the workers, whose arrival was registered by
an 'election.' Actually the election meant nothing, as there was
only one candidate, and he was sent from a higher body. Any
open criticism made by a worker of this state of affairs would
have been fruitless.

The authority of the trade unions was at a low ebb. Later,
in 1934 and 1935, the trade unions reorganized their work and
began to carry on activities which won back the respect and
support of some of the workers. They did this by building rest
homes, insisting on the observance of labor laws, even if it
meant that the jobs suffered for the time being, giving out theater tickets, organizing schools and courses of all kinds, and sending workers and their wives and children to sanitariums.

VII

I LEFT the meeting
and joined Popov and several other welders who were turning
their steps toward home.

'How much overtime did you put in today?'

'Three hours,' answered Popov. 'Alexander is staying on
for another shift. I worked two shifts yesterday and didn't get
my bread. Today I refused.'

We walked over ditches, across railroad tracks, and slid down
banks. It was already almost pitch-dark and very cold. We
had half a mile to walk before reaching the beginning of the
city. Popov looked around at a burner behind him. 'Hey —

your nose is white!' he shouted. The burner swore, took off his glove, and picking up a handful of snow, rubbed his nose vigorously with it. The rest laughed. 'Sasha always did have a bad nose ever since he was up north with the army, and got it half-frozen off,' someone said to me.

As we left the construction site, each of us gathered a little bundle of firewood. When possible we took scraps that were no good to the job anyway; when we could not find these, however, we split up planks and ties, anything that came to hand. We had to be warm in the barracks and the supply organization had no coal.

Before leaving the territory of the plant, we had to go around the guard, whose job it was to prevent wood from being stolen. He was an old partisan, with a rifle which might shoot, so we had to make a wide detour. According to a new law stealing Socialist property was a capital crime, and while everyone took wood home, it might just be someone's ill luck to be made an example of. We saw the old guard with his enormous sheepskin and long rifle silhouetted against the sky, but he didn't see us.

Having left the territory of the plant the group split up. Grisha had a pail. He took all the milk cards and went off to the milk station to get the half-liter (pint) of milk each which welders and burners were entitled to every day according to law. There was comparatively little chance that there would be milk there to get. The winter supply was very bad. Milk was brought in frozen lumps in bags from a neighboring state farm. However, it was worth trying. So every day the welders sent somebody, and occasionally, once or twice a week, he came home with a half-pail of milk.

Two of the welders took the wood from the whole group and started off toward the barracks while the rest of us went to the store to get bread and anything else which might be obtainable.

The blast-furnace construction workers' cooperative was a

large one-story affair, almost unheated and very dirty. As
we came near we saw that it was jammed full of workers and
that there was a line outside the door.

'Funny,' said Popov, 'they must be giving out something
special.'

We approached and asked the well-worn Russian question:
'Chto daioot?' ('What are they giving?')

'Only bread,' answered a worker who was standing in line.
'There wasn't any this morning. It just came in half an hour
ago.'

We got in line. The line moved forward slowly. It was ten
minutes before we got inside the door and twenty more by the
time we arrived at the counter. The shelves behind the counter
were absolutely bare save for four boxes of artificial coffee and a
display of perfume. The only thing being sold was black bread.
A sales-girl was cutting steaming fresh loaves with a cleaver.
She seldom had to put a piece on the scales twice. A store clerk
with a dirty white apron over his sheepskin was tearing off the
numbers on the workers' bread cards as they handed them to
him. A second girl took in the money, thirty-five kopeks per
kilogram (about fifteen kopeks a pound). Just when Popov
reached the counter, a tall fellow with Mongolian features
shouldered up and tried to get his bread out of line. There was a
storm of protest.

'If you're a foreman, go to the foremen's store! If you are attached to this store, then get in line!' said forty people at once.
The big Mongolian protested and expostulated phrases in
broken Russian about the rights of national minorities. He did
not get his bread out of line, however. Too many workers of the
minor nationalities had been trying to get things for nothing, or
out of line, or to obtain other privileges on the basis of the
Leninist national policy. It no longer worked.

Popov took out a ragged pocketbook and hunted for change

to pay for the bread. The pocketbook was full of money. He
had over two hundred roubles.[1] He had received his last month's
pay the week before, only ten days late, and there was nothing
to buy. He got bread for himself and for Grisha, who had gone
to the milk station, and Grisha's wife, and then shouldered his
way out of the store. He had five kilograms (twelve pounds) of
bread under his arm. This was two days' rations for two workers and one dependent. I got my bread and we walked across
the road to a drygoods store to try to buy a pair of woolen
inner-gloves Popov needed badly. The store was empty, however, and we saw through the window the little pile of silk
handkerchiefs and summer shirts which, for several days, had
been the only things on sale.

'Lousy business,' he said; 'in summer they have sheepskins,
in winter nothing but silk handkerchiefs. I guess I'll have to go
to the bazaar tomorrow for gloves and a pair of pants.'

VIII

W<small>E WALKED</small> on
up the hill for ten minutes between two rows of whitewashed
one-story barracks. The last on the right was home. It was a
low wooden structure whose double walls were lined with straw.
The tarpaper roof leaked in spring. There were thirty rooms in
the barrack. The inhabitants of each had made a little brick or
iron stove so that as long as there was wood or coal the rooms
could be kept warm. The low corridor was illuminated by one

---

[1] Nominally nearly one hundred dollars; equivalent in buying power, about ten
dollars.

small electric light bulb. Popov stumbled along in his felt boots
till he reached room 17, pushed the door open and went in. His
roommate, Grisha, who worked on the iron mine, was just
making a fire.

'Hello,' he said, without looking up.

'Cold,' answered Popov, putting his bread on the table and
unbuttoning his coat. The room was about six feet by ten and
had one small window, which was pasted around with newspaper
to keep the cold out. There was a small table, a little brick
stove, and one three-legged stool. The two iron bedsteads were
rickety and narrow. There were no springs, just thin planks
put across the iron frame. Popov hung up his coat and came up
to the stove to warm his hands.

Our room was considerably larger than Popov's, because
Kolya was a foreman and I was a foreigner. We had a table, two
stools as well as two beds, and a small closet. I lit a fire and
peeled some potatoes.

There were eighty men, women, and children living in our
barrack. The oldest man was thirty-four. Everybody worked
for the construction trust, which owned the barrack. Until 1934
we paid no rent. After that it cost us about ten roubles a month
each.

There had been a kitchen, but now a family was living in it
so that everybody did his cooking on his own stove. One of the
rooms was the Red Corner. Here hung the barrack wall newspaper, two udarnik banners, pictures of Lenin, Stalin, and
Voroshilov. Here, also, was a two-hundred-book library. Twice
a week classes for the illiterates were held in the Red Corner.
A few months before there had been seventeen illiterate adults
in the barrack, now there were ten. To be sure, one was considered literate if one could sign one's name and read a simple sentence in any language.

Most of the young workers in Barrack No. 17 were unmarried. This was due, in the first place, to a general shortage of women in Magnitogorsk, as in any large construction camp. In the second place, it was a reflection of hard living conditions. After doing two shifts of heavy physical work at low temperatures on a bad diet, little energy was left for making love, particularly if it had to be done out-of-doors or in overcrowded rooms.

IX

A<small>T</small> ABOUT six o'clock a dozen or so young workers, men and women, gathered in the Red Corner with a couple of balalaikas and a guitar. Work was finished for the day, supper was on the stove, it was time for a song. And they sang! Workers' revolutionary songs, folk tunes, and the old Russian romantic lyrics. A Tartar worker sang a couple of his native songs. A young Ukrainian danced. The balalaikas were played very skillfully. I never ceased wondering at the high percentage of Russian workers who could play the balalaika. They learned during the long winter evenings in their village mud huts.

Then a discussion sprang up. 'Why don't we get more sugar? We've received only two hundred grams' (half pound) 'per person this month. Tea without sugar doesn't get you anywhere.' Almost everybody had something to say. One young fellow explained that the sugar crop was bad this year. The sugar industry fulfilled its plan only fifty-some per cent. Somebody else pointed out that the Soviet Union exported a great deal of candy, which meant sugar.

'We still have to export a lot to get the money to buy rolling mills and other such things that we can't make ourselves yet.'

Some of the women remained unconvinced. There had always been sugar except during the war. There was no war now. There ought to be sugar. The older women particularly had not yet become accustomed to having money which could not buy what they wanted. Previously money had always been a measure of their material situation. A good payroll meant the best of everything. This had been true all through the late twenties, particularly in the industrial districts of the Ukraine where workers with jobs usually ate well. Now, however, the meaning of money had changed. The size of the pay envelope, the number of bank notes under the mattress, no longer determined living standards. Everybody had money, but what one ate or wore depended almost exclusively on what there was to buy in the particular store to which one was attached. If one were a foreign specialist or a party of GPU top flight functionary attached to the exclusive foreigners' store, one had caviar, Caucasian wine, imported materials, and a fair selection of shoes, suits, etc. Engineers, foremen, people like Syemichkin and Kolya, had cards for a technicians' store where they could buy bread and occasionally meat, butter, fish, and some dry-goods. The majority of the people, however, like Popov, were attached to workers' stores where bread was the only thing one was reasonably sure of getting with any regularity. Occasionally there was no bread for several days; but most of the workers, schooled in famine, had a small supply of hoarded crusts which tided them over temporary shortages.

I had a card in the workers' store and would have got along as best I could with that had it not been for Kolya, who insisted that I go get a book for 'Insnab,' the famous and fabulous foreigners' store. Kolya arranged it, though according to the letter of the law I was not entitled to it, as I had not come to the

Soviet Union under contract with Amtorg, but on my own hook. My main difficulty was in getting to Insnab to buy things. I usually arrived late and found the store closed. Still, what with my Insnab book and Kolya's many dining-room cards and technicians' store cards, we managed to eat fairly well, certainly better than most of the people in our barrack, and incomparably better than most of the workers in the sprawling city of Magnitogorsk.

Food conditions were the subject of constant discussion at spontaneous little meetings in the Red Corner at the barrack before or after dinner. There was nearly always someone to explain the official position and the majority was usually satisfied.

'Just wait five or ten years and we won't need one single thing from the capitalist world,' said Anya, a young woman welder. 'Then we won't have to export food. We'll eat it all ourselves.'

'In five or ten years there won't be any capitalist world,' said a young rigger, waving his hand. 'What do you think the workers in the capitalist world are doing? Do you think they are going to starve through another ten years of crisis, even supposing there is no war during that time? They won't stand it.'

'Of course they won't. They'll revolt,' said another. 'And we'll help them when the time comes.'

Then a more prosaic subject was discussed. Belyakov, the administrator of supplies in the Blast Furnace Construction Trust, was a bureaucrat. Everybody had a bad word for him. It was one thing to freeze your hand on the job or to do without sugar; such inconveniences were caused by distant and objective considerations like the climate and the general policy of the Soviet government, about equally removed from the will of the individual workers. But to have to put up with a bureaucrat like Belyakov, who seemed to take delight in acting like a gendarme or a mediaeval landlord, that was too much.

X

I⊤ was nearly seven o'clock when Kolya got home and stuck his nose into the Red Corner. 'Jack, we must go if we're going to be on time.' We went into our room to get our books. Kolya had already eaten supper at the technicians' dining-room down at the mill for which he had three cards.

'I stopped in at the hospital to see Vaska,' said Kolya as he changed his grimy work valinkis for another pair. 'He looks pretty low. The doctor told me he would probably die this week.'

Vaska was a welder who lived in our barrack and worked in our gang. He had fallen and crushed his chest two weeks before and had been lying between life and death in the hospital since. I had been to see him twice, but it was not a pleasant place, and I tried to postpone my next visit as long as possible. It was cold and dirty. The nurses were besheepskinned village girls who had become completely indifferent to the pain and suffering they saw around them in the surgical ward: men burned with pig iron, who invariably screamed for three days before dying, men rolled like flies in or under cranes or other heavy equipment; they were all just nuisances. Vaska was treated fairly well because his crushed chest permitted of no screaming and because he was a nice fellow, but some of the other patients were not so lucky.

'I haven't been to see him for four days,' I said.

We took our books, wrapped in newspaper, and started off for school.

Many people were leaving the barrack; some were going to

the cinema, some to the club, but the packages of books wrapped in newspaper under the arms of most of them told of their destinations. They were going to school. Twenty-four men and women in the barrack were students in some organized school.

I attended the Komvuz. The course took three years and included Russian, arithmetic, political economy, Leninism, history of the Communist Party of the Soviet Union, history of the revolutionary movement of the West, party structure, and dialectic materialism. Most of the graduates of this school became professional propagandists or functionaries in the local political or administrative organizations. Most of the students entered the Communist University as semi-literates. The entrance requirements were those of the fifth grade in elementary school, but actually only reading and writing were rigorously demanded. The academic level of the Komvuz was consequently low. Textbooks caused a great deal of trouble, particularly for subjects like dialectic materialism, where the only book in print was that of Bukharin, which had been declared 'opportunist' and banned for use in schools. To give students with a very limited general education 'Anti-Duehrung,' 'The Dialectics of Nature,' or 'Materialism and Empiro-Criticism' to read was only to invite blatant superficiality. The teachers were, therefore, in a difficult position. The dialectic materialism teacher in the Communist University was changed four times in the academic year 1933–34. In each case 'deviations' caused removal, and in two cases, arrest. 'Deviation hunting' was one of the main tasks of the director of the school. And if his efforts in this direction produced no results, he was liable to get into trouble himself for 'complacency' or 'harboring enemies.'

I entered the Komvuz when I had been in Magnitogorsk only three months in order to get some help in Russian. Then I became interested in the material of the courses. The history particularly was fascinating. Every experience in history was black or white, trends and tendencies were simplified. Every question had a perfectly definite answer. Not only that, the formulation of the answer must be thus and so. When you followed all the rules, everything made sense. It was a system built up like arithmetic. The only trouble with it was that often it did not always correspond to objective realities.

I remember one altercation about the Marxian law of the impoverishment of the toilers in capitalist countries. According to this law as interpreted to the students of the Magnitogorsk Komvuz, the working classes of Germany, Britain, and the United States, as well as those of all other capitalist countries, had become steadily and inexorably poorer since the beginning of the Industrial Revolution in the eighteenth century. I went up to the teacher after class, and told him that I happened to have been in Britain, for example, and that it seemed to me that conditions among workers there were unquestionably better than they had been during the time of Charles Dickens, or at the time when Engels wrote his treatise on the 'Conditions of the Working Classes in England.'

The teacher would have none of me. 'Look at the book, Comrade,' he said. 'It is written in the book.' It mattered nothing to this man that 'the book' would be declared counter-revolutionary next month. When it happened he would be given another book. The party made no mistakes. He was given a book by the party. That was enough.

Kolya attended the Technicum, a school with slightly higher academic standards than those of the Communist University. The entrance requirements were seven years of schooling and the applicants were weeded out by competitive examination. The curriculum included algebra, physics, chemistry, mechanics, strength of materials, mechanical drawing and designing of structural steel, reinforced concrete and wooden structures, with emphasis on those types of construction needed for Magnitogorsk. Most of the teachers were engineers working in the designing office or on the job. They came to do their teaching after a day's work and were often tired and unprepared. The strain on the students was even greater, inasmuch as they studied four nights a week, whereas the teachers usually taught less. The student body was picked without regard to party affiliation. A komsomol, a non-party worker, were admitted on the same basis as a party member. 'Class enemies' and members of their families, however, were rigorously excluded. Shabkov, whose father had been a kulak, could not enter the Technicum. This deprivation of rights of higher education to 'lishentsi' (disfranchised citizens) was enforced till 1936, when a decree from Moscow granted equal educational rights to all.

Half a dozen other schools were attended by workers from Barrack No. 17 every evening: the chauffeur's school; an 'Osoaviakhim' course, including various military subjects; special courses to train economists, planners, midwives, post-office workers, and telegraph operators. These schools were run by various trusts and organizations.

School expenses, lighting, heating, teachers' salaries, and sometimes even books and paper for the students, were met from the large fund for training technicians and skilled workers. The students paid nothing. They even got special privileges, longer vacations, time off from work during examinations.

At this time Magnitogorsk boasted very few full-time adult schools. Most of the workers, like Kolya and myself, studied in the evenings. There was too much work to be done, the pressure was too great, to release several million young workers from Soviet industry and send them to school. Within five years, however, the evening professional schools practically disappeared and were replaced by bona-fide full-time institutions, whose academic standards were much higher. Students of these institutions received allowances from the State, ranging from forty to five hundred roubles a month. This was true until 1940, when the government, faced with the necessity of raising billions for armaments, instituted tuition for all schooling over the seventh grade.

The tremendous investment made by the Soviet Union in education was necessitated by the lack of trained people in every conceivable field. The Revolution, civil war, and mass emigration of 'old' elements left Russia in the early twenties even more illiteracy and fewer trained people than she had before the war. The increasing complexity of economic, commercial, and political life in the early thirties made it absolutely essential for the government to create a Soviet intelligentsia. This was the basic reason for the tremendous effort to educate and train which found expression in Magnitogorsk in the allocation, according to the general construction budget, of almost one hundred million roubles to the training of skilled workers. This sum was conceived and listed as capital investment just as was the similar sum spent on blast-furnace equipment.

The necessity of training a Soviet intelligentsia had even more sweeping effects than the outlay of millions of roubles for education. The graduation of wages, the increased differential between the wages paid to skilled and unskilled, educated and uneducated, was largely an attempt to stimulate the desire to study. In doing this, the lethargy and traditional sluggishness of the Russian peasantry had to be overcome. The population, and in particular the peasants, had to be made to want to study. To some extent this desire was already present as a reaction to centuries of deprivation of educational opportunities and as a result of the natural curiosity of man. But additional stimulus was necessary. If pay were the same for shepherd boy and engineer, most peasants would graze their flocks and never trouble Newton and Descartes.

In 1933 wage differentials were approximately as follows: The average monthly wage of an unskilled worker in Magnitogorsk was something in the neighborhood of 100 roubles; a skilled worker's apprentice, 200; a skilled worker, 300; an engineer without experience, 400 to 500; with experience, 600 to 800; administrators, directors, etc., anywhere from 800 to 3000. This heavy differentiation, plus the absence of unemployment and the consequent assurance of being able without difficulty to get a job in any profession learned, supplemented, and stimulated the intellectual curiosity of the people. The two together were so potent that they created a student body in the Magnitogorsk night schools of 1933 willing to work eight, ten, even twelve hours on the job under severest conditions, and then come to school at night, sometimes on an empty stomach and, sitting on a backless wooden bench, in a room so cold that you could see your breath a yard ahead of you, study mathematics for four hours straight. Of course, the material was not always well learned. Preparation was insufficient, conditions were too bad. Nevertheless, Kolya, after having studied two years in the Technicum, could design a truss, calculate volumes, areas, and do many other things. Moreover, he knew from personal experience the concrete practical application of everything he had learned.

Kolya and I walked down the hill toward school. It was cold, the wind bit our cheeks, and within five minutes the moisture from our breath began to freeze on our eyebrows and eyelashes. We walked fast, as it was nearly seven o'clock.

'What do you have tonight?' I asked.

'Mechanics,' Kolya answered.

'Did you do your problems?'

Kolya swore under his breath. 'When the hell do you think I could have done them?'

We went on in silence. The Komvuz school building was a

barrack very similar to the one in which we lived, except that it was cleaner and the rooms were larger. As we approached the door, we heard Natasha, the janitress, come out of her room with her cowbell in her hand, ringing it vigorously. Just in time. Kolya went on to the Technicum. I went into my classroom. There were twenty-four students in the group. The age range was from fourteen to forty-five. The teacher was a sharp-looking little man with glasses who worked as a designer during the day.

We began with party structure. Before five minutes had passed the big riveter sitting in front of me was sound asleep with his chin on his collarbone. There had been some emergency work to do in his gang and he had had no sleep for forty-eight hours.

Popov did not go to school. He went to the miners' club which was a ten-minute walk from Barrack No. 17. There was to have been a cinema, but for some reason the film had not arrived. He spent a half-hour in the clubroom reading a story in the literary newspaper, then went to the district bathhouse for a shower. The queue was too long, however, he would have had to wait at least an hour, so he trudged home to write a letter to his brother in the Red Army in Kazakhstan.

XI

I T WAS a little after eleven when I got back to Barrack No. 17. Kolya had come in ten minutes earlier, and had started a fire. 'Hungry, Jack?' I was. We boiled a half-dozen small potatoes, and ate them with salt. They tasted very good indeed, but before Kolya had finished his last one he fell asleep squatting on his haunches in front of the little home-made iron stove.

Outside of the barrack the wind howled dismally, but in our little room it was warm. Strips of newspaper pasted around the window-panes and frames, as well as over cracks in the plaster walls, kept out the cold. The dying wood fire cast a red glow around the room.

I began to doze off when a particularly obstreperous louse bit me in the small of the back. I found the little fellow, and snapped him between my thumbnails in good Russian style. Then I woke Kolya, and we both went to bed.

PART THREE

PART THREE The Story of
Magnitogorsk

I

IN THE SPRING OF
1933 I received a bad burn in the mill. For two weeks I went
around with my arm in a sling. Nearly every day I walked to
the clinic and let the old doctor with the white beard dress my
hand. We struck up quite a friendship and I called on him frequently in the medical workers' barracks near the hospital.
He lived alone, his family being in France as nearly as I could
gather.

The doctor had been practicing medicine in the Urals since
the turn of the century. Since the very beginning he had been
a Socialist, but since 1905 had adhered to Martov's Menshevik
group. In Magnitogorsk he was under surveillance, for he was
known as an ex-Menshevik who had never found it necessary
to repudiate his position. He never discussed politics and spent
his life working in clinic and hospital, setting broken bones,
healing the sick. In his free time he worked on a monumental
opus on industrial hygiene which was only half-finished, though
he had been at it for the best part of a decade.

Long before the Revolution the doctor had worked in Ufa,
some two hundred miles west of Magnitogorsk, and had oc-

casionally come on horseback across the steppe to the old village of Magnitnaya. He told fascinating tales. With his help
I jotted down a short outline of the history of Magnitogorsk.

II

THE 'MAGNETIC
Mountain,' iron heart of Magnitogorsk, is situated on the eastern slopes of the Ural Mountains, some seventy miles east of
the watershed which separates Europe from Asia. The surrounding countryside is barren steppe — rolling hills so smooth
they remind one of a desert. The summers are hot and dusty,
and only about three months long. The winters are long, cold,
and windy. There is very little rainfall.

About five miles west of the Magnetic Mountain the Ural
River wends its way. It is, or rather was, before the dams were
built, a mere creek, except during a few days in spring. During
the summer months it almost dried up and in winter it froze
solid.

The 'mountain' itself is really two big hills, rising eight
hundred feet above the level of the river. They are smooth,
bare, and uninteresting.

Such is the geography of Magnitogorsk. Such it was centuries
ago, when Mongols and Tartars swept back and forth from
Central Europe to the Pacific, and when nomads first watered
their flocks in the headwaters of the Ural River. It was at some
time during these restless centuries that a little village grew up
on the river just a few miles below its source. The Bashkir in-

habitants engaged mostly in cattle-raising. The village was very small, and made up of crude earth huts.

The villagers noticed the two smooth hills, which lay some eight miles away from their dwellings on the same side of the river. They called them Eye-Derlui and Atach, but paid little attention to them. They were more interested in the bare valley, which was just grassy enough in some places to graze stock.

The bitter, stormy winters and the hot, dusty summers came and went. Centuries passed and there was very little change in the lives of the villagers. The rainfall was so slight and the soil so poor that not even grass grew well. Gradually, nevertheless, the villagers took an interest in agriculture. They learned to plant grain on the flat places near the river where it was not so much work to irrigate by hand. In this way their culture developed very slowly. It was reaching the agricultural stage, in the beginning of the eighteenth century, when the first Russians arrived. A military outpost was organized in Chelyabinsk, about one hundred and twenty miles to the northwest. From this center the Russians came, prospected, made maps, and tried to collect taxes. Sometimes they succeeded. Sometimes they were killed by the herdsmen. They never stayed for long.

Then one of the Russians noticed that his compass needle was strangely affected by this mountain Eye-Derlui. He called the near-by village 'Magnitnaya' or 'The Magnetic,' and went away. He returned the next spring with a party of men, with shovels and supplies. They dug into the sides of Eye-Derlui and found rich iron ore. Some of the men stayed all the summer and dug. The villagers were curious at first, then they lost interest.

In 1747 an enterprising Russian landlord and industrialist, Myasnikov, came in and began mining operations. He brought serfs with him from Central Russia. He fed them with meat bought from the Bashkir herders for a song. The serfs worked long hours and slept on the ground in summer. Myasnikov did well.

During the warm months of the year the ore was dug out of the side of the hill and left in piles. When winter came, it was transported on sleighs over the snowy steppe to Beloretsk, a distance of over seventy miles. Here it was smelted with charcoal in little 'teapot' blast furnaces which produced a few tons of iron a day.[1]

In 1753 Myasnikov and his partner Tverdishev received the whole Magnetic Mountain as a gift from Czarina Elizaveta Petrovna. It cost a great deal to line the pockets of all the people in between, but it was worth it.

A few years later the mine and the smelting plant in Beloretsk were sold, and after some shady transactions finally became the property of Vogau and Company, a metallurgical corporation, the greater part of whose stock was owned in France and Belgium. The mining activities became more business-like. As much as two hundred tons of ore was mined and transported per year. The cost of production and transportation of the ore was three to four kopeks a pood, or something under two roubles a ton.

For a century and a half the mineral riches of the Urals were 'worked' by young industrial capitalism. By 1913 the work had been rationalized and production brought up to a peak of fifty thousand tons of ore a year. (This much is now produced in two days.) Serfs were no longer used as labor. Instead the local Bashkirs and Kirghizi, as well as transient Russian workers, were employed on a wage basis.

Although the work was better organized than previously and some machinery installed, the essential processes were the same as those utilized in the eighteenth century. Transportation was furnished by horses and sleighs. Men and animals were the

---

[1] Up to forty tons.

only sources of power. There were no railroads, no electricity, no modern equipment at all. The work was carried on barbarously; ore was taken from the surface and no attempt was made to develop the mine and create more advantageous conditions for future extraction of the ore. The top soil was thrown off and dumped near-by, only to be moved again whenever the mine was enlarged.

III

THE inhabitants of the village of Magnitnaya and a very considerable part of the working force on the mine before the war were the Bashkirs and the Kirghizi. Both were Asiatic peoples whose historical and cultural inheritances came from the Turks, Mongolians, Tartars, and Russians. Their languages were similar and akin to the Turkish.

Kirghizia is fifteen hundred miles southeast of Magnitnaya. It is a wild, mountainous country with many lakes and several glaciers. Before the war there was almost no agriculture there at all. The masses of semi-nomadic Kirghizi made their living tending flocks and herds. They were subjected to the double exploitation of the local Kirghizi beys and of the Russian colonists and tax collectors. The cultural level was very low. There was no written Kirghiz language. The population was over ninety-five per cent illiterate. There were no doctors, no schools, no cultural institutions.

At the beginning of the eighteenth century an obscure but

bloody war ravaged Kirghizia, and sections of the Kirghiz herders emigrated to other parts of the country. Some went north and mingled with the Bashkirs, Tartars, and Kazakhs who inhabited the country north and northwest of Kirghizia. In this way the section of the southern Urals in which Magnitnaya was located came by its old stock of Kirghiz blood.[1]

So it was that the village of Magnitnaya was made up of Kirghiz and Bashkir herders who were just beginning to till the soil — illiterate, uncultured, wild, and with a tradition of resistance to outside influence.

They resented the iron miners when they first made their appearance on the sides of the mountains overlooking the Ural River. Later many of them went to work hauling iron ore to Beloretsk, thus becoming proletarians, wage-workers for absentee capitalism, while their cultural level was still somewhere between barbarism and civilization. They did their work, received their wages, and found they could buy vodka, cotton print material, and tobacco with the money. They acquired a taste for all these things and never returned to their flocks. They became drivers, miners, laborers, and remained such until the construction of Magnitogorsk, when many of them learned trades and became skilled workers and technicians.

These tribesmen remained very conscious of their nationality. They taught their children only Kirghiz and Bashkir, and tried hard themselves to learn only as much Russian as was necessary to work. Even today the children go to school largely in their own languages (for which the Bolsheviks made alphabets). To a great extent they retain their national dress. They remain by and large an unassimilated element in the great agglomeration of Russians, Ukrainians, Jews, Letts, Finns, Germans, and others who came in to build Magnitogorsk.

[1] See Appendix 1.

IV

THE Revolution of 1917 had no immediate effects on the miners and herders living in the neighborhood of Magnitnaya. They went about their business as usual, though it was harder to buy things and transportation went to pieces.

Then came the civil war. The Russian miners came with rifles on their shoulders and strange talk about the Soviet power, expropriation of capitalists, and seizure of the land by the peasants.

Some of the younger villagers went off and joined the Red guerrillas. A few joined Admiral Kolchak's White Army which invaded the Urals from Siberia. Not much action occurred in the neighborhood of Magnitnaya, however. Both sides preferred fighting where there was wood to burn and more to eat.

Finally Kolchak, reinforced by Czechs, Japanese, and others, advanced, taking the region as far east as the Volga, and incorporating it into his Siberian empire. The villagers found themselves set upon with unprecedented restrictions and deprivations. Their property was confiscated, their men were taken into the White Army, and their herds eaten by the soldiers of many nationalities trying to destroy the Bolsheviks and reestablish a feudal-capitalist system in Russia.

Fighting went on with equal violence on both sides of the Kolchak lines. Iron-ore production stopped completely. The population was even more impoverished than it had been before. No one knew what historical issues were at stake. They all knew that Kolchak represented the landlords and capitalists while the Red Army gave the land to the peasants and the mines and factories to the workers, that the Red Army drove the hateful tax collectors and epauletted White officers away or shot them.

After three years of civil war, Kolchak and his army were driven out of the Urals and back to the Pacific Ocean. The village of Magnitnaya did not know until afterward of his final defeat. They knew only that they were free of him. They collected their diminished and scattered herds, rebuilt their houses, and tried to reestablish their lives on some basis which would ensure them a living. It was, however, very difficult. The industrial machinery of the country was paralyzed. The transportation system was in a state of complete collapse. There were no reserves of materials or supplies. Seven years of war, revolution, famine, and civil war had reduced the country to the condition of a man beaten to within an inch of his life.

In 1924 the general industrial production of Russia was between ten and fifteen per cent of the level of 1913. For the next four years the country struggled back to its feet with the help of the New Economic Policy. Foreign concessions and the partial development of private enterprise in industry and commerce facilitated this recovery.

During this period, while old capitalist forms were successfully utilized to strengthen Soviet economy, a bitter struggle was in progress between various factions among the leading groups of the Soviet Union. Stalin emerged victorious, annihilated his enemies, and proceeded to force the realization of those measures which he considered necessary.

Stalin's program was essentially nationalistic. It was dedicated to the proposition that Socialism could and would be constructed in one country, in the Soviet Union. Whereas Lenin had counted on revolutions in Central Europe to aid backward Russia on its difficult road to Socialism, Stalin counted on the ability of the Soviet Union to equip and defend itself.

In order to construct Socialism and defend it against the attacks which Stalin felt sure were coming, it was necessary to build Russian heavy industry, to collectivize and mechanize agriculture. These monumental tasks were undertaken in the late twenties. The first Five Year Plan provided for the reconstruction of the national economy and the creation of whole new industries, new industrial bases. One of its most important projects was the creation of a heavy industry base in the Urals and Siberia out of reach of any invader, and capable of supplying the country with arms and machines in immense quantities.

This project had several very outstanding advantages. In the first place, the iron deposit of Magnitogorsk had been known for years as one of the richest in the world. The ore was right on the surface and tested up to sixty per cent iron. The coal deposits in the Kuzbas in Central Siberia were almost unique. In some places the coal lay in strata three hundred feet thick. By connecting these two great untouched sources of raw material into one immense metallurgical combine, the country would be ensured of an iron and steel base, not inferior to that of the United States, to supply the growing needs of the country for decades to come. In the second place, both Magnitogorsk and Kuznetsk were in the center of the country, some two thousand miles from any frontier, so that new interventionists, which, Stalin felt, were bound to come sooner or later, would be unable to reach them, even with their best airplanes.

So great were the expenses and so enormous the technical difficulties that no one in the pre-revolutionary days had ever undertaken to project a Ural–Kuznetsk metallurgical base. The capital investment necessary was much more than any firm, or even the Czarist government itself, could afford. 'Too large and difficult for the capitalists, the task was left to the workers,' as the doctor said.

It was necessary to start from scratch. There were no supply bases, no railroads, no other mills in or near Magnitogorsk or Kuznetsk. But Stalin and his Political Bureau decided that the job must be done, and so in 1928 the first serious attempt was made to project the Ural-Kuznetsk Combine and a powerful, modern metallurgical plant in Magnitogorsk.

Stalin was probably one of the few men in the Soviet Union who realized how catastrophically expensive it was going to be. But he was convinced that it was just a matter of time until the Soviet Union would again be invaded by hostile capitalist powers seeking to dismember and destroy the first Socialist State. Stalin considered it his sacred obligation to see to it that when the time came the attackers would not be able to accomplish this. The fulfillment of this task justified all means.

As the doctor told me, there had been many discussions among scientists and economists about the desirability of going headlong into the construction of the Ural-Kuznetsk Combinat with its galaxy of machine-building and armament plants. Initial costs stood twice as high as those in similar units built in the Ukrainian or Donbass industrial regions already equipped with railroads and power lines, and near bases of industrial and agricultural supplies. The regions around Magnitogorsk and Kuznetsk were as yet little known, geological surveys had been superficial. Would it not be better to build in the Ukraine, and wait with the Ural-Kuznetsk Combine until more thorough surveys had been made?

At many times during the late twenties and the early thirties such objections were raised. The tempo of construction was such that millions of men and women starved, froze, and were brutalized by inhuman labor and incredible living conditions. Many individuals questioned whether or not it was worth it.

Stalin suppressed such ideas with his usual vigor. The Ukraine had been invaded by the Germans in 1918. It might be invaded again. The Soviet Union must have an uninvadable heavy industry base, and must have it immediately, said the Georgian Bolshevik. His word was law.

In January, 1931, Stalin made an historic speech to a conference of business managers. In his inimitable, simple vernacular Stalin insisted on the necessity of increasing the tempo of industrialization. He warned the Russian people that they must make their country as strong as the surrounding capitalist states within ten years or Russia would be invaded and annihilated.[1]

Stalin's indomitable will and his ruthless tenacity were responsible for the construction of Magnitogorsk and the entire Ural and Western Siberial industrial areas. Without Stalin the job would not have been done.

V

As the Arctic winter broke suddenly into spring, Magnitogorsk changed beyond recognition. In early April it was still bitter cold; we had had hardly a single thaw; everything was still frozen solid. By May 1 the ground had thawed and the city was swimming in mud. Leaving our barrack we had literally to wade. Garbage heaps and outdoor latrines near the barracks thawed and the winter's accumulation had to be removed immediately to avoid contamination. Welding became next to impossible, as our ragged cables short-circuited at every step.

[1] See Appendix 2.

At about this time I noticed that my friend the doctor was unusually busy. He told me later what it was all about. Bubonic plague had broken out in three places not far from Magnitogorsk. The three villages had been surrounded by troops and isolated. Fifty years before every living thing in these villages would have been exterminated, the doctor told me. Czarist Russia dealt very summarily with bubonic plague, the troops burned the infected areas and everything in them. Now there was no killing, but the entire medical staff of Magnitogorsk was mobilized to prepare for a possible outbreak in the city. The resistance of the population was very low because of undernourishment during the winter and consistent overwork. Sanitary conditions, particularly during the thaw, were appalling.

The doctors had divided the city into eight areas and made arrangements for their complete mutual isolation. Much work was done, but the doctor told me that had the epidemic reached Magnitogorsk he believed it could never have been isolated within any one area of the city.

Within two weeks the sun had dried the earth and summer was upon us. By the middle of May the heat was intolerable. In the barracks we were consumed by bedbugs and other vermin, and at work we had trouble keeping to the job. Accustomed as we were to resisting cold, we were knocked out by the heat.

Actually the summer in Magnitogorsk is comparable with that of Washington, D.C., except that Magnitogorsk is dryer. For three months it did not rain. The Bashkirs and Kirghizi set to work with camels to do the excavating and hauling done by horses during the other seasons. The steppe dried up like a desert.

In the middle of June we passed our examinations in the Komvuz, which then closed until September, and I was delighted to find I had a good deal of free time on my hands. I took to visiting my friend André, a Ukrainian-American who had been sent to Magnitogorsk by the McKee Company, in the technical archives in the cellar of the Combinat administration building. It was the coolest place in Magnitogorsk. André was never too busy to stop for a cigarette and talk of this and that.

I became interested in the archives. An immense cellar had been divided into several rooms equipped with neat racks. Here more than one hundred thousand blueprints were filed. Engineers and technicians from all over the plant came to the archives every day to look up technical points, and André's staff of eight or ten was kept busy printing and filing flimsies and blueprints of each new aggregate as the project was received from Moscow or Leningrad or released by the project department of the Combinat. I spent two or three evenings going over the original projects for Magnitogorsk and became engrossed. I had Kolya put me on an evening shift, and for nearly a month I spent every afternoon in the archives or in the technical library in the same building ferreting out interesting facts about Magnitogorsk.

VI

$$T_{HE} \text{ first serious}$$

project for the Magnitogorsk Metallurgical Combinat was made in 1928 by the Gipromez, a Leningrad projecting organization for metallurgical plants.[1] This project envisaged a plant which,

[1] See Appendix 3.

although a big one for Russia, would have been far smaller
than the newer industrial enterprises of the United States both
in size and in technical efficiency. It would have been only
twenty per cent as large as the steel plant in Gary, Indiana.

Just a year later the party and the All-Union Council of
People's Economy passed resolutions to increase the capacity
of the future Magnitogorsk plant from 656,000 to 2,500,000
tons of pig iron per year. This decision was reached after a discussion of modern technical developments in the United States
and the necessity of fully utilizing these achievements in the
Soviet Union.[1]

Carrying out this general directive the representatives of
the Soviet Union signed a 2,500,000 gold dollar contract with
the McKee Company of Cleveland, Ohio, for the projecting of
the plant and for technical supervision of its construction.
It was necessary to give this contract to a foreign contractor
because of the obvious incapacity of any Soviet organization
then in existence to do the work.

At about this same time, thorough geological and topographi-
cal surveys of Magnitogorsk and the surrounding countryside
disclosed a richness of raw material far surpassing the hopes of
the most optimistic. The Magnitogorsk iron deposit was found
to contain 228,000,000 tons of ore, a great deal of which was
fifty-six per cent and more iron.[2]

While the iron ore obviously was the most important prerequisite for the metallurgical plant, other necessary materials were found: large deposits of fire clay, limestone, chalk-
stone, dolomite, magnetite, building sand, manganese ore,
and building stone. The Ural River flowing past the ore deposits at a distance of only five miles provided a water supply
which, though seasonally inadequate, could be made to suffice
by the construction of two artificial lakes. The deposits of

[1] See Appendix 4.   [2] See Appendix 5.

fire clay were sufficient qualitatively and quantitatively to permit of local manufacture of all the fire bricks necessary. The manganese deposits showed possibilities of producing more than enough ore to supply the Magnitogorsk open-hearth department.

In 1932 disagreements arose between the McKee Company of Cleveland and the Soviet engineers and administrators. The original contract was broken, the projecting of the rolling mill was given to the German firms 'Demag' and 'Klein,' while the detailed projecting of the coke plant went to the American firm Koppers and Company. The blast furnace and mining departments were left to McKee, while all the rest — open hearth, auxiliary shops, transport, water supply, etc. — were given to various Soviet projecting organizations.

To skip ahead of the story, by 1934 (when the whole plant as projected in 1928 should have been completed) a more or less finished project containing elements of a dozen different origins, often very badly coordinated, was finally achieved. This project stands more or less to this day, though the plant itself will probably never be completed according to its provisions.

According to this 1934 project Magnitogorsk was to comprise a 7.5 million ton iron mine, eight blast furnaces, eight batteries of coke ovens, thirty-six open-hearth ovens, and sixteen rolling mills.[1] Construction costs were to exceed 2.5 billion roubles.[2]

According to this project the finished Magnitogorsk should be the biggest continuous mine-to-rolling-mill metallurgical combinat in the world. In line with the decision of the Seventeenth Congress of the Communist Party of the Soviet Union in 1934, the plant should have been completed by the end of the second Five Year Plan — that is, December, 1937; and in addition a model Socialist city for two hundred thousand inhabit-

---

[1] See Appendix 6. [2] See Appendix 7.

ants costing in the neighborhood of a billion roubles was to
have been well under way.

These grandiose plans were fulfilled by only about forty-
five per cent. Four blast furnaces, twelve open hearths, a
dozen rolling mills, and a corresponding proportion of the
other aggregates on the list were constructed and in operation
by 1938, after which construction virtually stopped.[1]

VII

T HE history of the
actual construction of Magnitogorsk was fascinating. Within
several years, half a billion cubic feet of excavation work was
done, forty-two million cubic feet of reinforced concrete poured,
five million cubic feet of fire bricks laid, a quarter of a million
tons of structural steel erected.

This was done without sufficient labor, without necessary
quantities of the most elementary supplies and materials.
Brigades of young enthusiasts from every corner of the Soviet
Union arrived in the summer of 1930 and did the groundwork
of railroad and dam construction necessary before work could
be begun on the plant itself. Later, groups of local peasants and
herdsmen came to Magnitogorsk because of bad conditions in
the villages, due to collectivization. Many of these peasants
were completely unfamiliar with industrial tools and processes.
They had to start at the very beginning and learn how to work
in groups. Nevertheless they learned so well that the first dam
across the Ural River was finished the sixth of April, 1931, and

[1] See Appendix 8.

the lake began to fill up. Within two years it was five miles long and assured an adequate water supply to the city and plant for the first half of the construction work.

The first quarter of 1931 saw the ground broken for excavation and foundation work for the basic departments of the plant, while the iron mine went into production. A colony of several hundred foreign engineers and specialists, some of whom made as high as one hundred dollars a day and expenses, arrived to advise and direct the work. Money was spent by the millions (170,000,000 roubles in 1931).

Despite difficulties the work went on much faster than the most optimistic foreigners anticipated, although much more slowly than the chimeric plans of the Soviet government demanded. By the end of 1931 the first battery of coke ovens and Blast Furnace No. 1 were ready to be put into operation. The first of February, 1932, saw the first melting of Magnitogorsk pig iron.

The plan fulfillment for the first quarter of 1932 was 44.9 per cent. The city construction plan fulfillment was practically zero. Nearly all the workers were living in tents or temporary barracks. The government decision to finish the Magnitogorsk plant by the end of 1932 was still nominally in force, though actually anybody could see that it was a pure daydream. Various Moscow organizations criticized each other for sabotaging the construction of Magnitogorsk, and those directly responsible for the work both in Moscow and Magnitogorsk were removed. The administration was changed three times during the year. Each change meant the breaking-in of a new set of responsible executives, and usually the training of a whole galaxy of inexperienced functionaries. At the same time conditions in the country had become very difficult. There were prolonged and severe food shortages. Malnutrition reduced productivity of labor. Economic difficulties caused reductions of gold allocations for purchasing equipment abroad and often currency shortages and consequent salary delays in Magnitogorsk itself.

It became obvious to many of those on the job that it was absolutely impossible to carry out the resolutions of the Moscow organizations with regard to dates of completion of the various aggregates. However, the expression of such opinions was 'right opportunism' in the political lingo of the country; for members of the Communist Party it was sufficient grounds for expulsion and removal. The resulting dishonesty and hypocrisy, which characterized the methods of local political and administrative leadership, could not but have telling effects on the progress of the work itself and on everybody concerned with it.

During 1932 piece work was established in almost every type of work. Likewise, the financial accountability of individual administrative units was enforced. These measures were calculated to reduce costs, which everywhere were grotesquely high, and to increase the productivity of labor.

The results were not always those intended. Often foremen would write out the day's wages arbitrarily, rather than go to the trouble of measuring the work of each individual in his gang. Such measurements, when made, were frequently inaccurate, and while nominally on piece work, the worker's wages did not actually reflect the results of his labor. Often foremen desiring to increase their workers' pay grossly exaggerated the product of their work. Cases were known where wages were paid for tens of thousands of cubic meters of hand excavation work which was never actually done at all.

However, by and large, productivity rose gradually in every department. For example, the time required to lay the bricks of the open hearths decreased as follows (the number of bricklayers working was constant): Hearth No. 1 (June, 1933),

30 days; No. 2 (August, 1933), 28 days; No. 3 (October, 1933), 16 days; No. 4 (November, 1933), 14 days. Bricklayers were learning fast.

From the very beginning consistent attempts were made to mechanize various construction operations. Often, however, expensive imported equipment was not used with anything like the efficiency possible. Figures compiled by Soviet engineers in Magnitogorsk showed that their excavators did only thirty and forty per cent as much work as machines of the same size and type did in the United States.[1]

One of the most serious problems with which the administration of Magnitogorsk had to contend during the early thirties was shortage of labor. From 1928 till 1932 nearly a quarter of a million people came to Magnitogorsk. About three quarters of these new arrivals came of their own free will seeking work, bread cards, better conditions. The rest came under compulsion.[2]

There was a constant shortage of skilled labor. This was due largely to the bad work of the organization whose task it was to train skilled workers, and to the fact that industrialization in other parts of the country precluded large scale recruiting of skilled labor from other industrial centers. The following table gives an indication of the labor supply in the beginning of 1933:

	Demand	Supply	Per cent
Bricklayers	959	559	58
Riggers	1456	815	56
Firebrick layers	416	230	55
Carpenters	3111	2600	83
Ditchdiggers	3622	2200	61
Laborers (unskilled)	5013	9700	194

Obviously many of the laborers had to do the work of skilled workers. The result was that inexperienced riggers fell and untrained bricklayers laid walls which did not stand.

[1] See Appendix 9. [2] See Appendix 10.

The labor shortage was aggravated by extensive loss of labor time incurred in large measure by 'absenteeism,' an old Russian custom of just not coming to work, either on the morning after a drinking bout or simply because one did not feel like it. This practice was bitterly fought, but never completely liquidated. Another cause of loss of working time was bad organization of labor. Two brigades would be assigned to do a job where only one could work. A brigade would be sent to pour concrete foundations before the excavation work was finished. Workers would be sent to a job for which there were no materials or for which essential tools or blueprints were not available.[1]

Socialist competition between individuals, brigades, and whole departments was encouraged and was unquestionably instrumental in raising production and efficiency. It was a partially adequate substitute for the motives of capitalist competition operating in the rest of the world. Wages were paid twice a month, but delays were frequent due to currency shortage. Average daily wages for construction workers rose gradually from three roubles daily in 1929 to 5.50 in 1935. It must be borne in mind that whereas the nominal value of the rouble was about fifty American cents until 1935, an actual steady inflation beginning in the late twenties found expression in the 1935 edict devaluating the rouble to two-fifths its previous value. Thus it is impossible to say that real wages rose from 1929 to 1935 among Magnitogorsk workers. Rising prices more than neutralized the increase in money wages.

Low real wages and bad conditions led to a high labor turnover, a knotty problem. In one of his first speeches in Magnitogorsk, Lominadze pointed out that one locomotive working on the mine had had thirty-four engineers in one year. The workers let themselves be recruited and sent to Magnitogorsk, then, seeing conditions were bad, left and went elsewhere where they

[1] See Appendix 11.

were reputed to be better. The only solution to this problem, whose detrimental effects on an intricate and highly specialized industrial establishment were obvious, was the improvement of living conditions. This was pointed out by Heavy Industry Commissar Ordjonikidze on his visit to Magnitogorsk in 1933, and both Lominadze and Zavenyagin worked incessantly at it.

During 1932 and 1933 there was a natural tendency on the part of administrators and foremen simply to refuse to let their workers go. For some time, during 1933, it was almost impossible for a worker to get released from his job, though legally he had a right to leave whenever he wanted to, after fifteen days' notice. The trade unions were afraid to help the workers. They feared being branded by the administration and the party for 'failing to fight high turnover of labor,' and spent their time instead persuading the workers to stay. These abuses were more or less stopped by 1936, but began again in 1938 and were legalized in 1940 by a government decree depriving Soviet workers of the right to leave their jobs without permission.

Another disease which created much havoc, particularly in 1932, was the rising number of office workers. Every industrial organization acquired a budget department, a planning division, an economic department, a technical bureau, a large supply department, and a tremendous bookkeeping staff. This inflation of personnel was caused by bad organization and by the lack of competent office workers which necessitated putting ten semi-literate 'office rats' in a place which should have been occupied by one accountant. An even more important factor was the universal introduction of piece work in 1932. Complicated work such as toolmaking, which in the most efficient capitalist shops is paid on a time basis, was made the subject of piece-work experiments. The result was very often that there were as many bookkeepers as toolmakers. This situation meant increased difficulties in satisfying labor demands because so many skilled workers and engineers were engaged in non-productive office work.

VIII

ONE of the most difficult problems in Magnitogorsk was the obtaining of supplies. The city was far away from the nearest industrial center. It was connected with Chelyabinsk and with the rest of the Soviet Union by a single-track railroad. Furthermore, during the years of the first and second Five-Year Plans there was tremendous shortage in the Soviet Union as a whole of every variety of industrial construction material as well as of many food products.

In 1932–33, the last of the imported firebricks, small tools, motors, cement mixers, electrodes, wire, and a hundred other items was exhausted. The Russian workers became dependent on Soviet industry or on their own shops to produce everything that they needed save the most complicated and delicate machinery, such as pyrometers and rolling-mill motors which continued to be imported for several years. The workers of Magnitogorsk were faced with the necessity of supplying themselves with hammers, chisels, saws, bits, small castings, and other small tools which could be made in makeshift shops. Many materials, such as copper wire for rewinding motors, were simply not to be had. The workers swore at the foreman, the foreman complained to the superintendent, the supply department telegraphed to Moscow. There was no copper wire.

Supplying the job with lumber was the knottiest of problems.

In winter lumber disappeared by the ton into workers' homes to be used as fuel. There was nothing to build scaffolds with. An incoming carload of lumber became the subject of telegrams to Ordjonikidze and sometimes even to Stalin to decide which of the many competing organizations was to get the precious material.[1]

Organizational shortcomings often aggravated supply difficulties. Many materials arrived which were totally unnecessary or were not needed for years to come. Material and equipment of this kind figured on the books as 'supply plan fulfilled,' whereas their actual value was a minus quantity because they had to be stored and cared for. In 1933 the value of material on hand was sixty million roubles, about 60 per cent of the total construction budget for the year.[2]

Waste and loss took a heavy toll of material and equipment. In 1935 excavation began for the foundations of the second open-hearth department. When the work started, supply organizations sent men to the site to claim equipment. I watched them squabbling over rolls of steel cable, rails, angle irons, donkey engines, electrical equipment, cement mixers, which were dug up. This equipment had been buried owing to thoughtlessness and indifference in 1931 and 1932 when excavation work was going on for the first open-hearth department. When recovered, its value was usually greatly diminished. Electric motors cannot be buried for five years without heavy depreciation.

If lack of materials held up construction work, shortage of equipment did so even more.[3] On January 1, 1934, only 21 per cent of planned equipment had been received and erected. Alongside of this picture of an unfulfilled plan of equipment deliveries, one found an interesting phenomenon in the central equipment storehouse, known as the 'nyulevoy sklad,' or

---

[1] See Appendix 12.　　　[2] See Appendix 13.　　　[3] See Appendix 14.

'zero storehouse.' This contained a collection of equipment which had never been delivered and erected, either because there was no indication as to the addressee, or because the latter could not be found, or sometimes apparently for no reason at all. In this warehouse I saw a two-ton rotor made by Siemens-Schukert. There was no indication as to the whereabouts of the motor of which it was a part. It was bought in Germany, paid for in gold, and then spent years deteriorating in the Magnitogorsk zero warehouse. Along with it I found shoe manufacturing machinery, odd bearings, spare parts for all manner of motors, lathes, electrical equipment, milling machines, automobile parts, and a whole pile of castings, forgings, and machine parts at whose nature and purpose one could only guess.

Foodstuffs, indirectly very important for the construction job, were as hard to get as industrial materials and supplies. Every industrial organization was responsible for feeding its workers. It gave out food cards and then tried to supply the items indicated thereon. This, however, it often failed to do. In 1932 a rigger's food card entitled him to (per month):

Bread.................. 30 kilograms
Meat................... 3 kilograms
Sugar.................. 1 kilogram
Milk................... 15 liters
Butter................. ½ kilogram
Cereal grain........... 2 kilograms
Potatoes............... In proportion to supply

During the entire winter of 1932–33, however, the riggers got no meat, no butter, and almost no sugar or milk. They received only bread and a little cereal grain. In the store to which they were attached they could buy, without the use of their cards, perfume, tobacco, 'coffee' (surrogate), and on occasion, when there was any, soap, salt, tea, candy. These latter products, however, were almost never in stock; and when a shipment did come in, the workers sometimes left their jobs, spud wrenches in their hands, to fight their way to half a pound of rocklike candy.

In addition to supplies given out in the stores each industrial organization ran one or more dining-rooms where workers ate, likewise by card, once a day. The card system in the dining-rooms broke down very badly because foremen and administrators attempted to get their personnel to work better by giving them additional dining-room cards. In this way the Welding Trust in Magnitogorsk was serving two thousand dinners to eight hundred workers in 1933. However, inasmuch as the central supply office knew that the Welding Trust had only eight hundred workers and released them food enough for only eight hundred dinners the dining-room director had to dilute. So the quality of the dinners deteriorated. In the beginning of 1933 in Dining-Room No. 30 it was necessary to eat two or even three dinners to get a really adequate meal for a man working high at fifty below zero.

IX

THE financing of the construction was carried on by the Industrial Bank and the State Bank, both of which had tremendous staffs of experts who often stepped on the toes of the financial departments of the construction administration. Often the banks did not receive as much money as they were supposed to, owing to currency hoarding and to the fact that the Magnitogorsk production plan was not fulfilled and the planned amount of iron and steel

produce was not shipped out, which meant a deficit in Magnitogorsk's account in the Moscow State Bank. Consequently
there was often insufficient currency on hand to meet the payroll, let alone pay for city construction and a hundred other
details the plan provided. Furthermore, construction organizations consistently overspent their budgets.[1]

At the mill, on the job, in the city, I was surrounded by
sweat and blood going into the construction of Magnitogorsk.
In André's archives I found these things crushed into statistical
generalizations. Whenever I got irritated with something —
a two weeks' delay in getting paid, for example — I went to the
archives and found solace in the information that Magnitogorsk was losing millions of roubles a month and that the Bank
had been four million roubles short on its currency receipts for
the month because there was nothing to buy in Magnitogorsk
and the workers were sewing their money up in their bedclothes
or else sending it home to their villages. I found satisfaction
likewise in the knowledge that despite incredible difficulties
Magnitogorsk was already producing nearly ten per cent of the
country's output of pig iron.

X

THE supreme com-
mander of Magnitogorsk was the plant director. He functioned
through the plant administration. Abraham Pavlevich Zavenyagin was director of Magnitogorsk from 1933 till 1936. He
was born in 1901 in the family of a locomotive engineer. In

[1] See Appendix 15.

1918 he carried out responsible party work and was a member of the military revolutionary committee of his district. In 1919 he was made editor of a district newspaper in Ryazan. Until 1923 he worked as party functionary, then was sent to Moscow to study in the Mining Institute. He spent seven years in this institution as student, dean, and then director. He was an excellent chemist and a good organizer. For three years Zavenyagin held various responsible posts in the mining and metallurgical industries, and in August, 1933, was made director of Magnitogorsk, where he showed himself a capable executive. The Seventeenth Party Congress[1] elected him candidate to the Central Committee, and in 1936, after three years of rather successful work in Magnitogorsk, he was appointed assistant to the People's Commissar of Heavy Industry.

In 1933 Zavenyagin was virtual dictator of Magnitogorsk. He controlled supplies, all plant administration, city construction and maintenance, public services, school construction, health service, and transport. Many of these functions the plant administration had usurped from other organizations (the Commissariat of Health, the City Soviet, the Commissariat of Education, etc.). This abnormal condition was the result of the fact that the plant administration had the money and the personnel at least to attempt to build the necessary schools, hospitals, streetcar lines, etc., while the City Soviet, for instance, was chronically bankrupt and incompetently directed.

[1] February, 1934.

XI

O<small>NE</small> afternoon I was sent to the large Trade Union Hall to hear a speech by Lominadze, the secretary of the party. I was one of several foreigners picked out because of knowledge of the Russian language to attend and then to tell the others what the party chief had said.

Lominadze's speech was the usual pep talk, sprinkled with interesting examples of shortcomings. But afterward I had a chance to meet the man and established an acquaintance which lasted until his death nearly two years later.

Lominadze, former head of the Young Communist International, was an enormous Georgian, whose huge body was covered with rolls of fat. He was very shortsighted and squinted continually. His biography was an interesting one. He had done underground Communist work in Germany, had helped to organize political strikes in Canton in 1927, where, according to his own words, he spent the best days of his life. Returned to Moscow after the fall of the Canton Commune he became leader of the YCI (Young Communist International), which position he held until 1930. At this time he developed deviations. He and Sergei Sertsov were the leaders of the 'right-left bloc,' the last opposition group which made any attempt at open activities inside the Central Committee of the Party. The issues on which they disagreed with Stalin were relatively unimportant questions of policy in the villages. There were other differences, however. Lominadze, Georgian though he was, had been in many countries and was a thoroughly cultured person. He knew German literature well, was a fine critic, and something of a writer. He had absorbed too much of Western European bourgeois civilization to be able to witness the ruthlessness and cold, colorless dogmatism of Stalin's leadership without protest.

Be this as it may, the 'right-left bloc' was suppressed in 1930. Lominadze was expelled from the Central Committee, relieved of his post in the YCI, and sent 'down' to a factory committee to work. He became the party organizer of an important aviation motor plant. He worked so well that in two years he received the Order of Lenin and was sent to Magnitogorsk as head of the district party committee. At the Seventeenth Party Congress he was permitted to read a self-abasing denunciation of his deviations. In Magnitogorsk, from the first day of his arrival, Lominadze worked like a beaver. An excellent orator, he made speech after speech to functionaries, engineers, and workers; explaining, persuading, cajoling, and encouraging. He demanded the greatest sacrifices from his subordinates. These, incidentally, he tended to choose from a circle of personal friends, many of whom had, like himself, at one time or another been associated with some opposition group.

As head of the party organization, Lominadze held in his hands a multitude of threads. Every shop, office, bank, railroad station, every school and mine had its party cell. Directors and managers of industrial units were usually party members. The authority of the party among the workers was high. Thus Lominadze could make his weight felt among hundreds of thousands of people in every walk of life. The party carried on ceaseless agitation and propaganda, teaching the workers what they were working toward, and showing them how to attain it. The party was the source of initiative and energy which drove the work forward. The party sometimes blundered, and often made trouble with its unnecessary intriguing and heresy-hunting, but by and large, Magnitogorsk would not have been built as quickly or as well without it.

The Young Communist League (Komsomol), the trade unions, and the Soviet organizations worked much less effectively than the party. These organizations did not hold membership meeting for months at a time. The leaders sat in their offices, almost completely out of touch with the memberships and passed resolutions. With the exception of the Barrack Soviet, a body of five elected by all the residents to decide domestic barrack questions, the Soviet meant little to the workers of Barrack No. 17.

The social insurance laws, whose application was directly connected with the trade unions, worked well. Paid vacations, sick money, free medical attention, rest homes, were universally enjoyed and taken for granted. This service was generally appreciated, but usually attributed to the Soviet power in general, to the Bolshevik régime, rather than to the trade unions.

XII

AN ORGANIZATION whose activities were important and far-reaching was the GPU (since 1934, NKVD), the State Political Administration or Political Police. This organization was charged with the surveillance of class enemies, the protection of political leaders against personal attacks, the discovery and prosecution of 'counter-revolutionary groups,' spy rings, sabotage organizations, speculators with foreign currency, and political malcontents generally. The 'spets-otdyel' or special department found in every organization in plant and city was directly connected with the district GPU and occupied itself with the surveillance of the personnel of the organization. Until 1935 the activities of the GPU in Magnitogorsk were almost entirely limited to this silent, unobserved control. There were few arrests. But material was accumulating in dossiers useful later in the great purge which struck Magnitogorsk with tremendous force in 1937.

Some fifty thousand Magnitogorsk workers were directly under GPU supervision. About eighteen thousand de-kulakized, well-to-do farmers like Shabkov, and from twenty thousand to thirty-five thousand criminals — thieves, prostitutes, embezzlers, who performed unskilled labor usually under guard — these formed the reservoir of labor power needed to dig foundations, wheel concrete, shovel slag, and do other heavy work. The criminals, known as 'Itekovtsi,'[1] were usually isolated from the rest of the city. They went to work under armed guard, ate in special dining-rooms, and received almost no pay, their living quarters and meals being furnished free. Most of them were serving short sentences, one to five years, and often good behavior cut these in half.

One of the welders with whom I worked in 1933 afterward became a functionary of the administration of the ITK, and I had a chance to look at the 'corrective' work which was carried on among these prisoners. They had drama circles, clubs, went to cinemas, attended courses where they were taught to read and write, to add and subtract. Their main function, however, was to work. A system of Socialist competitions made it a question of supreme interest to the various brigades to keep production high, as their rations, degree of freedom, and length of sentence often depended on the amount of work they did. They worked a legal eight-hour day which, in periods of stress, was lengthened to nine or ten hours at the discretion of the plant administration.

[1] ITK: Ispravitelnaya Trudovaya Colona — Corrective Labor Camp.

I saw a curious sight one day coming home from work. A brigade of forty or fifty orthodox priests and bishops wearing dirty, ragged, black robes and their black miter-like hats. All wore their hair long; in some cases it fell to their waists. They were hard at work with pick and shovel, digging away a little hill. A pugnosed plowboy sat on a near-by knoll with an old rifle on his lap and surveyed them placidly. I asked one of them what he was there for, but he did not even answer me.

XIII

ONE or two evenings a week I had no school. On these occasions I sometimes went to 'Berezki,' the little suburb inhabited by the valuta foreigners and the highest Soviet officials and functionaries. Berezki was a little world in itself. Most of the Magnitogorsk workers had no idea who lived there or how.

Berezki, or the 'American City,' as it was sometimes called, consisted of a group of some one hundred and fifty houses situated between two hills some five miles from the plant. The houses were well made, most of them had stone walls and metal roofs; all were equipped with running water and central heating. Here lived the three hundred or four hundred German and American specialists who were paid gold, working either for the Soviet government directly or for some foreign firm whose equipment they were installing. Every attempt was made to create for these specialists conditions approaching those they were accustomed to at home. The foreigners' store, Insnab, a branch of which was situated in Berezki, was stocked with a good quantity of all the necessary food products, such as meat, butter, eggs, milk, flour, bread, fish, canned goods, confectionery, and a fair variety of rather poor quality drygoods. The prices were much lower, sometimes only one-tenth of those which the Soviet workers had to pay for similar goods in their stores. Theoretically no Soviet specialists were attached to the Insnab; actually, however, the director of the combinat and his assistants, the secretary of the City Party Committee, the chief of the GPU, and a half-dozen of the best of the prisoner specialists were on the list along with the foreigners. The number of Soviet citizens attached to this store increased steadily until 1935, when all restricted stores were liquidated and special supply arrangements for foreigners discontinued.

The lives led by the people in Berezki were varied and in most cases approached the Western European standard. The Italian specialists gave Insnab candy to local collective farm girls, searched the steppes for flowers in summer, sang, and drank the various available Caucasian wines. The Americans played poker, read the *Saturday Evening Post*, and attempted to forget in their off-hours that they were in a Siberian waste on the other side of the world from home. The Germans discussed politics over cognac, there being no good local beer, and many of them attempted to establish contact with the Russian specialists and become acquainted with the Soviet workers and their lives.

Few of these foreign specialists had their wives and children with them. All had two- and three-room apartments and in general lived very decently, though they suffered from the cold and the lack of fresh fruit and vegetables. Ragged Tartars and Bashkirs from the near-by collective farms who came to beg in Berezki were usually generously treated and went home with fabulous stories about the sumptuous lives led by the foreigners. This rather discouraged the older men of these national minorities from working in the mills which the Soviet government was trying to induce them to do. Many of them preferred to beg, though there was enough work for all of them, and the militia (the police) often made roundups in order to keep able-bodied men who did not choose to work from living in the already crowded quarters of their friends and relatives.

In 1933 the foreigners began to go home and by 1936 only half a dozen valuta specialists remained in Magnitogorsk. As they left, their rooms were occupied by young Soviet engineers and functionaries like Syemichkin and Shevchenko. The better prisoner specialists like Tishenko moved into individual houses; automobiles which had previously been at the disposal of the foreigners were likewise given to the Soviet engineers.

The relations of the prisoner specialists with the foreigners were somewhat strained. The former were afraid of being accused of having too friendly relations with foreigners. However, some intercourse did exist. The chief electrician of the whole plant, one Tikhomirov, a taciturn, white-haired man of fifty who had worked for a Belgian firm before the revolution, traveled and studied in every country of Europe, and was now serving ten years for his activities in the 'Industrial Party' in 1929, was on excellent terms with many of the foreigners. The relationship was one of mutual respect. Tikhomirov conducted himself with great dignity. As a Russian he resented any derogatory references to his country, or to its government. While far from a Communist himself he often defended Bolshevik policies with intelligence and conviction. With reference to his own past he was silent. Occasionally he would let drop a remark which helped to form a picture of the long trial, the endless interrogations, the months in prison which had followed his arrest for activities in the Industrial Party and ended in his 'administrative exile' to Magnitogorsk. Tikhomirov was respected and feared on the job. His department was the best run in the combinat. In spite of primitive conditions, lack of fuel and of skilled personnel, the power supply of the plant almost never failed and its cost was consistently below plan.

Tikhomirov was a great friend of Tishenko. The two of them had studied together in Germany and worked together before the war. Now, while frequently together, they had begun to adopt essentially different lines of conduct with regard to the Soviet power. Tishenko was sullen, unenthusiastic, indifferent. He was a broken man who could not reconcile himself to doing his best for the Bolsheviks, while he saw no sense in fighting them. When on trial in 1929, Tishenko had refused to the bitter end to sign confessions; Tikhomirov, on the other hand, admitted on rare occasions that he had signed liberally, preferring to have it over with, and either be shot or get to work doing something, anything being preferable to the endless interrogations. The breach between the two grew. It culminated eventually in Tishenko's getting a second ten years, while Tikhomirov received a state pardon and the Order of the Red Banner. In 1933, however, their positions were formally the same. They lived in four-room cottages with their families, made from two thousand to four thousand roubles a month, had automobiles, and went hunting in the Ural forests seventy miles away on holidays. They were under GPU surveillance and could not travel except by special permission.

I used to visit André in Berezki. He was a great chessplayer, and we spent many a long evening over his chessboard, eating good Insnab toast and butter and sipping Caucasian wine.

XIV

Sotsgorod, or the Socialist City, was projected in 1931 and 1932 under the technical supervision of the famous German architect, Doctor Ernst May. Owing partly to May's blunders and partly to the failure of the construction workers to do the job as projected, Sotsgorod from the very beginning was a chain of mistakes. Its situation was such that the prevailing winds carried to it all the smoke from the plant. The seventy-odd houses were monotonously uniform and resembled match boxes on edge, laid out in long rows. Moreover, construction was always behind schedule. It was 1933 before the first house was occupied. The quality of the work was very bad. The roofs leaked, as did the water pipes. Foundations sank, walls cracked. Lack of various construction materials resulted in the most absurd shortcomings. For example, in some twenty houses the bathrooms were not supplied with electric light. The city construction organization was continually harried by government plans and schedules and by a consistent shortage of materials and labor.

The fortunate individuals who moved into the Sotsgorod houses as they were finished were predominantly maintenance and production rather than construction men. Some two hundred non-valuta foreigners were among the first to occupy these houses. Most of these men were German-speaking skilled workers who had come to the Soviet Union on contract, but received Soviet currency for wages. They were sympathetic to the Soviet régime and had come motivated, at least ostensibly, by idealogical enthusiasm and the desire to give their all to help in the construction of Socialism. They were treated well, having a branch of Insnab at their disposal and fairly good living quarters. Many of them were grossly overrated by the Russians and took advantage of the situation shamelessly. A draftsman from Amsterdam passed as a famous Dutch architect, had numerous assistants and a high salary; a lineman from Central Germany, on crossing the Soviet border had become an electrical engineer and worked as chief electrician of a department. Most foreign workers, however, were highly skilled, did their jobs well, and were instrumental in teaching many young Russians. Up until 1934–35 the Soviet workers were urged by consistent propaganda to learn from the foreigners; to master German and American technique. The overrating of the foreigners at the time was probably all for the best, as the available Soviet workers were even less well-qualified for responsible jobs than were the foreign pseudo-specialists. The foreigners, however, handicapped by the Russian language which most of them never learned and by a reluctance to study, were gradually overtaken by the young Soviet workers who surrounded them, anxious to learn and willing to work night and day. This was the background for the reaction which came with such force in 1936 and 1937, when foreigners were dismissed, demoted, publicly discredited, sent home, sometimes arrested.

XV

THIS was the Magnitogorsk of 1933. A quarter of a million souls — Communists, kulaks, foreigners, Tartars, convicted saboteurs and a mass of

blue-eyed Russian peasants — making the biggest steel combinat in Europe in the middle of the barren Ural steppe. Money
was spent like water, men froze, hungered, and suffered, but the
construction work went on with a disregard for individuals and
a mass heroism seldom paralleled in history.

PART FOUR

A Trip Through
Stalin's Ural Stronghold

I

I N MID-SUMMER I received my twenty-five days' annual vacation, increased by ten days' back overtime. Attempts to get a place in a rest home on the Black Sea coast were unsuccessful. I was casting around for something to do when Comrade Cherry, a functionary of the City Party Committee charged with political work among the foreigners, talked me into going to a near-by state farm for a few days to help repair tractors.

Fourteen of us — all Germans and Austrians except myself — set out in a one-ton truck supplied by the plant administration, armed with tool kits and two shotguns in case any rabbits or game birds put in an appearance. Cherry went with us, as did the manager of the farm, one Petrov, who had been in Magnitogorsk for a week or more trying to find someone to repair his tractors and attempting to bludgeon the plant supply department into giving him gasoline, tires, and some other things he needed.

Petrov talked all the way to his farm which had been organized the year before in an attempt to create a local source of supply of vegetables and grains for Magnitogorsk. The plant administration had furnished the money. Ordjonikidze in Moscow had arranged that they receive agricultural machinery, seeds, and building materials. Everything, in fact, had been thought of, he said, 'except good land and men to work it.'

So light was the rainfall and so thin the top soil that it was nearly impossible to raise anything. All shipments to and from the farm had to be handled by truck. There were no prospects of a railroad within the next ten years. This was all very well as long as gasoline and tires were available.

Petrov's main complaint was that he was unable to get skilled men to come and work for him. He offered twice the legal wage for mechanics and tractor drivers, but no one was interested.

We arrived at the farm in the middle of the day. The sun was boiling down like an electric arc. It seemed to be just a few feet over our heads. I have never felt such a hot sun except in Baghdad. We piled out of the truck and looked around the farm.

Petrov had an undefined tract of land in the middle of the Ural River valley. There was land aplenty. He had but to take what he wanted. It was flat and stone-free, and went as far as one could see in all directions. But there was very little top soil.

A half-dozen buildings had been constructed around a well. There was a store whose shelves were virtually empty, an administration building, a large dormitory, and a club dining-room. Over toward the river bed a cow barn and other farm buildings had been built. Most of the farm machinery stood out-of-doors. We saw it even before we alighted from the truck. There had not been enough lumber for buildings to house the machinery. Cows or men would die if they had no shelter in winter, but machines would not, said Petrov.

We were given a very good lunch, the best that I had had for months. Then we went to work. A dozen young open-faced boys took us out to show us the tractors. I remember the enthusiasm of one of them. 'Come on and fix this tractor first,' he told us, dragging us over to the corner of a ragged-looking wheat field where a tractor listed hopelessly against a little knoll. We asked him what was so urgent about this particular machine.

He grinned. 'Very good tractor,' he said, pointing to a hole in the top of the radiator beside the radiator cap.

We did not understand, to the obvious disappointment of the driver. 'How is it that these foreigners, these highly qualified specialists cannot see the technical possibilities of that hole?' he said in an undertone to another local farm boy. Then he told us. 'Marvelous for boiling potatoes. Even two or three at a time. We used to have fights to decide who would drive this tractor. Then it was decided that the driver who fulfilled his norm by the highest per cent would get it.'

Out of twelve tractors only three were working. The rest were in various stages of disintegration. Some had cracked blocks, stripped gears, burned-out bearings. Some were merely out of time, or the plugs were gummed up with carbon from the bad quality fuel. At the end of three days we had nine tractors running. These nine included the good parts from the other three. I remember Petrov's face when we showed him a pile of junk which was the other three tractors. To him it was quite normal to leave machinery out in the dust or snow all year round. But to dismember a tractor so that you could not even find it any more — that was dangerous. Suppose someone from the Control Commission came and wanted to see the twelve tractors? What then?

We would have turned our attention to some of the other farm machinery had it not been for the fact that several of the German mechanics were badly needed back in Magnitogorsk. Petrov reluctantly let us go. Before we left, we had a little class with the farm personnel, which consisted of a score of absolutely green shepherds, about half Russians and the rest

Bashkirs and Tartars. They had never seen any kind of machinery or equipment before coming to the farm. They had been taught that when you pushed the pedal the tractor moved. That was the extent of their technical education. Matters such as lubrication and timing were completely beyond their ken. We tried our best to explain some simple points, but I am afraid very little of what we said was understood.

Besides these plowboys, the farm boasted an agronomist, several supposedly experienced farmers, and one mechanic. The latter stayed out of our sight. The others were usually busy and had no time to come to our elementary class in care of machinery.

To run ahead of the story, I visited the same farm four years later and found astonishing changes. Petrov was gone, but several of the Tartar tractor drivers were still there and showed me with pride their new tractor barn full of comparatively well-cared-for machines. They had become fair mechanics and nearly all the machinery on hand was in working order.

The farm itself looked prosperous. They had one cabbage field that must have run close to one hundred acres. The potatoes and grains looked fair. The cattle were much better-looking than most stock in Russia. It was Petrov who had put the place on its feet. If a score of such farms could have been organized around Magnitogorsk, the city could have been provided with vegetables and dairy products from local sources entirely, thus solving one of the knottiest problems confronting the plant administration.

When I asked what had become of Petrov, people looked away and said nothing. When I pressed the point, the new director took me aside and told me that, to the astonishment of everyone on the farm, a GPU machine had driven up about a month before and taken Petrov away. The only information they could get was that 'he would not be back for some time.'

'I think I know what it may be,' said the new director. 'Petrov told me once that when he was a kid in the Young Communist League he had found himself on the same side as Zinovyev in the factional fight.'

II

Rᴇᴛᴜʀɴᴇᴅ to Magnitogorsk I went to the new Insnab restaurant for dinner and met a fellow American, an industrial chemist from New York. Mike was in his late thirties, and worked in the central research laboratories of the Eastern Metallurgical Trust in Sverdlovsk, the capital of the Ural Region, about three hundred miles north of Magnitogorsk. He had left America in 1931 under obscure circumstances. I gathered that he had been just one jump ahead of the sheriff. He and his wife were very comfortably fixed, he said, and he was thinking of becoming a Soviet citizen.

Mike was in Magnitogorsk on a 'Komandirovka,' a business trip, to inspect the new laboratories for the open-hearth department. He had one or two conferences with the chief chemist of the plant, a look around the new laboratories, and then spent four days waiting for a railroad ticket to go back to Sverdlovsk to report on his findings. This time we spent together looking around Magnitogorsk, trudging wearily over the iron mine and splashing around in the nascent lake which was already about five miles long and as many yards deep.

Mike suggested that I go back with him and have a look at Sverdlovsk. I agreed, and he ordered two tickets instead of one. We set out together one blistering hot day on the thirty-eight-hour trip to the capital of the Ural Region.

Mike was a foreign specialist, a consultant, and when he went on a 'Komandirovka' he took nothing but the best. We had a compartment to ourselves in the train and spent our time reading some new American books that Mike had in his suitcase.

The train banged along at the usual speed of from fifteen to twenty miles an hour over the three-year-old single-tracked Magnitogorsk–Kartaly Railroad which had been laid down on the steppe almost without ballast. There was nothing to see on either side but bare rolling hills. We both fell asleep. When we woke up, the sun was setting, the train was standing still, and we could hear all the passengers getting out. It seemed that there was a wreck ahead and the line was blocked.

We ran out and found a freight train piled up about a quarter of a mile ahead of us. Half a dozen cars were rolled up beside the track, and the engine lay on its side in a big hole right in the middle of the roadbed. Several hundred passengers from our train were gathered around gaping.

The wreck had occurred just at the bottom of a grade. I thought at first that someone had blown up the tracks and made the pit in which the locomotive was lying. But Mike, who had some experience in such matters, saw immediately what had really happened. The freight train had come along at a good clip, and at the bottom of the grade the sand ballast had sunk enough to part the rails at a junction. This had derailed the locomotive which had plowed a great hole in the ground, while the first half-dozen cars in the train had piled up after it.

The first to arrive on the scene of the wreck, which was ten miles from the nearest station, was a truck-load of GPU internal troops with fixed bayonets, sent to prevent looting. They stationed themselves around the damaged freight cars, some of which were spilling merchandise of various kinds on the steppe.

Next a section gang arrived in a repair train. They had half a dozen rails, some very elementary equipment, and a few ties. The foreman was a bluff young fellow with a good deal of sense. He looked the situation over and began reasoning out loud.

'The easiest thing to do,' said he, 'is to go round the engine,' and he waved his hand in the direction of the battered locomotive bedded in bent rails and débris. 'We could never get her out of that hole without a crane, and the devil only knows when a crane will get here.'

'Good idea,' said several authoritative-looking passengers at once. 'Of course, as a temporary measure.'

'Oh, of course,' said the foreman, and he set to work forthwith. The bent rails were removed, and a dozen men began clearing away wrecked freight cars on one side of the locomotive. Then the whole gang got together, and after shaking one of the ends of track loose of the sand ballast with crowbars and odd pieces of iron they tried to drag it over to one side. It hardly budged.

'Come on, comrades,' bellowed the foreman to the passengers from our train, 'get into this or you'll be here all week.' Several score passengers gathered together. There were not enough bars to go around, so many just took the rails with their hands, and within ten minutes one end of the track had been moved enough to clear the wrecked locomotive comfortably. By midnight both ends had been dragged over and ballasted down, and the foreman ordered his men to cut two pieces of rail to the necessary length to connect the two tracks on their new bed. Half a dozen men set to work with two hacksaws. They worked for an hour, taking turns, and cut less than half through the rails. I felt one of the blades. It had scarcely any teeth on it at all. By this time the new roadbed was made, the ties down, and it remained only to put the two odd-length rails in place. At this point Mike and I went to bed leaving the repair work to the more than adequate gang on the job.

We were awakened at five in the morning. The sun was shining, and our train was moving slowly. From our window we saw the repair train backing away in the direction of Chelyabinsk, while we pulled ahead at about two miles an hour past the wreck. We could have touched the prostrate locomotive with our hands from our window. Then we gathered speed and went banging along at the usual rate until we got to the next station, Djabik, I think it was called. Here we stopped for half an hour and the passengers raided the station in an attempt to buy something to eat. There was not a crumb to be had. A train running toward Magnitogorsk had stopped there during the previous night because of the wreck, and the passengers had bought out the town. Even tinned 'commercial' crab meat at nine or ten roubles a small can was sold out. Mike and I munched our Insnab bread contentedly and waited for the train to go on.

But we did not go far or fast. The schedule on the line was disrupted by the wreck, and we arrived in Sverdlovsk some twenty hours late.

The railroad line over which we were traveling was terribly overtaxed. A new road on a sand ballast should be used sparingly, several trains a day at most. But Magnitogorsk had iron and steel to ship out, while all sorts of construction materials and supplies as well as nearly two hundred carloads of coal had to be delivered to Magnitogorsk every day. More than thirty trains a day were run over the line. A railroad engineer on the train told us that wrecks like the one we had seen occurred frequently and were unavoidable when a new sand-ballasted line was used so heavily.

Arrived in Sverdlovsk we went to Mike's flat, in an immense stone apartment house, and I received a great surprise. He had four rooms, a large kitchen, running water, steam heat, and all the conveniences one could wish for. The building even boasted an elevator, though it had never been put in operation. I had not realized that such apartment houses existed in the Soviet Union except in Moscow. Mike's wife gave us a marvelous dinner, we had baths, and I went to sleep in a really clean bed for the first time in a year.

III

I SPENT a week in Sverdlovsk. Some engineers Mike introduced me to took me around the Ural Heavy Machine Building Works just outside the city. It was one of the best-looking plants I have ever seen. The first mechanical department was a beautiful piece of work. A building a quarter of a mile long was filled with the best American, British, and German machines. It was better equipped than any single shop in the General Electric Works in Schenectady. There were two immense lathes not yet in operation. I could not figure out then what they expected to make with lathes as long as ferryboats. Later I found out that they were used for turning gun barrels.

The foundry was likewise a beautiful job, completely mechanized and laid out according to the latest American technique.

The Ural Heavy Machine Building Plant was, like Magnitogorsk, a child of the first Five-Year Plan. It was even then equipped to make rolling mills, turbines, and other heavy machinery. Beginning in 1936 it turned out submarines which were shipped in sections either to the Pacific Ocean or the Black or Baltic Seas, thousands of miles away.

Supply conditions in Sverdlovsk were better than in Magnitogorsk. The city was surrounded by villages and farms which furnished vegetables and dairy products. Life went on more or less normally. Overtime was an exception. In Magnitogorsk it was the rule. There were theaters, and even a ballet performance, which I saw and liked immensely. Most families lived in houses or apartments, while many of the people of Magnitogorsk lived either in tents or in barracks.

I went to visit the house where the late Czar and his family met their death at the hands of a Red firing squad in 1918. Formerly a residence, it had been converted into a museum. The guides showed visitors the room in the cellar where the former sovereign was shot. I saw the holes in the wall which were made by Kolchak's soldiers, who, when they took the town shortly after the execution of Nikolai, dug out the bullets that had done the job to take with them as souvenirs.

It was a pleasanter life than I had been accustomed to in Magnitogorsk and I was tempted to stay and get a job in the big new 'URALMASH' plant which had so impressed me. But I resisted the temptation, partly because I had signed a contract to stay in Magnitogorsk until four blast furnaces were in operation. After a week with Mike and his wife, I started back toward home.

I had some money left over and decided to fly. Every morning two small local planes took off from Sverdlovsk, one bound for Chelyabinsk and one for Magnitogorsk. I went to the central ticket office and tried to get a plane ticket several days ahead. I was told that they were not allowed to make reservations in advance as many government or party officials always turned up at the last minute and demanded transportation, but that if I cared to go to the airport any morning I should almost certainly get a ticket a few minutes before the plane left.

So I took my little suitcase containing a shirt, some handkerchiefs, and several days' food supply, said good-bye and thank you to Mike and his wife, and started out. The planes left at five in the morning, and as I was afraid I should not be able to get there that early, I went out on the streetcar late the evening before and spent the night at the airport.

In those naïve days one could still wander around Soviet airports, look at planes, and talk to pilots; five years later, every aerodrome in the Soviet Union was surrounded by barbed wire and one was permitted to enter only a few minutes before the plane on which one had a ticket was scheduled to leave.

The Sverdlovsk Airport was about six miles out of town in the midst of a beautiful pine forest. Hangars snuggled in the trees beside the field itself, which was large and well kept. When one entered the territory of the airport, one seemed to step into a different world. Everything appeared to be in order. Equipment was well cared for. The mechanics and pilots, even the buffet waitresses and the scrubwomen, were better dressed and better fed than the run of skilled workers in either Magnitogorsk or Sverdlovsk.

I went into the waiting-room and checked my bag, then ordered a glass of tea, and got into a conversation with two other prospective passengers who, like myself, had come on the chance of getting a place on a plane the next morning. By midnight there were nearly a dozen of us, some waiting for the big East-and-West planes bound for Moscow or Novosibirsk, some hoping for a place on the little four-passenger planes to Magnitogorsk and Chelyabinsk. Only three or four had tickets. The rest, except myself, were armed with certificates from their offices or factories stating that they were traveling on business, and urging all transportation officials to assist them in getting to their destinations as soon as possible. These 'Komandirovka' slips were very useful, and on subsequent trips I always wrote myself out a very impressive one and had Syemichkin sign it and affix the Blast Furnace Construction Trust's seal.

Shortly after midnight we were joined by a half-dozen pilots. They were a clean-cut, fine-looking group, neatly dressed in the uniforms of the Civil Air Fleet, cleanly shaven and well fed. They contrasted strikingly with the run of people seen on the street, most of whom were unshaven, sloppily dressed, and often hungry-looking and dirty.

I had a talk with two of the pilots, and found to my surprise that they made from five hundred to a thousand roubles a month, and that their store was almost on a par with the foreigners' Insnab. They had had military training and were reserve army pilots, ready at any moment to join their air corps units.

After a little hesitation they took me out and showed me some of their planes and equipment. Not being an aviation specialist I could not tell much about the planes themselves. I did see, however, that the mechanics were furnished with neat and complete sets of all the elementary small tools, many of them imported and all in good shape. This would have been considered a matter of course in America or Western Europe, but in Russia in the early thirties almost no industrial or transport organization boasted good small tools — witness the hacksaw on the wrecking train.

Gasoline was kept in tank trucks which could be moved to any part of the field quickly and easily. The tanks were furnished with real screw-on caps, instead of being plugged up with rolls of old newspaper as similar containers were in Magnitogorsk. Everything was in its place, and the whole outfit had a well-kept and well-organized air which was completely lacking in other branches of Soviet industry at the time.

I was very much impressed.

I asked the pilots how many airplanes the Soviet Union had. They shrugged their shoulders. 'Very many,' they said. 'Many thousands.'

We went to the little bar and had a beer, the first I had drunk since leaving Moscow for Magnitogorsk a year before. The pilots plied me with questions about America and Germany. Their queries were intelligent and indicated that they had read a good deal about international affairs, and particularly about industry and aviation in Germany and the United States. Finally I got them back on the subject of Soviet aviation.

'You know what we do with many of our planes,' one said. 'They come out of the factory, are tested on the ground, then tested in the air very thoroughly, then they go back to the factory, where they are taken apart, put into crates, and sent off to storehouses near the place where they may be needed.'

I subsequently heard this story from other people, and am inclined to think it substantially correct. Particularly in the Far East, along the frontiers of Manchukuo, large numbers of crated planes were stored. Of course such a practice meant that Soviet planes would tend to be obsolete, but I think that until 1938 the Russians realized their industry could not hope to keep up with the West in retooling for new models. They, therefore, counted on the quantity rather than on the quality of their planes to overwhelm any possible enemy.

'In Perm we have an aviation motor factory which will make the largest plants in the United States look small,' said one of the pilots. 'And the new motor works in Ufa will make some aviation motors soon.' Perm was in the North Urals, while Ufa was roughly two hundred miles northwest of Magnitogorsk. The aviation motor plant about which the pilots told me was put into operation in the early thirties, and though I was never able to find out its exact size, it was reputed to be the largest aviation motor plant in the Soviet Union. The situation of both Perm and Ufa was ideal. Iron, steel, copper, aluminum, and nickel were produced within a radius of two or three hundred miles, while Ufa boasted good transportation facili-

ties, being on the main southern line of the Trans-Siberian, and
also at the intersection of the projected Moscow–Ufa–Magnitogorsk–Akmolinsk Railroad, part of which was completed in
1940. Furthermore, Ufa is near the new Ishembayevo oil
fields, which in 1940 already produced more than two million
tons of oil. In 1934, passing through Ufa, I saw the immense
plant, still under construction at the time.

At about two o'clock I turned in on a wooden bench and slept
until four-thirty, when I was awakened by the turmoil at the
ticket window.

The Magnitogorsk plane filled up long before my turn came
round. A high party official and a GPU functionary took two
of the four seats immediately, then the chief engineer of one
of the rolling-mill construction trusts who was returning from
vacation got a ticket, and the fourth place went to a rank-and-
file engineer who had nothing but the usual komandirovka, but
who was ahead of me in the queue. I stayed in the line from
pure inertia, and when I got to the window I found that there
was an empty place in the Chelyabinsk plane. I played the
important foreign specialist game, pretended not to speak
Russian, and finally went away with a ticket to Magnitogorsk
via Chelyabinsk with two days' stopover in that city, all for
the usual Sverdlovsk–Magnitogorsk plane ticket price — one
hundred and twenty roubles, I think it was.

Half an hour later I squeezed into a neat little four-passenger,
single-motor monoplane, and we took off.

IV

It was a beautiful day, but windy, and the little plane danced around spryly, much to the discomfort of the other three passengers, two of whom were State Bank functionaries. The plane gained altitude rapidly and we swept over the beautiful evergreen forests which surround Sverdlovsk. Then we skirted the foothills of the Urals for nearly half an hour as the country below got more and more barren. By six o'clock we were over the bare steppe. There were neither mountains nor forests in view, no living creature, no house could we see in any direction and the visibility was good. Only an occasional lake floating on the brown waste broke the monotony.

Yet the territory over which we were flying was extremely rich. Within an area of five hundred miles square in that Ural district, Nature placed almost all the minerals most prized by man — gold, platinum, silver, copper, nickel, lead, iron, and aluminum, as well as many precious and semi-precious stones. Ferrous metallurgical plants in Magnitogorsk, Tagil, Zlatooust; machine-building units of Sverdlovsk, Chelyabinsk, Orsk, Ufa, Perm; the precious stones and gold mines of Miass and Bashkiria; chemical plants in Berezniki and Solikamsk, and numerous nonferrous metallurgical units in and near Orsk as well as the new railroad car works in Nizhny Tagil and the Ishembayevo oil fields and projected Ufa oil refineries: these and many more comprised the new Ural heavy-industry base. This rich region lying in the center of the Soviet Union was and remains one of Russia's best guarantees against total military defeat.

I dozed off for a few minutes, and when I awoke my fellow passengers were pointing joyfully to a gleaming city some miles ahead of us. The immense Chelyabinsk tractor plant covered a larger area than the entire old city of Chelyabinsk. Around the plant we saw a 'Socialist City' of shining white apartment houses, spotted with parks and gardens. Farther away we could see the 'Stankostroi' factory, originally planned as a light-machine building plant, but reprojected in the early thirties to make tanks.

The plane came down in a perfect landing, and we got out and made our way to the city by bus.

Chelyabinsk was originally a fortified city, an outpost of Peter the Great's empire in the early seventeen-hundreds. Later it became a stopover point for convoys of exiles on their way to Siberia. During the eighteenth and nineteenth centuries these often made the journey on foot, and Chelyabinsk was one of the places where they were permitted to rest for a few days.

The old quarter of Chelyabinsk was more or less as it had been for many decades: small wooden houses, rather down-at-the-heel, narrow winding streets, and no modern conveniences. Two new housing developments, however, were outstanding: the tractor plant 'Socialist City' and the 'Gorodok OGPU' or GPU City. Streetcar lines had been run through from the old quarter to both these new developments, which were fast becoming the social and cultural centers of the city.

The Gorodok OGPU consisted of several huge blocks of houses six stories high and well constructed. Each block boasted all the communal services that one could desire: nurseries, laundries, kindergartens, tailor shops, dining-rooms, and clubs. The Gorodok had two cinema houses and one theater.

It seemed incredible to me that there should be enough GPU functionaries in Chelyabinsk to warrant the construction of such a monumental housing project just for these police officers. I found out, however, that party and Soviet officials also lived in these houses.

I took the streetcar out to the tractor plant. To my disappointment, on arriving at the gates I was stopped by a burly man with a gun at his hip — 'Pass!' He would not let me in, and I decided I had better go to the foreign office of the administration and announce myself before trying to get a pass from the factory commandant.

I was leaving the gate when I ran into a German machinist who had been transferred from Magnitogorsk some time before. He wore his day-off clothes. 'Just came to the plant for a technical conference,' he explained. 'On my way home now; want to come along?'

We walked together down the broad avenue connecting the plant with the apartment houses. It was a double boulevard, with a garden between the two lanes and streetcar tracks along the edges. The apartment houses were set back nearly a hundred yards from this avenue, and trees and shrubs had been planted everywhere. A large club and a clean-looking theater occupied prominent places in the layout of the development.

'Must buy some cigarettes,' said the machinist. 'Insnab is way down the avenue, so we often buy cigarettes here.' We pushed our way into a large well-constructed store. It was jammed with housewives and some workers standing in line, waiting for bread.

Just as we got in the door, the bread arrived. The crowd became animated immediately; everyone began to fish for bread cards and money. Toward the front of the line I noticed about twenty solid-looking men, standing patiently and silently waiting for their bread. They were Finns.

'We have about three hundred of them in Chelyabinsk,' my friend told me. 'They are good workers, but they drink too much. Most of them ran across the frontier in 1930 and 1931.

They were smugglers, many of them, and they stick together in a remarkable way. When they first arrived last winter, they were put to work on the power-house construction. There were not enough valinkis to go around, and the second day none of them came to work. The party and the trade union sent a man around immediately to find out what was wrong. The Finns were sitting at home and showed no signs of going to work. "Today is a working day," the party man told them. The spokesman of the Finns said that he knew it, but that they would not go to work until they had all received the valinkis they were entitled to according to the collective agreement. There was a terrible scandal, and in the end they dug up more valinkis for the remaining Finns.

We had just bought our cigarettes when a hullabaloo burst out in the bread line. A Young Communist League functionary came in and breezed to the head of the line to get his bread. The bovine Russian housewives took it as a matter of course. But not the Finns. They took the young Bolshevik and lifted him gently out of the way. The store clerk smothered a gleeful smile and began yelling for order. The komsomol was furious. He came back again. One of the Finns finally opened his mouth and boomed out in bad Russian, 'We stand in line; you stand in line.' Whereupon three or four of the burly Finns took him gently and put him down outside the door of the store. Most of the housewives were delighted. The komsomol gave up trying to get his bread, and we saw him walking down the street swearing.

We had lunch, and then at my request set out for the plant. The machinist fixed up a pass which permitted me to go anywhere except into the power house and substations. I spent all the rest of the day wandering through the immense plant.

The assembly line was interesting, but the conveyor foundry was the most fascinating thing I saw. Everything was working well, and the yard outside the assembly building was crowded with finished machines. These were heavy-duty caterpillar tractors which I had seen at work in Magnitogorsk, and which stood up very well.

I went back to my friend's apartment and after dinner some other German workers came in, and we spent an interesting evening discussing recent events in Germany. Hitler was consolidating his position. The Soviet press in general was somewhat indifferent and most of the Russians had no particular antipathies for the Nazis, but the Germans in Russia, most of them Social Democrats and Communists, were profoundly disturbed. It was a serious business, they said, the Russians would see.

After two days in Chelyabinsk, I took the plane to Magnitogorsk. It was a beautiful flying day, almost no wind and good visibility. For nearly two hours we sped along at a thousand to fifteen hundred feet over smooth, rolling hills, undecorated by any vegetation. An occasional lake spotted the steppe, otherwise it resembled a desert. About an hour out of Chelyabinsk we picked up the railroad line. It wound along endlessly, with a station and a small group of houses every ten or fifteen miles.

Finally a long pillar of smoke appeared in the distance and then a low range of mountains. The old magnetic mountains Eye-Derlui and Atach seemed to come up to meet us, while the column of smoke above the plant appeared to rise right up into the stratosphere. At that time the chemical plant in Magnitogorsk was not in operation and all the smoke from the coke ovens was released into the air. On a windless day it accumulated and piled up a veritable tower over the city.

Magnitogorsk from the air presented a very different picture from Chelyabinsk or Sverdlovsk. It displayed no glistening Socialist city, no shining whitewashed factory buildings. The four blast furnaces stood up like stately gentlemen, with mufflers around their necks. At their feet lay a wide construction camp which looked dirty and disorganized, even from the air.

We made a good landing in the airport, but then had difficulties. The truck which was supposed to meet the plane had not arrived. The chief of the airport said something about lack of gasoline and spare parts and disappeared into his office. We waited two hours and then decided to walk it. It was about six miles to the city, the road winding over the steppe. Frequently we were guided more by the pillar of smoke over the city than by the elusive tire tracks under our feet. It took us two hours. A bearded Soviet engineer who had been in the plane remarked bitterly, 'Two hours from Chelyabinsk to Magnitogorsk, a trip which takes twenty hours in the train — and then we spend four more hours to get from the aerodrome to the city. That's Bolshevik tempo!'

Nevertheless, when we arrived at the crest of the hill and saw Magnitogorsk spread out like a complicated differential geometry problem on a blackboard, crowned by its aura of thick black smoke, everybody in the party felt a distinct sense of pride. Here, hundreds of miles from the nearest center of human activity, a gigantic plant and city had been created within five years. Even the least important of the builders, even those who worked under sentence in expiation of alleged crimes, felt that in a very real sense the city was theirs because they had helped to build it.

PART FIVE

PART FIVE Masha

I

Back at my job I was immediately set upon by Kolya, who wanted a vacation himself. No one around the mill seemed capable of replacing him, except some of the engineers and technicians who had other work to do. And so, in spite of my reluctance, I found myself installed as acting foreman. It was difficult at first, but I did the job as well as anyone else available at the time could have done it.

When Kolya returned six weeks later, the gang was split into two and I continued as foreman of one, pushing twenty to twenty-five welders around the structural steel of the blast furnaces and their auxiliary equipment.

Two years passed, during which I became a husband and a father.

II

One evening I left the mill after working several hours overtime and staggered through the snow to the Komvuz as usual, only to find that I had heard the wrong whistle and had come an hour early. All the classrooms were dark and cold, and no one seemed to be around. I walked into the office, where the director, a very good fellow by the name of Jamarikin, and his two secretaries carried on their work of planning lecture hours, calculating teachers' pay, and checking the political quality of the academic material being poured into future party functionaries and administrators.

I said hello to Jamarikin, sat down on a stool next to the stove, and dozed off immediately, only to be awakened by Anya, one of the secretaries. 'Comrade Scott, do you know integral calculus?' she asked. 'Our new secretary studies in the mathematics institute and is having a hell of a time finding anyone to help her with her problems.'

I pleaded not guilty to calculus, and took a sleepy look at the new secretary, who was grinning sheepishly, as she penciled figures and symbols on a piece of ragged scrap paper. I saw an open-faced girl in her early twenties. She had a very ruddy complexion and wore her hair in two long pigtails down her back.

'This is Masha, our new part-time secretary,' said Jamarikin, with a grin.

Masha seemed to be a nice peasant girl, like so many others who had come from some village to work and study in Magnitogorsk. The fact that she was working over integral calculus in a town where very few people had any clear idea what algebra was intrigued me. But I was very tired, and whatever calculus I had ever known was hopelessly rusty. I made some apologetic remark and dozed off again.

Masha's first impressions of me were more interesting than mine of her. She wrote as follows in her haphazard diary:

'When I first went to work in the Komvuz I was filing a pile of applications from the previous year when I came across one written in such an impossible handwriting that I could hardly read it. I finally made out the name John Scott, and further learned that he was an American and had recently arrived in the Soviet Union. I had never seen an American and was much interested by the prospect of seeing this John Scott, who had, no doubt, come from the land of capitalist oppression to find a home in the land of Socialism. I imagined him as being tall, handsome, and very interesting. I asked Anya, the other secretary, to point him out to me.

'The next evening a stringy, intense-looking young fellow came into the office and sat down near the stove. He was dressed in ragged brown working clothes and had a heavy brown scarf around his neck. His clothes and his big tattered valinkis were absolutely grimy with blast-furnace dust. He looked very tired and lonely. When Anya told me in a whisper that it was John Scott, I didn't believe her at first. Then I was very disappointed, and then I became sorry for him.

'The first American I had ever seen, he looked like a homeless boy. I saw in him the product of capitalist oppression. I saw in my mind's eye his sad childhood; I imagined the long hours of inhuman labor which he had been forced to perform in some capitalist factory while still a boy; I imagined the shamefully low wages he received, only sufficient to buy enough bread so that he could go to work the next day; I imagined his fear of losing even this pittance and being thrown on the streets unemployed in case he was unable to do his work to the satisfaction and profit of his parasitic bosses.'

III

I saw Masha in
school from time to time, but got to know her only in the
spring, when the snows melted and warm winds began to blow,
and when the pressure of work in the mill decreased. We went
to the theater once or twice; she took me to the Central Hotel
where she lived with her sister and brother-in-law; and we went
for walks over the steppe. I found that she was three months
my senior, and had been born and brought up in a village under
circumstances as strange and incredible to most Americans as
my actual background was to her.

Her father was a poor peasant. He went to war in 1915,
leaving behind his wife and eight children, the oldest of whom
was fourteen. The mother was left to get along as best she
could. 'Zhivi kak khochesh,' or 'Live as you like,' as the Russians say in such cases. The children, six of whom were girls,
worked in the fields as soon as they were old enough to hold a
hoe or a pitchfork. They lived in a one-and-a-half-room
wooden hut, and Masha remembers that they were happy when
there was as much bread and salt as they wanted. Tea, sugar,
and meat were great luxuries.

The family lived in the Tverskaya Gubernia, roughly halfway between Moscow and Leningrad, a part of Russia where
poor soil and long winters have always kept agricultural production low and the population correspondingly poor. Masha's
mother and father were both descended from serfs, and were
both illiterate. They were determined, however, that their
children should go to school, and so, often barefoot and ragged,
Masha and her brothers and sisters started to study in the local

village school, which went as far as the fourth grade. By the time Masha went to school, in 1920, her oldest sister was the teacher.

During the civil war there were no military operations in Masha's village, but her elder brother went to the front, and her father arrived home, wounded and sick with a trench malaria which never left him. The village livestock was requisitioned and sent off to Moscow and Leningrad to feed the revolution. Masha's second brother worked for a while in the town of Udomlya, some five miles from home, taking care of the requisitioned stock until it could be shipped off. Every evening he would come home with a pail of milk, which was drunk dry immediately by the many children.

The new Bolshevik government sent inspectors to every village to look for hoarded bread. There was famine in the country, and foreign and white armies were pressing upon it on many fronts. The inspectors found nothing in Masha's hut.

In 1924, just as the civil war gave place to Lenin's New Economic Policy, Masha finished the four-year village school. She wanted to study further. Her older brothers and sisters had gone off to distant towns to go to schools, which were now everywhere free. They lived as best they could.

Masha and her third sister decided that they too would go to Vyshny-Volochok, get jobs as maids, and study in the evenings. But they had neither clothes nor money. They went to work cutting wood for the local kulak. In two weeks they earned three roubles, at that time about seventy-five cents, and started off with all their belongings in a torn burlap bag, and lapties, homemade bark sandals, on their feet. It was about forty miles to Vyshny-Volochok, and it took them three days to walk it.

They spent some time in Vyshny-Volochok, but found that it was impossible to work as maids and study at the same time.

They spent their money on two cotton dresses and some bread, then returned to their village.

Shortly a 'secondary' school was organized in Udomlya, and Masha enrolled. It was five miles each way every day, and when she was fourteen Masha got her first pair of shoes.

During the middle twenties things got better. Masha's older brother and sister were finishing college and working, he as engineer, she as teacher. The redivision of the land had given Masha's father better fields, and he was no longer chronically in debt and hungry. Masha got a new dress every year, and her little niece got what no one in the family had ever had — a store-made doll.

From the incredible poverty and suffering of the civil-war period, the Russian people were working their way up to a higher standard. All Masha's family were enthusiastic. Several of the children joined the Komsomol, and after years of argument, the mother succumbed to the pressure of her children and took down the icons from the walls of the hut. Then she too decided to study. Masha's mother learned to read and write at the age of fifty-five. She was taught by her youngest daughter.

On finishing the eight years of the secondary school in Udomlya, Masha decided to go to Moscow to continue her studies. One brother and one sister were there already, and had secured a room in a cellar. One by one during fifteen years the younger brothers and sisters came to Moscow, and lived in that little room while they went through one of Moscow's many higher educational institutions. Masha went to the capital in 1929. At that time the industrialization of the country was just beginning. Russia's rapidly expanding economy was crying for every kind of professional skill, for engineers, chemists, teachers, economists, and doctors. The higher schools paid stipends to their students, and aided them in every way to get through their courses and out to factory and laboratory. Masha finished up her preparatory work, and then entered the Mendelyeyev Institute, where she worked part-time as laboratory assistant to make a few roubles for bread.

In 1932 Masha's second oldest sister graduated from the Moscow University, married, and went off to Magnitogorsk. The following year, for personal reasons, Masha followed her. She went into the junior year of the Magnitogorsk Teachers' College, majoring in mathematics and physics. She lived with her sister, and got a job in the local Komvuz, where she spent four hours a day, most of it engaged in preparing her lessons for her next day's classes.

Masha was very happy in Magnitogorsk. She felt that the world was at her feet. She slept on the divan of her sister and brother-in-law's tiny hotel room, she had two or three dresses, two pairs of shoes, and one coat. In two more years she would graduate from the teachers' college. Then she would teach, or perhaps take graduate work. Not only this, she was living in a town which had grown up from nothing just as she herself had. Living conditions were improving as the pig-iron production of the mill increased. She felt herself a part of a going concern. Hence her spontaneous pity for me, whom she first saw as a cast-off from a bankrupt and degenerating society.

IV

MASHA bowled me over. After some trouble I secured a small room in a permanent apartment house in Sotsgorod. Then one day I asked

Masha to marry me. She agreed, and the next evening after work her brother-in-law Max as a sort of gesture walked up with us from the hotel to Sotsgorod carrying Masha's little suitcase containing her worldly belongings.

The next day we made a date to meet at the office of the ZAGS, or Bureau of Civil Acts, where the marriage bureau was located. With some difficulty I got away from the mill and puffed up to the little wooden barrack where one could marry or divorce, only to find that Masha had forgotten her passport. We had to postpone the ceremony until the next day.

When we got there the next afternoon, we found quite a queue, and had to wait for nearly half an hour. The couples were in their early twenties, most of them simple peasants-become-workers with blue eyes and rough hands. When our turn came, we signed our names in a registration book, I produced three roubles, and we received a piece of rough wrapping paper which had been mimeographed into a marriage-license blank, which declared us man and wife until or unless either of us should go to some ZAGS anywhere in the Soviet Union and pay three roubles for a divorce.

We began our life together almost casually. For both of us family life was definitely subordinate to work and study.

V

LATE in the summer we both took a vacation and went to the village to see Masha's family. Masha's mother and father were more than cordial, though I am sure I was something of a disappointment.

Old Ivan Kalinovich, her father, was a kindly, bearded peasant with a deep voice and horny hands. He was a member of the local collective farm administration, and was heart and soul for collectivization. He spoke slowly and simply to me of what the collective farm had done in the village. Everyone had bread. The flax crop was larger than ever before, and there was more livestock. To be sure, there was some resistance. Some of the old peasants still preferred individual farming, but they would learn.

The village and the fields looked poor. There was no machinery at all. Tractors and combines were being sent to the grain regions in the Ukraine and Siberia where better soil and larger agricultural units made them more effective.

Masha's mother was the most remarkable member of the family. She had given birth to nine children, and had never needed the services of a doctor or a midwife. They were all born at night, Masha told me, and the mother never woke anyone up. The next morning she would get up as usual and make the fire before daybreak, then she would go to work in the fields as though nothing unusual had occurred. She was in her sixties, had never seen a dentist, and had all her teeth. She had a sharp tongue in an argument, but shed copious tears whenever one of her children came home or went away. Her hut was spotlessly clean, and she still worked in the fields and took care of a flock of collective-farm sheep.

From the standpoint of agricultural technique and material standards, the village functioned and lived more or less as it had during the years before 1914, I learned, although there were two new elements. In the first place, many of the young people went off to the cities to go to school and then worked in industry, leaving the village short-handed. In the second place, there was a new spirit in the village. They were working, not only for themselves as they had during the first years of the revolution, but for the Kolkhoz, for their collective benefit. They were working together. Little fields had been made into big ones, work was done by brigades. On the other hand, whereas before the revolution they had worked twelve or fourteen hours a day, now they put in eight hours. What was gained by collective effort was spent in decreased working hours. Production was about the same as it had been twenty years before. This, incidentally, was true by and large of Soviet agriculture as a whole, though in some sections like the Kuban and Western Siberia numerous new large tractor-worked agricultural units produced many times more than previously.

I should have liked to stay in the village for a month or so, but our vacations were limited, and Masha and I returned to Magnitogorsk. We settled down to working and studying, and were so busy that a year went by before either of us was thoroughly used to the idea that we were married.

VI

DURING this time Blast Furnaces Nos. 3 and 4 were put into operation, as well as eleven open-hearth furnaces and a half-dozen rolling mills.

It was not only in the mill that changes were noticeable. The city of Magnitogorsk grew and developed from the dirty, chaotic construction camp of the early thirties into a reasonably healthy and habitable city. A streetcar line was constructed and went into operation. New stores were built, and supplies of all kinds made their appearance in quantity and at reasonable prices. Fuel, clothing of all kinds, and other elementary necessities became available. It was no longer necessary to steal in order to live.

Improved living conditions in Magnitogorsk were a reflection of a similar trend throughout the Soviet Union. Collectivization was producing results. Many collective farms in the Urals became quite prosperous. Food cards, restricted stores, and other expressions of deficit economy disappeared. Insnab was liquidated, but the foreigners missed it only in that prices there had been lower. Similar grocery products and drygoods could be bought in 1935 and 1936 in open stores, often without even the inconvenience of a queue.

My work was irregular and strenuous. I remember particularly the erection of a gas-pipe line connecting the blast furnaces with the power plant, a distance of roughly a mile. The six-foot-diameter welded steel pipe, set up on columns of various heights, made many twists and turns in order to circumvent railroad lines and various industrial aggregates which, according to the project, were to be built. Standing on the top of the huge pipe at its highest point, nearly one hundred feet up in the air, and looking along its tortuous track over the bare steppe one got the impression that some obscure designer had gone mad, and we pawns were blindly executing the senseless pattern of his pen.

This pipe line was absolutely unprotected from the wind. During the winter the workers nicknamed it 'Sakhalin,' after the Soviet Union's icy Pacific island. The north wind would race across the endless barren steppe and sway our columns back and forth like reeds. Once two columns and a section of pipe fell and a rigger and a welder were killed. But the line was finished nonetheless, and went into operation in due course of time.

I came to work one autumn day just in time to see a sixty-foot column knocked out from under our pipe where it crossed the main railroad line connecting the blast furnaces with the pig machine. One of our columns was situated between the in- and out-bound tracks. A careless engineer ran past with a train of empty slag ladle cars, one of which had not been turned up- right after having been emptied. This ladle stuck out too far, and as it passed it caught our column, wrenched it loose from its foundation and from the gas pipe overhead, and flung it a dozen yards away on the ground. Our welded pipe, designed to rest on regularly spaced columns, was suddenly left without one of its supports. My heart was in my throat for half an hour until a crane was brought up to take the strain from the pipe while a new column was being constructed. Our welding held better than could have been expected. We were officially com- plimented by the plant administration, and every one of us felt proud of our work.

VII

In 1935 I had my first siege with a Soviet dentist. Galya was a nineteen-year-old girl. Born in a village, she attended a country school for three years, then moved to a town where she worked as a maid, and finally took a two-year rush course in dentistry. Thus equipped, she was sent to Magnitogorsk to help in the monumental task of repairing the teeth of a quarter of a million Russians and others. She meant well, but obviously lacked training, and furthermore did not have at her disposal the equipment, both mechanical and pharmaceutical, considered necessary in most

countries for the practice of dentistry. I do not remember what
it was she used to extract a nerve from one of my teeth, but it
certainly felt like a hacksaw.

Another tooth, Galya said, must come out. She told me to
report at the clinic at a given time, when the specialized ex-
tractor of teeth held sway. I came a few minutes early and
found a queue of some twenty people sitting on chairs along the
side of the corridor leading to the dentist's office. I took my
seat at the end of the line and waited. Every minute or so the
door would open, a pale patient would come out, spit furtively
into a large blood-bespattered spittoon near the door, and leave
the clinic sucking his handkerchief. The next in line would get
up unsteadily and disappear into the dentist's office. When I
was halfway down the line, a nurse in a dirty white apron approached me surreptitiously with a large hypodermic syringe
in her hand.

'Which tooth, comrade?' she said. I showed her and she put
a shot of something into my jawbone that made my head spin.
When I was two places removed from the door, the dentist himself emerged. He was a husky, black-haired man of thirty-five
— sleeves rolled up, horn-rimmed glasses splattered with blood.
He walked to the end of the corridor, took half a dozen drags at
a cigarette, then stalked back without looking to either side.

When my turn came, I went in, and before I had had time to
sit down in the dentist's chair a nurse had brought a tray on
which a newly sterilized pair of dental pliers and several other
instruments lay, while another nurse had tied a dirty apron
around my neck.

'Which tooth, comrade?' said the dentist, picking up his pliers
in one hand and a chisel in the other. I showed him, and before
I had time to collect myself the tooth was lying on the tray
with the pliers, the apron had been taken from my neck, and
still another nurse had made her appearance bearing a tray with

freshly sterilized instruments for the next patient. I went out of the door and spat into the spitoon.

From the standpoint of dental technique I suppose the extraction was very well done. The dentist certainly had plenty of practice, and elementary rules of sterilization had been observed. But psychologically, it was a grueling experience. There were not enough dentists in Magnitogorsk, or, for that matter, in the Soviet Union. Most of them worked two shifts a day and earned eight hundred to twelve hundred roubles a month.

VIII

Masha and I lived busily, happily, simply.

In the fall of 1935, however, something happened which complicated our lives to a considerable degree. Our first daughter was born. Neither of us knew anything about children, and, what was more, we were both interested in our jobs and our studies. It was several months before we recognized the necessity of modifying our lives in the interests of the second generation.

We found an ideal maid who took over our haphazard household and made it function. Vera was sixteen, daughter of a disfranchised kulak living in the special district in a barrack near Shabkov's. She had arrived in Magnitogorsk in 1930 with her mother, father, sister, and two brothers. They spent the first winter in a tent. The mother, one son, and one daughter died. Vera survived, and went to school for two years. Then her father was hurt and could only work as a watchman. They had not enough bread and Vera had to get a job.

She was a wonderful maid. She took the responsibility for buying groceries, cooking, and taking little Elka out for walks. The only thing she insisted on was time off to go to school every afternoon. She and Masha made arrangements so that one of them was home all the time, and everything went smoothly. For three years Vera was with us, and became almost a member of the family. It was a great shock to us when, in 1938, after I had moved to Moscow, the police made Vera and several thousand other disfranchised minors move to Chelyabinsk on twenty-four hours' notice. Labor power was needed to build a new armament factory in Chelyabinsk. Theoretically the ex-kulaks and their families had equal rights in 1938, but actually, when it was a question of securing labor power for an important military factory, the authorities did not bend over backward to live up to the letter of the laws. Vera received a mimeographed notice, and was herded off in a freight train the next night. We never saw her after that, but I am told that the plant in Chelyabinsk was constructed on schedule and went into production in 1941.

While Vera was with us everything went smoothly. Late in 1935, after a long campaign with the plant administration, I secured an order for the room next to the one we already occupied in Sotsgorod. One Sunday afternoon I went to work with a saw and wrecking bar, broke through the wall, hung a door, and we were the proud possessors of an apartment, an unusual thing for a worker or junior executive in Magnitogorsk at that time.

This gave us a chance to isolate the baby, so that we could all get some studying done. It also made us accumulate a whole household apparatus which we had not boasted before — furniture, rugs, pots and kettles were bought at high prices piece by piece, and began cluttering up our flat.

Masha graduated from the college a few months after Elka's birth, and went to work teaching mathematics in the secondary school which had just been organized in the special district inhabited by disfranchised elements. She taught five hours a day on the average, and received something over five hundred roubles a month, which was as much as I was earning. She liked her work, and was a successful teacher. The school where she worked had the highest scholastic average in the city, which was what might have been expected. The sons and daughters of the disfranchised lishentsi had gone through a rigid natural selection. The weakest and least resourceful had been eliminated, and those who remained were hell-bent on getting an education. Their fathers had been, for the most part, the most energetic and clever elements in the villages from which they had come. They had been liquidated as a class, in the interests of the worthy cause of agricultural collectivization. Their children were determined to become leaders in some other field of endeavor.

Masha's work was not limited to teaching. She was personally responsible for a group of about twenty-five children. If they had poor marks, were late, absent, or ill-behaved, it was Masha's duty to find out why, and to try to remedy the situation. She also took them in groups to the theater, to lectures, and to meetings. This social work took her an hour or two every day.

Not satisfied with this, she took up chess seriously, and for a while was women's champion of Magnitogorsk. Later, when a local music school was organized, she enrolled and began to learn to play the piano.

Masha was typical of a whole generation of young Soviet women who had received and utilized extensive educational opportunities, and became professional women whereas their parents were barely literate. This group, and Masha along with them, were steeped in the slogans of equality of opportunity for women. They had been raised on the propaganda of the twenties about the elimination of the bourgeois family as an institution. They wanted to have as little as possible to do with cooking, washing dishes, and changing diapers. These were the functions of servants who did not have intellectual qualifications, or had not yet received sufficient training to permit them to practice a profession.

As I pointed out to Masha many times, this psychology was in some respects similar to that of the women in Left aristocratic families before the revolution. Moreover, I assured her that, if ever we went to America, she would find that many professional women in the United States washed their own dishes. Masha was skeptical about our ever going to America, and, moreover, my argument seemed illogical to her. She taught mathematics, earned five hundred roubles a month. Vera was paid fifty roubles a month, which was high. Why should Masha wash dishes? It was not efficient division of labor.

This tendency caused no trouble as Vera did most of the housework, and furthermore, when it was necessary for some reason, Masha always did whatever cooking and washing came along. I think she actually enjoyed it sometimes, but ideologically she found it insupportable.

We lived very happily. We were both engrossed in our work. We had as much money as we needed, and usually spent less than we earned; the household ran smoothly as material conditions in the city as a whole improved. Little Elka gradually emerged as a personality, and Masha and I fell head over heels in love with her. By the time her little sister was born, I knew that she and Masha and Elka had become the most important considerations in my life.

John Scott, 1940, Moscow.
Provided by Maria Scott.

Masha Scott, early
1940s. Provided by
Maria Scott.

Masha, little Elka, and John, December 1938. Masha is pregnant with their second daughter, Elena. Provided by Maria Scott.

Digging the ditch for the main water line to the factory, 1930. From I. F. Galiguzov and M. E. Churilin, *Flagman otechestvennoi industrii* (Moscow, 1978).

The first and second blast furnaces under construction, 1931.

A brigade working on blast furnace construction, early 1930s. John Scott is seated, far left, second row, the only one smiling. Provided by Maria Scott.

Assembly work high on Magnitogorsk's sister plant in Kuznetsk. Such work was common in Magnitogorsk, and, as a result, accidents were frequent. Below, a view of workers' barracks, many of which were located on the territory of both factories. From Central State Archives of Film and Photo Documents (TsGAKFD), Krasnogorsk, USSR.

Cement pouring in winter conditions. Work on the factory went on beyond the traditional spring and summer construction season. From Galiguzov and Churilin, *Flagman*.

Socialist competition blackboard dividing brigades into airplanes, carts, and tortoises, according to norm fulfillment percentages. From *Iunost' Magnitki* (Moscow, 1981).

The record-setting Galiullin brigade, whose exploits in laying the foundations for the coke and chemical plant served as the inspiration for Valentin Kataev's 1933 novel, *Time, Forward!*, based on his experiences at Magnitogorsk.

The coke and chemical plant, where John Scott became an operator, as it looked in 1934.

A panorama of the chaotic site, showing the two blast furnaces and coke plant. From TsGAKFD.

Agitation point in the tent settlement, 1930. From Iu. Petrov, *Magnitka* (Moscow, 1971).

Steel workers reading the city newspaper, *Magnitogorskii rabochii* [The Magnitogorsk Worker], 1936. Illiteracy, widespread in the early 1930s, was greatly reduced by the end of the decade. From TsGAKFD.

One of the first barracks built on the site in 1929. Later most barracks, although still made of wood, were covered with stucco. This and the six following photographs are from the Magnitogorsk City Museum.

Interior of an exemplary "shock workers'" barracks.

Flower gardens adjacent to barracks.

Store for hygiene products in the open steppe.

The staff of a cafeteria for shock workers, apparently located in a barracks.

Party lessons.

Children carrying a banner: "Under the hammer and sickle Lenin calls us: He is my greeting. I am the successor of the current shift. I am bold and young. I am a pioneer." Banner above reads: "We demand attention to ourselves."

A cottage in Berezka, the secluded settlement where first the foreign engineers and then the local Soviet elite lived. From V. I. Kazarinova and V. I. Pavlichenkov, *Magnitogorsk* (Moscow, 1961).

The "socialist city," where John and Masha obtained an apartment, as it looked in 1935. Provided by Maria Scott.

Fountains on the pedestrian mall between the apartment buildings of the socialist city, 1938. From TsGAKFD.

PART SIX

PART SIX The Battle of
Iron and Steel

I

During the early
thirties the main energies of the Soviet Union went into construction. New plants, mines, whole industries, sprang up all over the country.

All too frequently, however, the new aggregates failed to work normally. Semi-trained workers were unable to operate the complicated machines which had been erected. Equipment was ruined, men were crushed, gassed, and poisoned, money was spent in astronomical quantities. The men were replaced by new ones from the villages, the money was made good by the State in government subsidies, and the materials and supplies were found somehow.

Beginning in 1935, the main energies of the country were transferred from construction to production.

Russia needed enormous amounts of iron, steel, and machinery of all kinds to satisfy the expanding demands of the country's consumers' goods market, and, not less important, for the Red Army, Navy, and Air Force; for guns, munitions, planes, cruisers, and tanks. Every Soviet newspaper, radio program, and public speech emphasized the vital importance of production.

In Magnitogorsk, Zavenyagin turned his attention to the problem of producing iron and steel and coke and ore. He left construction in the hands of subordinates. Production workers' wages became higher than those of the builders; the press, supply organizations, the party, all turned their eyes toward production. I had worked three years welding blast furnaces and climbing structural steel. I decided to go over to production.

My graduation from the Komvuz was a contributing factor in this decision. After being ceremoniously graduated, I was urged by local party authorities to go into propaganda work. However, as I showed no inclination either to join the Communist Party or to renounce my American citizenship — steps necessary for anyone to become a party functionary in the Soviet Union — the party authorities found it necessary to tell me what no employment of a political nature was open to me.

I was very glad. I had learned a great deal in the Komvuz — my Russian was good and I had a clear idea of the theories of Marx, Lenin, and Stalin, upon which the social and economic structure of the Soviet Union was presumably based. I knew all the answers, or at least most of them, and could enumerate the errors and infamies of the Trotzkyite and several other oppositionary groups with a speed and accuracy which made my teachers smile with pride.

But to become a professional propagandist I had no desire. It is all very well to be taught things one does not believe or accepts with reservations; it is quite a different matter to teach these things to others. I wanted to study sciences which I could accept more fully, learn lessons I could master and repeat without any feeling of intellectual hypocrisy. I wanted to go to engineering school. Magnitogorsk boasted but one such — the Mining and Metallurgical Institute — entry to which was open only to production workers in the mill.

After a great deal of difficulty the Construction Trust accepted my resignation as of the termination of a six weeks' vacation. During this time I set out to find a berth in one of the production units which would interest me, leave me more or less free for evening study at the Institute, and pay enough to meet current expenses.

II

I spent two days stumbling around the immense iron mine which was producing upwards of five million tons of ore a year — nearly twenty-five per cent of the Soviet Union's total output.[1] Twenty-five imported electric locomotives were at work pulling modern fifty-ton dump cars from cutting to crusher and thence to the agglomeration plant. I watched the electric excavators shoveling ore at the rate of fifty tons per minute, or else standing with their arms extended awaiting the arrival of empty cars to fill — a sight which always reminded me of a man surprised while eating, frozen with his fork halfway to his open mouth.

The mine did not appeal to me as a place to work. I went back to the blast furnaces to survey the possibilities there.

I had seldom seen any but the seedy side of the blast furnaces. Our gang of construction workers was called in only to do repair work when something went wrong.

During the winters of 1933 and 1934 the whole blast-furnace department was periodically shut down. The cold winds played havoc with the big furnaces. Gas lines, air lines, water pipes, all

[1] See Appendix 16.

froze. Tons of ice hung down all around, sometimes collapsing steel structures with their weight. One of the four furnaces was shut down for general repairs most of the time.

One job we all remembered vividly was the demolition work after the disastrous explosion on No. 2 in 1934. We were kept busy night and day for two months. Owing to incorrect handling of the tapping hole a water jacket burned through and several cubic yards of water came into contact with the molten iron. The resultant blast blew the roof off the cast house, badly damaged the side of the furnace, and seriously injured everybody who was near-by at the time. No. 2 was shut down for two months for repairs, which cost the country some fifty thousand tons of iron. The repairs themselves cost a million and a half roubles, and occupied construction workers who could have been doing other things. Several people were tried in an attempt to fix responsibility for this accident, but there were no convictions. For two weeks previous to the disaster everybody connected with the furnace had known that the tapping hole was in bad shape. The foreman told the superintendent, who told the director, who told Zavenyagin, who telephoned Ordjonokidze, the People's Commissar of the USSR for the whole industry. Nobody realized the dangers of a bad tapping hole, and no one wanted to take the responsibility for shutting down the furnace prematurely at a time when the country needed pig iron very badly.

Inexperience and carelessness took a heavy toll in the blast-furnace transport system also. There were never enough ladles, mainly because of the fact that the railroad workers failed to put them squarely under the iron spouts or else neglected to take them away in time. In either case the ladles were inundated with hot iron, which ate through axles, wheels, and rails.

During the first years of blast-furnace operation, when watching a gang at work in the cast house I frequently got the impression that they were big children playing with a new toy. I remember vividly a big, sparsely-bearded Mongolian puddling around in the trough of white-hot iron with a sixty-pound crowbar, smiling and swearing to himself with glee. A young komsomol brigadier came up to him, slapped him on the back. 'Iron, see?' The Mongolian smiled, undoubtedly thinking of his dinner with half his mind while he contemplated this strange new world of blast furnaces and pig iron in which he found himself. Such scenes should have stimulated (whether they really did or not still remains to be seen) the development of a new romantic proletarian literature, but they definitely did not lead to efficient blast-furnace operation.

By 1935 conditions were much improved. When I went scouting for a job I was struck by the appearance of No. 2. It was clean as a billiard table, the walls were whitewashed, tools hung neatly in their places. The gang went about its work quietly and efficiently.

The personnel was getting enough to eat. Everybody had given up trying to idolize proletarian labor on a komsomol blast furnace (work on any blast furnace in any country is hot, unhealthy, dangerous, and gruelingly hard). The workers were enjoying some of the good things of life outside the mill. Their living conditions had improved, so that their attention could be focused on these things and their work regarded more realistically, as necessary labor which must be done efficiently and well in order to make possible the sunnier side of life. This point of view made possible strict labor discipline and efficient work.

Furthermore, the technical leadership had learned a great deal. The first foremen to work on the Magnitogorsk furnaces were oldtimers who had had their training on little 'samovar' furnaces producing forty to fifty tons a day, where all work was done by hand. The Magnitogorsk furnaces were equipped with the latest mechanical devices. The Brosius mud gun, for instance, the latest thing in American blast-furnace technique, was installed by the American engineers and then lay idle because the oldtime Russian foremen preferred hammering clay by hand.

Gradually these old foremen were replaced, partly by young Soviet engineers and partly by workers who had been pushed forward as being more eligible for the job because of their willingness to learn and to work hard.

The blast furnaces were doing very well. They often exceeded the American project capacity of one thousand tons per furnace daily.[1] The iron was of good quality.

Costs were still high, fifty-five roubles a ton in 1935, and productivity lower than in the United States; for example, while an American furnace of one thousand cubic meter volume was tended by seventy to eighty men, in Magnitogorsk it took one hundred and sixty-five. Still, enormous progress had been made. Magnitogorsk produced more pig iron in 1935 than all the mills in Czechoslovakia, Italy, or Poland.

I should have taken a maintenance job in the blast-furnace department, probably, as I knew the layout like the palm of my hand and had grown accustomed to the incessant roar and the sparks as big as tea kettles that flew around the cast house at tapping time; but Kolya had recently taken the job of foreman of maintenance welders, and, what with Masha expecting a baby any day, I could not see taking a welder's job at four hundred roubles or so a month.

So I went to the rolling mills to look at the situation there.

The rolling-mill department consisted of a blooming mill, the mechanical parts of which were made by the German firm Demag, the electrical equipment by General Electric, theoretical productivity 900,000 tons a year; intermediate mills '450'

[1] See Appendix 17.

and '630,' equipped with flying shears, mechanical equipment by Demag, cross-country merchant mill '500'; a 300 mm. light merchant mill; a 250 mm. wire mill.

I knew a number of people working on the rolling mills, and one afternoon I set out to visit some of them. I walked down the immense blooming mill, where eight-ton ingots were tossed and shot around by mechanized cranes and power-driven rollers, and entered the operator's cabin where a close friend of Masha's worked.

Shura was an operator. She sat in a white cabin with large double glass windows directly over the rolls of the mill, and operated a score of control buttons and a dozen foot pedals. One set in motion the rolls which brought the ingots to the mill; another regulated their speed; several more controlled the large mechanical fingers which turned the ingot over; others reversed the direction, and so on. Shura had under her control a ten-thousand-horsepower direct-current motor which reversed its direction of rotation every ten or fifteen seconds and which had received the full benefit of several decades of the best electrical engineering experience in the United States, and a score of auxiliary motors of various kinds. The place was as clean as the operating room of a good hospital, and before I was fairly inside the door an electrician came up and told me no one was supposed to come in because it might upset the operator. They were trying to make a record, he told me. According to the project they should roll an ingot in less than a minute. Actually it took 3.2 minutes on the average and the record for an eight-hour shift was only two minutes, and an average of fifteen per cent of their production was not up to specifications. The electrician made a whole speech until a shortage of ingots caused a shutdown and Shura left her levers and came and talked to me.

She was a village girl who had been very sick, which had been the cause of her taking the operators' course instead of doing more active work. She was twenty-three, had the high cheek-bones and open features of peasant stock, and the rather pale, nervous expression which had come as a result of her months in the hospital and subsequent work as blooming-mill operator. She came to work always with a red kerchief around her head, and the same serious, high-strung expression. She was never late, did not have to take time off for a smoke like many of the men, and never came with a hang-over. Moreover, she had learned the technique of operating the blooming mill. She understood the electrical controls which she operated, and while her knowledge of theoretical physics was not extensive (she had gone to school only seven years), she knew enough to be a thoroughly competent operator. Beyond this it was a question of a simple mechanical and nervous dexterity, and at this she was a master. She was one of the best operators in Magnitogorsk.

In many jobs, such as crane operating, mill operating, and so forth, where reliability, dexterity, and consistency were required rather than physical strength, women largely replaced men in Magnitogorsk. Their only disadvantage was that, with a birth rate in 1937 of thirty-three to one thousand, they were prone to be running away for maternity vacations too frequently, and losing the knack of their work.

Like the blast furnaces, the blooming mill had worked very badly at first. Monthly plans were fulfilled by twenty and thirty per cent, and there were continual costly shutdowns. For instance, in December, 1933, the blooming mill was shut down forty-four per cent of the time. The causes were the following: lack of gas or electricity or water, thirteen per cent; electrical equipment out of order, two per cent; mechanical equipment out of order, nine per cent; ingot fouled in the mill, fourteen per cent; sundry, six per cent.

However, by 1935 it was working so well that it rolled all the steel the open hearth produced.

III

F ROM the blooming mill I walked down to the 500 mm. merchant mill, or 'Mill 500' as it was called. I was particularly attracted to Mill 500 because of its size, and also because Mitya Glazer, the party secretary there, was an old friend of mine, having been one of the teachers in the Komvuz. Mitya was twenty-seven, son of a Ukrainian Jewish tailor, and a komsomol and party functionary for ten years. He was businesslike and very capable.

Mitya showed me around the mill. When I told him I was looking for a new job, he produced a bright idea — he knew that I wrote short stories in my spare time.

'Why not write a pamphlet about Mill 500?' he asked enthusiastically.

It was an intriguing idea. I spent two weeks studying the mill and organizing the material gathered. Mitya, in the meantime, was 'seeing about having it published.'

Nothing came of it, of course, but some of the material gathered is of interest today.

Mill 500 cost 12,240,000 roubles. Nearly sixty per cent of this money was paid in gold, and it bought the best the world had to offer in rolling mills. The entire process was mechanized. When running normally, the steel traveled along about as fast as a man can run, billet following billet not more than a few inches apart.

The mill was manned by seven hundred and twenty workers, engineers, and sundry white-collar men. About two-thirds of these were Russian, the rest were Ukrainians, Tartars, Bashkirs, and Jews.

Of the whole personnel, twenty-nine per cent came to work on Mill 500 directly from the villages. About twenty per cent were old rolling-mill men who had been sent to Magnitogorsk from mills in the Donbas in the South or from other small mills in the Magnitogorsk plant. Of these, however, approximately three-quarters had come from the village not long before.

The administrative structure of the mill was as follows: The 'natchalnik' or superintendent was a young Soviet engineer named Weissberg. He had three assistants. One was respon-sible for equipment, one for production, the third for living and working conditions of the workers and sundry questions. A master mechanic and a master electrician were responsible for respective equipment. The factory clerk with two assistants kept account of the orders, types of metals to be rolled, load-ings, and shipments. The bookkeeper and three assistants calculated the wages of the workers and the financial operations of the mill generally. The trade union and party organizers occupied themselves with educational and propaganda work among the whole personnel, questions of labor discipline, and inner party and inner trade-union questions. One man in the personnel department kept a record of the workers. Four men in the technical bureau studied the technical processes of pro-duction, figured out rationalization schemes, ways to save time and money, and calculated materials, equipment, and spare parts needed. Two workers in the labor bureau fixed the norms and studied the labor processes involved in production. In ad-dition to this there were two girls who answered the telephone and did a little typing. This completed the list of the white-collar workers.

In addition to these the following people directed the pro-cesses of production, though they themselves did no manual la-bor; five shift foremen, five shift engineers, and one general fore-man. This made a total of about thirty-five not directly engaged in the process of production. The remainder were all 'workers' (as opposed to engineering and technical personnel) — electricians, rollers, repair mechanics, gas men, and so on. These workers were divided into categories, according to their qualifications. The categories ran from one to eight, and when graduating into a higher category, a worker had to pass examinations, both theoretical and practical. Any worker had the right to ask for a higher category at any time, and if he could pass the examinations, to receive it. The administration, with the approval of the trade union, could reduce a worker's category if he proved himself incompetent. The foremen did not have the power to change workers' categories, nor to hire and fire, although naturally their opinion was taken into consideration by the superintendent and union functionary when they were deciding questions of this kind.

In Mill 500 only a handful of workers had the first and second categories, which correspond to apprentice or laborer. The average category was the fifth.

During the whole of 1934 the output of the mill was negligibile. Production was ten, fifteen, twenty per cent of capacity. The reasons for this, though many, could all be put under one heading: the workers had not yet learned how to run the mill. Things were always getting out of order, and there was nobody at hand who could fix them.

The planning department of the plant gave the workers of Mill 500 very easy plans, forty to fifty per cent of project capacity, but even these were not fulfilled. People got discouraged, but little by little, month by month, the workers learned their jobs better; output increased until, beginning in January, 1935, the project capacity was attained and then surpassed.[1]

I made something of a study of wages in Mill 500, which I offer as a typical example of the way in which piece-work and a

[1] See Appendix 18.

bonus system were utilized in Magnitogorsk in the middle thirties to raise production.

As a matter of basic policy, the party and the administration tried to fix wages in such a fashion that each individual would be paid in proportion to useful work done.

The engineer and technical personnel were salaried. Foremen received approximately 550 roubles per month; general foremen, shift engineers, master mechanics, and electricians about 800 roubles; bookkeepers about 450; superintendent's assistants about 1000, and the superintendent about 1200 roubles per month. These basic salaries were fixed by the labor bureau when the employee was hired. They could be raised by the superintendent within certain limits, and theoretically could not be lowered by anybody.

These employees, however, actually often received two or three times their salary, while occasionally they only got seventy per cent of it. They received bonuses for production according to the following scale: [1]

Production per cent of Plan for Month	First Group (per cent)	Second Group (per cent)	Third Group (per cent)
Less than 100............	75	75	75
100....................	100	100	100
101 to 120..............	130	120	112
121 to 130..............	170	150	140
131 to 150..............	200	180	155
151 and up	300	250	200

The first group included the superintendent and assistants, general foremen, chief mechanic, and electrician. The second group included shift engineers and foremen. Their wages were based on the plan fulfillment of their shift only. The third group included all the other employees, bookkeepers, and so on. As an example of the application of this system, for the month

[1] Condensed. The original table was eight pages long, containing separate salary percentages for each individual per cent of plan fulfillment.

of October, Foreman Shevchug's shift fulfilled its plan by 162 per cent. For the month, Shevchug received 250 per cent of his basic salary (800 roubles), or 2000 roubles. The same general idea was carried through in the wage system of those workers directly engaged in the process of production. Each category had what was known as a 'tariff,' the wage received if the plan was fulfilled by an even one hundred per cent. Here are the tariffs for rollers by categories, in roubles per eight-hour day:

Category	2nd	3rd	4th	5th	6th	7th	8th
Roubles	9.00	9.93	11.20	13.25	15.88	19.94	23.94

These figures represented the daily wage of the worker whose shift fulfilled its plan by exactly one hundred per cent. The plan was fixed by the planning department of the Magnitogorsk Mill, on the basis of project capacity, directives from the Commissariat of Heavy Industry in Moscow, and any special conditions which might be present (lack of materials, and so forth). Thus, supposing that the plan for a given shift was 100 tons of metal, a roller of the eighth category would get 23 roubles, 94 kopeks, or approximately 24 roubles per 100 tons. If the shift rolled only 50 tons, then the roller would get only 12 roubles. If, however, they rolled more than 100 tons, progressive increases began to make themselves felt. Between 100 and 120 per cent of plan they got price-and-a-half per ton. For every ton between 120 and 130 per cent they got two prices; more than 130 per cent, three prices. Thus, if 140 tons were produced in his shift the roller of the eighth category would get twenty-three roubles, 94 kopeks for the 100 tons, plus three prices per ton or 72 kopeks per ton for the remaining 40 tons, or about 55 roubles for the day.

The question arose: 'Was it profitable for the State to pay so much for production over plan?' The answer was unquestionably 'Yes.' [1] The fixed charges were so much greater than the

[1] See Appendix 19.

labor cost that the actual wages paid out were easily covered by the increased production obtained for the same fixed costs. Of course, it would have been still more profitable for the State to obtain the increased production without paying the increased wages. Decrees providing for reduction of progressive bonuses did come out in 1937 and 1938.

When the mill was shut down for any reason not under control of the workers, they received two-thirds of their tariff, the bill theoretically being footed by the organization responsible for the shutdown. Thus, if Mill 500 shut down for lack of coke gas, the coke-oven department theoretically paid the wages of the idle rollers. Actually, however, this interdepartmental financial juggling did not take place, owing to the refusal of the debtor to pay.

On the other hand, if Mill 500 shut down because of a breakdown of some part because of the carelessness of some of its own workers, then they got nothing for this time.

Overtime was forbidden in general. In emergency cases it was permitted and paid time-and-a-half, double time for holidays. All night work was paid time-and-a-quarter. Work between 11 P.M. and 7 A.M. was, by definition, night work.

The trade-union secretary was a comparatively unimportant figure. Although virtually everybody in the mill was a member of the union, its activities were limited to educational and 'cultural' work. The union organizer of Mill 500 had at his disposal five permanent seats in the City Theater and five similar seats in the circus. He also controlled a fund whose size varied with plan fulfillment, for the satisfaction of the cultural needs of the workers in the mill, decorating the club room, newspaper subscriptions, and so on.

The trade union exercised at intervals a certain actual disciplinary power by the use of 'comradely courts.' For example, if a worker, through carelessness, damaged some equipment, regularly came to work late, drank at work, or in any other way acted as a disorganizing influence, one of several things could happen. If the matter was potentially or actually serious enough to be of political significance, it probably merited the attention of the Secret Police, who dealt with it independently of any mill organization. If, on the other hand, as was usually the case in 1935 or 1936, the Secret Police did not interest themselves, the worker was often brought to trial before his own comrades and shopmates, who elected from their number for the occasion a judge and prosecuting and defending attorneys. The decisions of these 'comradely courts' had no formal legal status. The maximum sentence was fifty roubles fine, to be given to the cultural fund by the convicted defendant, or a recommendation to the administration that the defendant be fired. The propaganda value, however, was very great. Often, after such a comradely trial, a heavy drinker, who was prone to let his excesses disorganize work in the mill, would change his ways to a greater extent than he would have after serving ten days at hard labor.

The Party Cell in Mill 500 included fifty-six members and candidates and twenty-one sympathizers. (Before one can become a full-fledged party member, it is necessary to go through the preliminary stages of sympathizer and candidate.) Weissberg, two of his assistants, three of the four shift engineers, four foremen, and the general foreman were all members of the party. Party members were privileged in that it was easier for them to get scholarships to schools, obtain new apartments, or get vacations in August instead of November.

But, on the other hand, a great deal more responsibility was put on them. If something went wrong and the brigade spoiled a job, a worker who was a party member was held as much or more responsible than the non-party brigadier. In case of vacancies in administrative posts, a party member was usually advanced faster than a non-party member of the same capabilities.

Mitya, as party organizer, probably more than any one person was responsible for the production successes in Mill 500. He had an efficient tongue, and knew how to talk to the workers, making them ashamed of bad work; getting them to try harder by making them understand what they were working for. He was fired with such tangible ardor for the construction of Socialism and everything connected with it that it impressed and influenced everyone with whom he came in contact.

Administrative and technical questions were discussed at regular closed party meetings, and inasmuch as most of the administrators were party members, important decisions could be, and were, made.

The development of 'vigilance' was a major party task. All party members had to be on the watch all the time for sabotage, spying, propaganda of the class enemy, counter-revolution, and similar phenomena. This boiled down to a rather abnormal interest of party members in other people's business and continual 'tattletaling,' and resultant suspicion and distrust particularly among the administrative personnel.

The party made every attempt to surround itself by a circle of 'non-party Bolshevists' who, though without party membership cards, carried out all party decisions and did a good deal of party work.

The work of the party was theoretically supplemented by that of the Komsomol. This organization, however, as in the earlier days of construction, was sadly deficient. This was partially due to the fact that practically one hundred per cent of the workers of Komsomol age (sixteen till twenty-six) studied in some formal school, which usually took up almost all of their spare time. Another reason was that the apparatus of the Komsomol had been filled with incompetent, ambitious, and politically irresponsible elements ever since the beginning of construction. A half-dozen secretaries of the City Committee of the Komsomol had disappeared ignominiously one after the other; one having been arrested for embezzlement of funds, another publicly denounced for debauchery, and several accused of political double-dealing of various kinds.

The Komsomol as an organization had very little influence in Mill 500, although many of its individual members were outstanding workers.

Until October, 1935, Mill 500 ran at a loss and lived on government subsidies like many other new industrial units. During the first half of the year, however, losses diminished as production increased.[1]

During this period the cost of production went down. At the beginning of the year it was 250 roubles a ton, and in October it was 130 roubles, 44 kopeks.

Productivity of labor increased, wages rose, and the cost of the finished product fell. The result was that in October, 1935, the mill made a profit of 960,000 roubles. This money, of course, belonged to the State, but ten per cent of it was turned over to Weissberg to be used for premiums to the workers of the mill.

IV

W<small>HEN</small> it became obvious that my story of Mill 500 was not to be published, I gave up ideas of writing for a living and resumed my search for more prosaic employment.

[1] See Appendix 20.

I ran into Syemichkin, my old superintendent, in the street-car, and he suggested I come to the chemical department. The new benzol department was to go into operation soon and he was trying to pick up forty or fifty suitable workers around the plant somewhere, as the administration would not give him any money to bring trained people from the Ukraine.

After looking it over, I took the job, and for the next two years I operated benzol stills amid the thick smoke of the coke plant. Syemichkin, who had become superintendent of the chemical plant, was my direct chief, which was fine because he gave me books on coke-chemical by-products industry and helped me to find my way around. His chiefs were old Tishenko and Shevchenko. They had gone over during the previous year from construction to production as building work tapered off and construction budgets were cut.

The Magnitogorsk coke and chemical plant was built principally according to the technical project of Koppers and Company, but, unfortunately, elements of the McKee project crept in, as did the influences of several Soviet projecting organizations. The benzol department was redesigned completely when it was found that the tar produced in the condensation department gave no oil fractions suitable for the benzol absorption from the coke gas, and it would be necessary to bring gas oil from the Caucasus to be used for this purpose. Gas oil is lighter than water while coal oil is heavier, so that all the apparatus, designed for use with coal oil, had to be rebuilt.

In the late years of the first Five-Year Plan emphasis was put principally on iron and steel production. Coke was necessary to smelt the pig iron; therefore, work on coke ovens was forced. Construction on the less important chemical plants, however, was allowed to lag. The result was that, while all four Magnitogorsk coke-oven batteries were in operation by the beginning of 1934, several of the chemical departments had not been completed. For two years, 1934 to 1936, some twenty-five million gold dollars' worth of valuable chemicals were allowed to escape in smoke every year. Incidentally, this delay in putting chemical plants into operation was one of the main charges made by the prosecution against Rataichak and other leaders of the chemical industry of the Soviet Union in the Zinoviev trial of 1937. I can testify to the unquestionable existence of this lag, but that it was the exclusive result of conscious sabotage seems doubtful.

Notwithstanding delays and difficulties, by 1935 the Magnitogorsk coke plant had attained large dimensions and was functioning well. Four batteries of ovens were in operation; sixty-nine ovens per battery with a capacity of fourteen tons charge per oven and a coking time of twelve to thirteen hours. The mechanical and electrical equipment of the ovens was mostly imported and worked very well, largely because of the tireless efforts of the master mechanic, one Farberov, a young Soviet engineer who went to work in the coke plant in 1932 and for five years tenaciously stuck to his job of making the mechanical equipment of the plant work.

Eighty-five per cent of the coal consumed was brought fifteen hundred miles from Kuznetsk in Central Siberia, and the remainder came six hundred miles from Karaganda in Kazakhstan and from the local Chelyabinsk deposits.

The chemical plant contained the following departments: A shoddily projected but fairly good condensation department, with four German exhaustors, handled some sixty million cubic feet of gas a day. A sulfate department, with three saturators and a maximum output of sixty tons of ammonium sulfate a day, went into operation in 1935. The well-equipped benzol department, with four stills and capacity of sixty tons a day, went into operation in January, 1936. All the pumps and most of the apparatus of the benzol department were imported.

Some distance away from this part of the chemical plant stood the tar distillation and the benzol rectification units which went into operation in 1934 and 1936 respectively. Both were well equipped and when properly operated turned out benzol, tuluol, naphthaline, and other products of tremendous value. They were profitable enough to make up the deficit that the coke ovens habitually ran, leave a substantial figure in the blue in the ledger of the coke and chemical plant, and even offset in part the enormous deficits of the open-hearth department.

Coke production mounted steadily from 1931 till 1936, when it reached 1,977,000 tons.[1] The cost of production of coke in 1936 was 37 roubles, 10 kopeks a ton. However, the State paid half the coal transportation bill, a very large item in the cost of production. This arrangement was made in order to enable Magnitogorsk to compete in production costs with the southern mills, whose sources of raw materials were, so to speak, in their front yards.

The entire coke and chemical plant employed about two thousand workers. Of these, some ten per cent were so-called engineer and technical personnel, including foremen, superintendents, planners, and so on. Wages in the coke plant were high because of the fact that during 1935 and 1936 the plan was fulfilled better than in most other departments; the workers overfulfilled their norms; pay was correspondingly good. The wage scale and the system of progressive premiums were similar to those on Mill 500 described above.

I was nervous for the first few weeks about the danger of fire and explosion. I was used to working where smoking was forbidden, but to have to wear special rubber-soled shoes, to use copper hammers and wrenches to avoid striking sparks which might ignite the benzol fumes, was a different matter. I gradually became accustomed to it, and concentrated my entire atten-

[1] See Appendix 21.

tion on the apparatus, trying to squeeze every drop of benzol out of the coke gas. Before a year was up, we were producing up to one hundred tons of raw benzol a day, or nearly twice as much as the project capacity of the aggregate.

Then for several months we shut down — the railroad did not send enough tank cars to take away our finished products, including tuluol and aviobenzol. Every container available was full. We stopped producing benzol because there was literally no place to put it.

In September I entered the Institute and began the four-year course in metallurgical engineering. The hardest thing about my studies was that I worked on a rotating shift in the mill, which meant missing a quarter or a third of all the lectures.

V

Oₙₑ night in the winter of 1936 my assistant did not show up. I telephoned Syemichkin.

'Oh yes,' he said, 'the Labor Department has decided that the operators will have to get along without assistants. Shevchenko O.K.'d it. Nothing I can do. Get along as best you can.'

My protests fell upon deaf ears.

About a week later, at the end of my shift I turned the plant over to the oldest operator in the place, one Kuretz, and went up to the Institute. Kuretz told me he was going to try to fix the pump in the storage room. This he did, and some time about eight o'clock was overcome by the fumes and fainted. There being nobody there to help him or to call assistance, he lay there two hours and was dead when found by the foreman. After criminal proceedings had been taken against the foreman, who was accused of negligence, and subsequently got two years, the Labor Department put the assistants back on again, fearing that the prosecutor might get around to them.

However, in spite of many such examples of rationalization and intensification of labor at the cost of men's lives, many men who actually were not necessary were taken off, and the productivity of labor increased.

One of our biggest headaches was loading and unloading tank cars quickly. Speed was necessary because the railroad levied enormous fines for holding up rolling stock. In 1937 Magnitogorsk as a whole paid 1,700,000 roubles to the railroad in fines. The system was inaugurated to help the railroads keep their stock moving, but it turned into one of their greatest financial assets. For some time the rectification plant was idle because there was no place to put finished products, the railroad having failed to send tank cars to take the current production, and every inch of space being filled. Finally the railroad sent fifty cars all at once. The norm for loading tank cars was three hours. According to the law, rolling stock held up for longer than the time norm for its loading or unloading involved paying X roubles (from one to ten roubles, depending on the type of car) for the first hour, 2X for the second hour, 3X for the third hour, and so on. In three hours only three of the fifty tank cars had been loaded, the department being equipped to load only one car at a time. It was a day and a half before the last of the fifty was out. The fine involved in this transaction was almost as big as the monthly payroll. The system did, however, result in people being careful about holding up rolling stock unnecessarily. It was the cause of my freezing my hand badly one night trying to help the sulfate department operator unload ten tank cars of sulphuric acid in three hours.

The coke plant spent considerable money on 'cultural' equipment and activities. An enormous bathhouse-dressing-room-restaurant was constructed for the use of the coke and chemical workers. The place was well equipped, and made it possible for the workers to come home clean and avoid the monotonous dirt in which miners and coke workers often live year in and year out in England and Germany, and even in the United States. A club house was built and equipped with a good library, billiard room, music room, children's room, and other rooms. The money for all this came out of the fund placed at the disposal of every plant which makes a profit in the Soviet Union, for use in bettering the cultural conditions of its workers.

Much was said but, unfortunately, not much done to make the working conditions in the coke plant more healthful. Ventilation systems often did not work, and sanitary inspectors found themselves powerless to force the administration (which had other more pressing duties) to take effective action. There were numerous accidents, though the number decreased with the years. Beginning with 1936 any fatal industrial accident became the subject of criminal investigation. Often they tried the wrong people, but in Russia this is relatively unimportant. The main thing was that the technicians and workers alike began to appreciate and correctly evaluate human life, both their own and other people's, and this was extremely important in a country where tyranny, war, famine, and strife had made life very cheap.

VI

Tʜᴇ manager of the coke and chemical plant, Shevchenko, the same who had been assistant construction director in 1933, had since received the Order of Lenin, been made a member of the District and Regional Party Committees, had received an eight-room private house, and regularly made several thousand roubles a month. He worked hard and drove those under him relentlessly. By and large his departments functioned well. But he, himself, had remained a sharp boor, a dishonest careerist. Occasionally, in little things, he would betray himself. For instance, on the first of May, 1936, the coke and chemical plant received fifty gramophones to be given to the best workers as May Day premiums. Shevchenko appropriated ten of these and sold them, putting the money in his pocket. It was not that he needed money. He had all he wanted. He was just that kind of person.

Shevchenko's chief engineer, the old prisoner specialist Tishenko, still worked without enthusiasm, more and more disdainful of Shevchenko, though fearful of his power. Partially because of his own lack of initiative and his failure to stand by his technical opinions and push them through, and partly because of Shevchenko's lack of confidence in the 'ex-wrecker,' Tishenko's authority declined steadily. Workers and foremen did not listen to him, knowing that he had no real power. He shrugged his shoulders and let things slide. His life at home was monotonously comfortable.

Three years had changed Syemichkin a great deal. Technically, he had gained experience and confidence. He worked hard, and had none of the 'bourgeois' background of Tishenko to overcome, while he had what Shevchenko lacked, a sound technical education. His life was much simpler than that of either of his chiefs. He had a three-room apartment, rode to work on the streetcar, and had to stand in line to buy shoes.

The superintendents and engineers on the coke ovens, where the work was administrative rather than technical, were almost entirely young fellows whom Shevchenko had put in because he knew them personally and could trust them. Shevchenko had no trouble in finding such.

During 1936 the Stakhanov movement was much talked of, not only throughout the Soviet Union, but in other countries as well. It was an interesting and important development in Soviet economy.

VII

T HE Stakhanov move-
ment took its name from a Donbas coal miner and became very important after Stalin addressed the first Stakhanovite con-
ference and pointed out that improved living conditions and technical training of industrial personnel had created the basis for drastic increases in productivity, which should be realized without delay.

It was true. Life had become 'better and more joyful' as Stalin put it. There was more to eat, more to wear, and every indication that the improvement would continue.

The Stakhanov movement hit Magnitogorsk in the fall of 1935 and was immediately made the subject of various meetings, press notices, administrative orders, and endless conver-

sations, private and public. Brigade and shop competition was intensified. Banners were awarded to the brigades who worked best, and monetary remuneration accompanied the banners. Everyone went nosing around his department, trying to uncover 'reserves of new productivity.' Wages rose. Production rose. Magnitogorsk was animated by a boom.

The Stakhanov movement in Magnitogorsk produced very marked results during the latter half of 1935 and almost all of 1936.[1] The coefficient of blast-furnace work, furnace volume divided by daily production, improved from 1.13 to 1.03; the production of steel per square meter of hearth increased on every single hearth, the average improvement being by 10.5 per cent, from 4.2 tons to 4.65 tons. On the rolling mills productivity rose and costs fell.

As a result of the improved work, the Magnitogorsk combinat showed a profit for the last quarter of 1936 of 13,800,000 roubles. Even before this, in October, 1935, the combinat had made a few thousand roubles' profit, and Zavenyagin with a quixotic gesture had expressed his confidence in his ability to get along without State subsidies, which were immediately discontinued, and without which the finances of the combinat suffered seriously through the first half of 1936. The plant's most serious liability was the open hearth, which, in the words of Zavenyagin, 'ate up millions every month.' In February alone the combinat ran a deficit of 4,000,000 roubles. Zavenyagin had to cover this by taking money from city construction budgets. But by and large, 1936, the Stakhanovite year, was a great success. The nominal profit for the year was 112,000,000 roubles. (It is difficult thoroughly to credit these figures, because of the numerous systems of bookkeeping in use for different purposes. This figure, however, appeared in the *Magnitogorsk Worker* for December 24, 1936.)

While this improvement was going on, negative forces were

[1] See Appendix 22.

being created. In the first place, the norms were raised in the fall of 1936 after a publicity campaign and a speech by Stalin himself. This created a restlessness among many workers who had received the impression that all improvements in production would reflect themselves in direct wage increases, and that the norms would never be changed.

Technically, also, many things were done which stored up trouble for the future. Equipment was overtaxed, current repairs were neglected. It was decided, for instance, to put two hundred and forty tons of steel into the Magnitogorsk open hearths, which were projected to hold one hundred and fifty tons. This necessitated a certain amount of reconstruction of the hearths themselves, and endless difficulties with the ladles and ladle cranes. It was found necessary to pour the melting out into two ladles at once with the help of a Y-shaped canal. One side of the Y continually got blocked and the steel was spilled all over the shop a hundred times.

Transport equipment, both rolling stock and rails, was sadly overtaxed. This was seen not only in Magnitogorsk inner plant transport, but in the transport system of the Soviet Union as a whole, where daily carloadings rose to 100,000 in a Stakhanovite boom under Commissar Kaganovich, and later went down to 75,000 where they still hovered in January, 1939. (After 1939, no figures were published.) All the rolling mills were given very hard plans, repair time was cut down, and equipment suffered accordingly.

In March, 1936, a conference of leaders of metallurgical industries from the whole Union met in Moscow to redefine the project capacities of various aggregates in the light of the achievements of the Stakhanov movement. On the basis of these new project capacities, new norms and plans were worked out for every unit of each combinat in the Union, including, of course, Magnitogorsk.[1]

[1] See Appendix 23.

VIII

IN THE coke and chemical plant, the Stakhanov movement brought about sweeping changes in some technical processes and was often unquestionably instrumental in raising efficiency in production. Suggestions of improvements of all kinds were made by workers and technicians alike and were often acted on and aided in bringing up production. Regular production meetings were held in all the shops and departments. Here the workers could and did speak up with the utmost freedom, criticize the director, complain about the wages, bad living conditions, lack of things to buy in the store — in short, swear about anything except the general line of the party and a half-dozen of its sacrosanct leaders. These meetings discussed the plan, passed the list of Stakhanovites for the month, and decided local shop issues.

The technical results of the Stakhanov movement were sometimes involved and of doubtful general benefit. For instance, due to the Stakhanov movement, the coke ovens produced some twenty per cent more gas than had been projected. It became the task of the Stakhanovites of the condensation department to suck all this gas into the chemical department without letting a single meter escape. The gas lines were big enough to carry the additional load, but the exhaustors, unfortunately, were machines to which it was hard to apply the Stakhanov movement. An induction motor of the type which ran the exhaustors (two pole) makes three thousand revolutions per minute, working on a fifty-cycle alternating current. Nothing that the Stakhanovite machinist or foreman could do could increase this speed. The alternative was to put more load on the exhaustors while maintaining the same speed. This was done, but only by dint of violating the most elementary technical rules. The motors were of German make and designed to take not more than ninety amperes. However, with the load imposed by the Stakhanov movement, they often ran up past one hundred amperes. It was plainly written on every motor in German and Russian that if the load exceeded ninety amperes the motor should be turned off. This was ignored, and it became the task of the assistant machinist to hold the breaker with a broomstick to prevent its kicking off when the load became too heavy. This practice went on for years. As a result a motor was burned out every two weeks or so. Nobody ever figured out how much it cost to rewind the motors.

The effects of the Stakhanov movement were felt particularly in the finance department. The Stakhanovites' wages rose very high. Often the increased receipts from the margin of the increased production did not equal the increased wages. Result — a deficit on the books.

The Stakhanov movement produced striking results on the iron mine. In 1937, 6,500,000 tons of ore were produced. In the same year Germany produced 4,700,000 tons, England 4,-200,000 tons, and Sweden 8,500,000 tons. The productivity of labor had risen from 2017 tons per average worker per year in 1935 to 3361 tons per average worker per year in 1937. This increase in productivity was the best indication of increased efficiency.

In 1937 finished blast-furnace ore cost three roubles, fifty-three kopeks a ton, which made it by far the cheapest ore in the Soviet Union and, even accepting the nominal rouble-dollar exchange, as cheap as ore from the best mines in the United States.

The ore mine made a considerable profit every year beginning
in 1935. The excavators produced more. In 1932, working
three shifts a day, the average excavator mined 446,000 tons
of ore; in 1934, 1,111,000 tons. In 1937, working only two shifts
a day, just under 2,000,000 tons.

The productivity of the electrical locomotives increased
likewise. In 1934 the average locomotive hauled 34,000 tons of
ore a month; in 1937, 57,000 tons.

The quality of the ore produced was excellent. The average
iron content for 1937 was 60.1 per cent.

IX

In the hottest days
of the Stakhanov movement I was brought into contact with
an interesting development in the open-hearth department.
Masha's brother-in-law Max was assistant manager of the department, and through him I became acquainted with the details of the fight for steel.

The open hearth was the largest single department in the
whole plant, and probably the most complicated and difficult
to run well. The whole plant and its equipment were the best
that money could buy for the production of a high-grade product at a low cost. The open-hearth department, however,
worked very badly, and counted its yearly, and sometimes its
monthly, deficit in millions. Furthermore, work in the open
hearth eased a number of promising young engineers and
technicians into hospitals, sanitariums, and jails.

Open-hearth plants all over the Soviet Union produced better results than in Magnitogorsk. For three years Zavenyagin nursed along the ailing department, changed the personnel, gave automobiles and motorcycles to the best steel-makers, and had the worst indicted for criminal negligence; but when he left in 1937, the open hearth was still very sick, and represented, in the opinion of many people, Zavenyagin's worst failure.

The cause, generally speaking, was bad organization. The open-hearth process was very complicated. Molten iron lay in a flat basin and was played on from above by a gas flame which burned out excess carbon. Other necessary materials, such as manganese ore or dolomite, were thrown in through small windows. The iron lay thus from eight to twenty hours, during the course of which time it became steel. In order for the department to operate successfully, the twelve open hearths must receive coke and blast-furnace gas, pig iron, both hot and cold, iron ore, manganese ore, dolomite, chalk, limestone, ingot molds, all at the right place at the right time. Moreover, a laboratory must give quick and accurate analyses of the steel while it was being made, and some twenty-five or thirty cranes of various types and sizes had to work smoothly and continuously, move from hearth to hearth, always at hand when needed.

This never happened. One of the materials was always lacking, a crane broke down, the laboratory gave an incorrect analysis, or else people just got confused and did the wrong things.

The open hearth was tremendously overstaffed. In America hundred-and-fifty-ton hearths are manned by forty-five to fifty men. In Magnitogorsk it took one hundred to one hundred and ten men. One could find laborers, under-brigadiers, brigadiers, under-foremen, foremen, general foremen, shift engineers, block engineers, chiefs of shifts, managers of auxiliary shops, technological observers, all getting in each other's way, and most of them not doing any productive work.

One man in the open-hearth department had sufficient fore-sight and knowledge to know what to do, though he lacked the personality and the administrative talent necessary to put his ideas across and have them realized. An efficiency expert by training and with some experience in heavy industry, this mid-dle-aged Soviet engineer, my brother-in-law Max, saw that the road toward improvement lay in synthesizing the work of the twelve hearths and the enforcing of a strict production sched-ule, so that the equipment would be able to perform the neces-sary operations on all the hearths, one after the other, instead of having nothing to do for two hours, and then being called to three places at once.

If properly organized, this project would eliminate the de-vastating current shutdowns, Max reasoned. (In 1936, one fourth of the total hearth hours of the year were spent shut down.) Max planned his work well. After making a survey of the open hearth, he went to Zavenyagin, who enthusiasti-cally approved his plan, then returned to the open hearth as as-sistant manager with Zavenyagin's blessing, though with the enmity of some of the oldtime steel-makers, who considered that this efficiency upstart did not know what he was talking about. For two months preparations went on: lectures for the workers, large dials indicating what stage of the production process each hearth should be in at a given time Max slept and ate at the mill, often not coming home for days at a time. Again and again he was forced to go to Zavenyagin to get authority to buck the oldtime leadership of the department who thought the old ways were best and that it was not natural for an open hearth to work by schedule. The day of the trial came, production rose for two or three days, and then fell down below the previous level. The schedule had been blatantly sabotaged by many of the responsible leaders of the department, while it had been met with the indifference or quiet disapproval of the ordinary workers, who preferred to do things when they wanted to or when they were ready, rather than at a specifically indicated time. For several months Max fought on for his schedule, on numerous occasions almost coming to blows with his associates. Finally Zavenyagin had to make a choice between Max and the oldtimers. Lacking confidence in the younger and less experienced engineer, Zavenyagin removed Max from the post of assistant director, and attempts at working on schedule were given up. Max was subsequently dealt with in the good old Russian fashion — that is, released from the plant in disgrace — while all the failures and shortcomings of the last few months were attributed to him in order to build up the authority of the administration and the workers' confidence in it. The open hearth went back into the old chaotic rut: in 1937, 12.7 per cent scrap costing a million roubles, and so on. The total deficit of the open-hearth department for the first quarter of 1937 was three million roubles.

At about this time one of the crack journalists of the *Magnitogorsk Worker* wrote a full-page story entitled 'The Sad History of Melting No. 1372.' This melting started out on the desk of the chief of the open hearth, who, after examining the orders for steel, wrote out the order: 'Melting No. 1372, auto-tractor-axle-steel.' The order was taken out to the dispatcher, who gave it to the chief of shift, who took it to the dining-room with him and spilled soup on it, and finally delivered it, partly legible, to the manager of Block No. 1, who, after certain delays, got it to the hands of the steel-maker of Hearth No. 4, who had just come to work. To make a long story short, the steel-maker couldn't read the order very well, and feeling in need of practice decided to make a melting of high-speed steel. There was, however, not enough of this and not enough of that, and by the time the hearth was charged it would have been difficult to determine just what kind of steel it contained. The laboratory failed to exercise accurate control, and one hundred and eighty tons of bastard steel were poured into the ingot molds after sundry minor shutdowns, waiting for the pouring ladle crane, waiting for the laborers to clear away the slag that had been spilled on the rails from the next hearth, and so on.

Eighteen ingots were registered on the dispatcher's book and shipped off to the stripper crane. On the way three ingots were lost. In the stripper crane two ingots were found to be welded in the molds and were scrapped. The thirteen remaining ingots started for the blooming mills. Here two of them were mixed with other ingots in the soaking pits, and lost track of. Eleven ingots went through the blooming mill, where one of them was scrapped. Finally, after having passed through the first two rolling mills, nine ingots came to rest in the intermediary stock yards. Here an analysis was made, and the results were compared with the original order for Melting No. 1372. They were declared not up to specifications and scrapped.

Despite these discouraging examples of bad organization and stupid leadership the Magnitogorsk open hearth made real progress. Thousands of tons of steel were produced every day.[1] After 1937, moreover, production increased steeply, while quality improved noticeably. During the five years from 1937 till 1942, Magnitogorsk furnished roughly ten million tons of steel to Russia's machine-building plants and construction jobs. It was expensive steel, both in terms of roubles and human lives, but ten million tons of steel will make a great many tanks whose military effectiveness bears no relation to the price paid for the steel.

[1] See Appendix 24.

PART SEVEN

PART SEVEN Administration
and the Purge

I

THE October Revolution brought about a complete change in the ruling class of Russia. In addition to the aristocracy and the big capitalists, some three million business men, bankers, engineers, doctors, army officers, postoffice and railway officials, and other small 'chinovniki' perished or emigrated. After the civil war in 1923 the Bolsheviks were faced with the task of reorganizing a country covering a sixth of the earth's land surface, with a population of one hundred and sixty millions, all completely disorganized and exhausted by nearly a decade of war, revolution, famine, and civil war. The old executives and administrators were gone. Raw peasants, a small industrial proletariat, a Bolshevik Party whose total membership at the time of the revolution was about twenty thousand, and a handful of professional revolutionaries of long standing were the only reservoirs from which to draw statesmen, ambassadors, financiers, factory directors, and even station masters and professional men. The Bolsheviks had to produce their leaders almost overnight.

The organizational task which the new rulers of Russia set

out to perform, particularly after the beginning of the Five-Year Plans, was one of unprecedented difficulty. The People's Commissariat of Heavy Industry, for example, ran thousands of mines, shops, and mills throughout the country. This commissariat was created by a stroke of the pen and was expected to begin functioning immediately. It did not have a chance to grow up over a period of several decades like the comparatively small organizations of Henry Ford, Andrew Carnegie, and Krupp. The result was what might have been expected: tremendous enthusiasm, boundless devotion, and hard work; and unbelievable confusion, disorder, and stupidity. The situation was aggravated by the presence of numbers of people hostile to the Soviet power and ready to sabotage wherever possible, particularly when they felt that they could do so safely.

In the late twenties, just as things were getting started, the Soviet power disfranchised, dispossessed, or 'liquidated' more than a million kulaks, or rich peasants, and their families. These kulaks had usually been the most skillful farmers, hence the local leaders; while their sons and daughters had gone to school and become the post-revolutionary bank cashiers, trained nurses, and even engineers, doctors, and administrators. The sons and daughters were disfranchised along with their fathers when it was found out that they were of kulak derivation.

With the exception of slight letups in the middle twenties and again in the early thirties, few foreign specialists were allowed to come to the Soviet Union.

Thus the Bolsheviks were forced to organize and run industry, finance, transport, and commerce with untrained, inexperienced executives and administrators.

This process developed in microcosm in Magnitogorsk, where within five years a tremendous industrial plant was constructed and began to operate. By 1934 most of the foreigners had left,

The plant remained in the hands of representatives of the new Soviet intelligentsia, aided by a score of prisoner specialists. Zavenyagin, the director of the combinat, was thirty-four years old, and, until being sent to Magnitogorsk as director, had had almost no industrial experience. Under him was a heterogeneous collection of engineers, superintendents, and functionaries, most of whom were unfit for their jobs, lacked experience, and often natural ability. Zavenyagin had to leave them in their positions because no one more able was available to take their places.

Whereas most of the workers in the mills were fairly well trained by 1935, had acquired the knacks of electric welding, pipe-fitting, or what not, most of the administrators were far from having mastered their jobs. They had not one quarter the practical experience of men occupying similar positions in industry in America or Western Europe. In order to give the reader an idea of local administrative problems I shall briefly describe a half-dozen Magnitogorsk executives, their lives and work.

II

I HAVE already spoken of Shevchenko, who by 1936 was running the coke plant with its two thousand workers. He was a gruff man, exceedingly energetic, hard-hitting, and often rude and vulgar. When anything happened in the plant he would come down himself, plunge into acid, flame, and dirt, get down and do the job with his own hands if necessary, in order that it should be done quickly and well. He was distrustful of those around him. He had a working axiom which he would express often with vehemence, 'Vsye lyudi blyadi — all people are prostitutes — except you and me. Work on that basis, and you won't make any mistakes,' he would say. He was contemptuous, often disrespectful, of his engineer subordinates and colleagues (though jealous of their technical knowledge). He was sweet as honey with Zavenyagin and his other administrative superiors.

Within certain limitations, on the face of it, Shevchenko was not a bad plant director. The workers respected him, and when he gave an order they jumped. Besides this, his readiness in making decisions and his cocksureness were often assets. For example, at one time the water settling basin connected with the benzol department clogged up with naphthylene. Resulting shutdowns cost the plant thousands of roubles daily. There were many suggestions as to what to do. Tishenko, the chief engineer, made two or three, Syemichkin, the head of the benzol department, made others. A half-dozen engineers, each defending his own plan, were standing around the ailing basin. Shevchenko came up with his usual bluster, and pushed his way to the center of the group. 'Do it this way!' he shouted, taking hold of the first plan in the chief engineer's hand, 'and be quick about it —— your mothers, or you will stand around all day, the lot of you, and make fifty suggestions, and never do anything.'

Shevchenko made this decision without any consideration of the merits of the various plans. He was incapable of such consideration. It was necessary to make people stop talking and get to work. Shevchenko attained this end very well.

In June, 1935 a serious explosion in the machine room of the chemical plant killed four people and injured eighteen others. Shevchenko was in the building, but miraculously escaped unscathed. I was in the plant at the time and am convinced that this accident was the result of technical stupidity, largely on Shevchenko's part. However, the latter was in the good graces of the powers that be and got off scot free, while Tishenko, who was at home eating dinner at the time of the explosion, got two years (in addition to the ten he was already serving), and the machinist and the head of the machine room, both of whom were killed, were picked out by the press as having been the ones really responsible for the accident.

The affair was gradually forgotten, but Shevchenko's dossier in the NKVD files had grown heavier, and he knew it.

Shevchenko came from a little village in the Ukraine. In 1920, Denikin's White Army occupied the territory, and young Shevchenko, a youth of nineteen, was enlisted as a gendarme. Later Denikin was driven back into the Black Sea, and the Reds took over the country. In the interests of self-preservation Shevchenko lost his past, moved to another section of the country, and got a job in a mill. He was very energetic and active, and within a surprisingly short time had changed from the pogrom-inspiring gendarme into a promising trade-union functionary in a large factory. He was ultra-proletarian, worked well, and was not afraid to cut corners and push his way up at the expense of his fellows. Then he joined the party, and one thing led to another — the Red Directors Institute, important trade-union work, and finally in 1931 he was sent to Magnitogorsk as assistant chief of construction work.

In 1932, however, misfortune overtook him. The wooden structure built over the coke batteries during the laying of the fire-bricks (in order to equalize the temperature) caught fire. Everyone lost his head. Firemen ran in, and with bull-headed stupidity insisted on pouring water on the burning structure, in spite of the frantic objections of the foreigners and several Soviet engineers present. Had the fire been allowed to burn itself out, a wooden structure and a few days would have been lost. Damages would have been limited to a few thousand roubles. By turning the cold water on the hot walls, 1,200,000 gold roubles' worth of the best imported fire-brick was ruined, and the job set back by several months. There were telegrams and telephone calls to and from Moscow. The next day Shevchenko, who was responsible administrator, and who had been on the scene of the fire, together with his subordinates and the chief fireman were arrested.

But Fate intervened in the form of the construction director, one Maryasin, who telephoned Moscow, pulled various strings in higher government circles, and got the men released.

Shevchenko was promoted to the post of manager of the coke and chemical plant. He was ardent, fluent, politic. He received the Order of Lenin and was made a member of the District Party Committee.

In 1935 Maryasin, already working on another job, was arrested as 'an agent of the Japanese secret service' and an active Trotskyite. From that time on Shevchenko was worried. He worked harder, took to drinking rather more than was good for him, and made even more ardent speeches at meetings.

Then a worker arrived from some town in the Ukraine and began to tell stories about Shevchenko's activities there in 1920. Shevchenko gave the man money and a good job, but still the story leaked out. One day Shevchenko was called before the District Party Committee and questioned. Hiding one's past counter-revolutionary activities from the party was a very serious crime in the Soviet Union, but in view of Shevchenko's good work the District Committee suppressed the story and the offender stayed in his position and in all his honorary offices, though from that time on the NKVD had enough material to send him up for many years, and he knew that this would be done if his work became unsatisfactory, or if any of his superiors, for personal or other reasons, chose to prefer formal charges.

One night he threw a party which was unprecedented in Magnitogorsk. He sent a special agent south to buy fruit and champagne, he hired the best musicians in the city, and invited the cream of Berezki society. Zavenyagin himself appeared at the party only at one A.M., but such was the general tenor of relations between these people that neither Shevchenko nor any of his guests began either eating or drinking until their chief appeared. The latter, rather disapproving such an orgy, stayed half an hour and left. Shevchenko and his pals were busy the rest of the night and most of the next consuming the remains. All of this was common knowledge among the engineers and administrators at the plant, though the workers were unaware of it. To them Shevchenko was still the 'iron Bolshevik,' the 'Red director,' the infallible.

One day about a year after the explosion in the machine room, Shevchenko was removed from his post, along with a half-dozen of his leading personnel. They stayed home fidgeting for several days, then were arrested. Shevchenko was tried fifteen months later and got ten years.

Shevchenko was at least fifty per cent bandit — a dishonest and unscrupulous careerist. His personal aims and ideals differed completely from those of the founders of Socialism. However, in all probability, Shevchenko was not a Japanese spy, as his indictment stated, did not have terrorist intentions against the leaders of the party and the government, and did not deliberately bring about the explosion referred to above.

The 'Shevchenko band' was composed of some twenty men, all of whom received long sentences. Some, like Shevchenko, were crooks and careerists. Some were actual counter-revolutionaries who set out deliberately to do what they could to overthrow the Soviet power and were not particular with whom they cooperated. Others were just unfortunate in having worked under a chief who fell foul of the NKVD.

Nikolai Mikhailovich Udkin, one of Shevchenko's colleagues, was the eldest son in a well-to-do Ukrainian family. He felt strongly that the Ukraine had been conquered, raped, and was now being exploited by a group of Bolsheviks, mostly Russians and Jews, who were ruining the country, indeed the whole Soviet Union, with their stupidity, bull-headedness, and greed. He felt, furthermore, that the capitalist system worked much better than the Socialist system. He expressed these opinions to his intimate friends.

Here was a man who was at least a potential menace to the Soviet power, a man who might have been willing to cooperate with the Germans for the 'liberation of the Ukraine' in 1941. He, also, got ten years.

Farberov, the master mechanic of the coke and chemical plant, likewise sentenced with Shevchenko, was a devoted rank-and-file Communist, businesslike, punctual, and fair with his subordinates. He was quiet and unobtrusive. He, more than any other one person, was responsible for the real successes achieved by the coke plant during 1935 and 1936. I do not know the concrete charges against Farberov, but I am convinced that he was the victim of unfortunate circumstances and did not deserve the sentence he received.

III

LATE in 1934, Sergei Kirov, Stalin's right-hand man and the head of the party in Leningrad, was assassinated by a former Komsomol oppositionary. Two weeks later Lominadze, the secretary of the

Magnitogorsk party organization, received a summons to appear before the District Chief of the GPU in Chelyabinsk. He got into his car and drove off, and halfway to his destination put two bullets into his abdomen. He was a big man and was still alive when the chauffeur brought him back to Magnitogorsk. He died that night in the hospital. No exact explanation of this unexpected suicide ever reached my ears. Lominadze had worked night and day for years in the revolutionary movement in China and Germany, and then in Soviet industry. To me it is absolutely incredible that he should have been in any way connected with the assassination of Kirov, particularly in view of the fact that later the Moscow trials seemed to indicate that the assassination had been engineered by Henry Yagoda, then the Chief of the GPU. It seems to me that such was Lominadze's temperament that he preferred death to the complications and suffering which an ordeal with the District GPU would entail.

But a number of people in Lominadze's apparatus did not commit suicide. They were nearly all arrested in 1937 and 1938. Most of these people had probably been unaware of any illegal ideas or activities on the part of their chief and had always adhered to the party line. Such was Dmitri Glazer, the secretary of the party unit of Mill 500, who was removed and arrested. Often these removals took place in the most nonchalant manner. The following is a quotation from the *Magnitogorsk Worker* for December 21, 1937, on page 4 in small type:

> The 16th and 17th of December the plenum of the Magnitogorsk City Committee of the party took place. The secretary of the Chelyabinsk district committee of the party, Comrade Ogurtsov, and the chief of the Chelyabinsk district administration of the NKVD, Comrade Chistov, took part in the meeting.
>
> The plenum removed its secretary, Berman, from his post, and from membership in the plenum and in the bureau of the city

committee, for not ensuring the necessary leadership to carry on
the struggle against the enemies of the people.

The plenum also relieved of their posts the following functionaries — Larin, Gaineman, Kaligortsev, Goltsev, and Yefanov.

The bureau of the city committee resolved to remove Larin
from his post as secretary of the Stalin Party section and expel
him from the party for association with enemies of the people.

The plenum gave over the post of secretary of the city committee temporarily to Comrade K. M. Ivanov.

In this way, in two days the whole leadership of the Magnitogorsk Party organization was changed. The operation was
performed principally by the District NKVD Chief and District Party Secretary in closed meetings. In most of the above
cases removal was followed by arrest.

While the activities of Glazer, Shevchenko, and others above
described probably do not coincide with most Westerners' ideas
of wrecking, there unquestionably was wrecking going on in
Magnitogorsk. Here is an example: Two German gas holders,
the largest of which had a volume of one hundred thousand
cubic meters, were imported and erected by German specialists
at a total cost of about two and a half million gold roubles (over
a million dollars at that time). They were erected in 1934 and
were still standing in 1940, unused.

After the money had been paid to the German firm and the
erection nearly completed, someone thought of inquiring
whether the extreme cold of Magnitogorsk would have any
adverse effects on the operation of these tanks. The question
was put to the German erection engineer. He answered bluntly
that operation was guaranteed down to fifteen degrees below
zero centigrade. In Magnitogorsk the thermometer goes down
to forty below zero almost every winter. At this temperature
the water vapor in the gas would condense on the thin steel
walls of the tank and freeze, forming a layer of ice whose weight
would collapse the tank.

The tanks stood unfinished for a year while investigations and discussions went on. Then the Germans finished them as per contract and went home. It was decided after much argument that the only thing to do was to build another thin wall all around the tanks, and heat the space in between the two walls with steam. All this would cost millions of roubles, and the financial plan of 1938 still did not allocate any money for it. The tanks stood idle, save for having slogans painted on them every first of May, while the work of the whole combinat was complicated by the lack of a gas reserve.

The investigations of the NKVD in this case were not, of course, published. It seems, however, that even that organization, with all its experience and talent, did not succeed in apprehending the wreckers responsible for this outrage. The German firm had received the order, been paid, and done the work according to the terms of the contract. Most of the Soviet organizations involved, Mashinoimport for example, had been liquidated or given over to other commissariats and it was impossible to find, or at least indict, the men who had signed the contracts.

Mikhail Jakovich Jaffe was the head of the AXU, or administrative and economic direction of the plant. The functions of this organization included care of all plant administrative buildings, all hotels, living quarters, rest homes, together with all the furniture and other appurtenances, plant automobiles, roads, and so forth — in short, everything which one would expect to belong to the City Soviet, or to some city or industrial organization. Mikhail Jakovich was short, rotund, rather inflated-looking, with an agile sly mind, hands, and features. He staged himself in the middle of an enormous office at a large U-shaped desk. Here he sat in a special easy-chair, surrounded by square yards of green velour-covered and paper-strewn desk surface, flanked by half a dozen telephones. When-

ever one went into his room, it was full of people. They were
asking for rooms, cars, paper to keep the books on, paint for the
porch of the new hotel, bicycle tires for messenger boys, trucks,
and almost everything else one could think of. The first answer
to every request was, 'Come and see me tomorrow,' or 'Go see
So-and-So.' Jaffe was always talking to three people at once,
and not understanding any of them properly. He was in a per-
petual whirl of petty intrigue. — If he was to get lumber for
that new building from the supply department, he had better
give the secretary of that organization a room she had been
asking for for some time. — Here was an automobile that was
left free by the arrest of So-and-So, perhaps the best thing
would be give it to the director of the circus, whom he had to
approach continually for good seats for visiting firemen and
others.

Again and again, in the newspapers, at various meetings,
Jaffe was attacked for bureaucracy and inefficiency. Most of
these accusations were well-founded, but Jaffe stayed on the
job between the devil and the deep blue sea, harried by requests
of all kinds on one side, and limited by a shortage of everything
on the other.

Jaffe made a thousand roubles a month, had a small house in
Berezki, an automobile at his disposal, and a fabulous wealth of
good-will. This expressed itself in many ways. The department store director, who was anxious for living space for his
employees, would call up to inform Jaffee that a new shipment
of women's shoes and yard material had arrived, and that if he
cared to send his chauffeur down, there were some very nice
articles which it would be dangerous to put on sale over the
counter to the general public, because it might start a riot.
Jaffe always made use of these little tips.

Many people in Magnitogorsk, arrested and indicted for
political crimes, were just thieves, embezzlers, and bandits, and

would have been dealt with as such in any other country. The political tags were put on their crimes for purposes of propaganda and education.

The director of the construction organization engaged in building individual dwelling houses was not satisfied with his salary of a thousand roubles a month and his two-room apartment. He built himself a house, the construction of which went on all through 1936. When he moved in, he was able to furnish the five large rooms with silk hangings, a grand piano, and other luxuries. Then he began riding around in a motor car, when it was well known that his organization had none. At this time his construction outfit was fulfilling its plan by about sixty per cent. When asked in the newspapers and in meeting what the trouble was, he blamed the lack of building materials, labor, and transport facilities.

The NKVD investigated the case and found that the director had systematically embezzled State funds, built his own house on the material plan of other jobs, sold building materials to State farms and other organizations and pocketed the proceeds, and that some of his subordinates were receiving money regularly to keep still about all that was going on. There was a public trial, which for several days monopolized the local press. They even broadcast the most important speeches over the radio. The case made against the defendant was not stealing, or bribing, or embezzling — but wrecking. He had sabotaged the construction of workers' houses at a time when they were very much needed. He was convicted after a full confession backed by all kinds of documentary evidence, and shot.

Thus Magnitogorsk had some of the same thieving and banditry which are found in any Western city. A difference was that in Magnitogorsk it was more difficult to embezzle on a large scale than in New York or Chicago; and if caught, one was likely to be accused, not of stealing, but of sabotage and counter-revolution, and had relatively little chance of buying one's self out.

Unquestionably some genuine sabotage went on in Magnitogorsk. Here are two examples which I knew of personally:

A certain foreman in the blowing house of the blast-furnace department was rather outspoken in his criticism of the Soviet power. He was a heavy drinker, and under the influence of vodka his tongue would sometimes run away with him. Once he boasted openly in the presence of several foreigners that he would 'wreck the works.' One day not long afterward a heavy stilson wrench was found in the mashed blades of one of the imported German gas turbines. The frame of the machine was cracked and the whole thing ruined, involving a loss of several tens of thousands of roubles and a good deal of labor. Several days later the foreman was arrested and confessed that he had done the job. He got eight years.

Another case I ran into personally which would be termed sabotage in any country, was the following:

The second part of the power house in Magnitogorsk was under construction, and two large (24,000 kilowatt) turbines were being installed. The reinforced concrete work — foundations, walls, and grouted roofs — was done by ex-kulak labor. As on many Soviet construction jobs, the erection of the equipment started before the building was completely finished. Consequently, when the big turbine was already in place and the mechanics working on it, the ex-kulaks were still around pouring concrete.

One morning the mechanics found the main bearings and some of the minor grease cups of the big turbine filled with ground glass. This substance will ruin a bearing very rapidly. Investigations were made immediately, and several pails of the glass were found near the shack where the ex-kulaks reported when they came to work in the morning. It was there for the electric welders, who used it, mixed with chalk and water, to coat their electrodes.

Obviously one of the embittered, illiterate, dekulakized laborers had taken a pocketful of the glass and put it into the bearings. Unnoticed, this act would have caused great loss. The action was clearly deliberate and malicious wrecking, and the motivations of the wrecker were easily understood.

During the late twenties and the early thirties the rich peasants, or kulaks, were liquidated. Their property was conficated and given to the collective farms. They were shipped out to some construction job for five years or so, to be re-educated. Some of the young ones, like my friend Shabkov, lent themselves to this re-education; but most of the old ones were bitter and hopeless. They were ready to do anything, in their blind hatred, to strike back at the Soviet power.

But the Soviet power was not around to strike. There were only workers and engineers and other ex-kulaks building a steel mill. But the machines were symbolic of the new power, of the force which had confiscated their property and sent them out onto the steppe to pour concrete. And they struck at the machines.

IV

THE purge struck Magnitogorsk in 1937 with great force. Thousands were arrested, incarcerated for months, finally exiled. No group, no organization was spared.

This purge was part of a vast Union-wide storm which went

on from 1935 until 1938. The causes of this purge have been
widely discussed — I offer the following:

1. The October Revolution earned the enmity of the old
aristocracy, the officers of the old Czarist army and of the various White armies, State employees from pre-war days, business
men of all kinds, small landlords, and kulaks. All of these people had ample reason to hate the Soviet power, for it had deprived them of something which they had had before. Besides
being internally dangerous, these men and women were potentially good material for clever foreign agents to work with.

2. Geographical conditions were such that no matter what
kind of government was in power in the Soviet Union, poor,
thickly populated countries like Japan and Italy and aggressive
powers like Germany would leave no stone unturned in their
attempts to infiltrate it with their agents, in order to establish
their organizations and assert their influence, the better to chip
pieces off for themselves. They sent fifth-columnists of all
kinds into Russia, as they did into every other country. These
agents bred purges.

3. For centuries Russia was governed and administered with
the help of a secret police. Their methods were traditionally
clumsy, brutal, and inefficient. It was considered worth while
to condemn nine innocent defendants in order to get one guilty
one. Sometimes whole villages of innocent people were de-
stroyed in order to get some 'guilty' peasant leader. For centuries the attitude toward foreigners was one of fear and mis-
trust.

The October Revolution changed many things in Russia,
but the abovementioned century-long traditions and habit
patterns are still present in the Soviet Union. They condi-
tioned the character and the successful execution of the purge,
which might well have caused an insurrection or a civil war in
England or the United States.

A large number of spies, saboteurs, and fifth-columnists were exiled or shot during the purge; but many more innocent men and women were made to suffer.

4. Bolshevik intolerance toward opposition leads to conspiracy and purges. To enlarge, twenty years of underground activity under the despotic conditions of Czarist Russia, the arrests, the Siberian exile, the *agents provocateurs* were dominant factors in determining the form and character of the party of Lenin. At the Second Party Congress in 1903 in London, Lenin demanded a 'party of a new type,' which was not to be a discussion group, but a disciplined army of revolutionary soldiers; members must work actively in some party organization; they must obey the decisions of higher party organs; after a vote the minority must stop talking and get to work — carrying out the decisions of the majority. Lenin's group became the Bolsheviks, and these general principles have dominated the Bolshevik Party ever since.

In England or the United States, if a member of the government disagrees with its policy he can object, appeal, protest, resign. He can then take the matter to the voters, and theoretically, at least, has a chance of coming back after elections with a majority on his side, and putting through his ideas. This opposition function is recognized as an important feature of government.

But in the Bolshevik Party there is no appeal after a decision has been reached. There is no protesting, no resigning. The only chance of the opposition, after they have been voted down, is conspiracy.

This method of dealing with opposition sowed the seeds of purges.

V

Soviet purge technique was highly developed. All arrests were made at night. Surprise was always sought for; people were arrested when they least expected it, and left alone for weeks when they expected every night to be taken. The arrests were made by agents having no idea of the accusations against the person being arrested. They arrived, usually a sergeant in uniform and two plain-clothesmen, in an automobile, knocked at the door, politely presented an order signed by the prosecuting attorney or by the head of the city NKVD, authorizing them to search the apartment and arrest a certain person. The door was then locked; no one could come or go during the search. A civilian witness was taken at random from an adjacent apartment. He or she watched the search going on, then was requested to sign a paper stating that the authorities had not abused their power; that is, beaten anybody up or stolen anything. Everything confiscated was listed and a receipt given. The search finished, the polite and completely uncommunicative agents departed with the arrested person. Probably no one in the house except the witness was aware until the next morning that anything had taken place.

After someone's arrest, the family was usually left completely in the dark for several weeks, while the 'arrested' was put in the Magnitogorsk prison to cool off and think things over prior to the first interrogation. This jail was very crowded. Cells meant for twenty people were occupied by fifty. (The crowding naturally put pressure on the authorities to speed up the investigations and get people shipped out.) Several weeks

after the arrest, the family usually received a formal notice
that the husband or brother had been arrested, and that the
family could come at such-and-such a time with a package.
They suggested that the package should contain warm clothes,
clean underwear, sugar, onions, and garlic. The latter were to
combat scurvy which became rather common in the prison
owing to the predominantly bread-and-water diet and the lack
of fresh air.

After the arrest of a husband, the wife sometimes lost her
job, and the family often faced a sort of social ostracism.
Everyone feared having anything to do with them because of
possible subsequent accusations of 'connections with enemies
of the people.'

In rare cases the family was informed as to the exact charges
against the arrested one, and was even permitted to see him.
These visits were usually arranged in the interests of the investigation. A husband was permitted to see his wife and child,
in the presence of an investigator, of course, in order forcefully
to bring to his mind the existence of his beloved ones, whose life
and happiness depended on his 'making a clean breast of his
crimes, and helping the investigation apprehend and convict
his accomplices.' Sometimes, naturally, the visits had effects
other than those desired by the investigation. Husbands whispered little things into their wives' ears. It was in this way that
Shevchenko's story and many others became known.

The interrogations usually took place at night and were
nerve-wracking ordeals, sometimes lasting weeks, and often
pursued between long intervals of cooling off in the prison.
The words 'wrecking' and 'counter-revolutionary activity,'
as used in the Soviet Union, mean much more than they would
in America. The criminal code of the R.S.F.S.R., Article 58-1,
reads:

> Any action is counter-revolutionary which is directed toward

the overthrow, undermining, or weakening of the power of the
workers and peasants ... or directed toward the weakening of the
external security of the Soviet Union, or the administrative, or
national gains of the proletarian revolution.

For a definition of wrecking, we turn to Article 58–7 of the
same code, which reads in part:

Undermining of state industry, transport, commerce, monetary
circulation, or credit system, as well as of the cooperative systems,
committed for counter-revolutionary purposes by counter-revolutionary use of state institutions or factories ... or interference
with their normal activity, as well as use of state institutions
and factories in the interests of their former owners ... involves
... supreme measure of social protection — shooting ...

Article 58–12 was the article on which many wives were indicted. It reads in part:

Failure to report definite knowledge of preparation or commit-
ment of a counter-revolutionary crime, involves ... deprivation
of freedom for not less than six months. (June 6, 1927.)

In almost no case did the accused see a defense lawyer during
the interrogations. He was pitted alone against one or more
experienced, smooth, literal-minded NKVD investigators.
Though, according to the code of procedure, the investigation
should not last more than two months, the accused sometimes
languished for months and years in the prison occupied by men
and women under investigation. This, obviously, gave the investigator a very potent whiphandle, ' ... if you don't want to
confess ... go back and think it over; if you do confess, you
will get a quick trial — a couple of years in Siberia, where you
will have a good job, receive wages, live at home, have the comparative freedom of the town, and perhaps see your family....'

The denunciation of one accused by another or of both by a
third party still formed the basis for a great many indict-
ments and convictions. A denounces B as having said that

Stalin is a son-of-a-bitch and should be shot. B, arrested, finally admits making the statement, and further asserts that C was present, and agreed with the opinion expressed. C, arrested, denies everything; then, confronted with B, admits that there was some such conversation, but insists that A was the initiator. A is arrested, like the others for terrorist intentions against the leaders of the party and government, but begs off on the ground that he did it all in order to expose to the authorities the counter-revolutionary activities of B and C. After six months of bantering and badgering, A, B, and C are sent for ten years to the Kamchatka.

During the rush years of 1937 and 1938 the methods used in the investigations were indefensible according to most civilized standards. Even physical coercion was employed in obtaining a confession from the accused. Promises were made to the accused that if he confessed, his wife would be let alone and permitted to keep her job. The confession signed, the wife was likewise arrested and shown the confession, and told that if she confessed connivance both would get light sentences. She confessed, and both got the limit, and went to Angarstroy to work on construction. Such methods are, of course, taken for granted in criminal proceedings almost all over the world. In the Soviet Union, however, the situation was somewhat different in that the NKVD made a play for, and to a large extent received, the support and cooperation of the population, in their work of defending the country against the inroads of foreign agents and attacks of the old bourgeoisie. Cases like the above cited shook the confidence of many Russians in the NKVD.

The trials were almost always *in camera*, and usually *in absentia*. There were almost no acquittals in Magnitogorsk in 1937, nor were there more than half a dozen death sentences. After the trial, the operative department of the NKVD turned the convicts over to the ULAG (criminal camp administration), whose job it was to get certain construction work done, using the labor of the convicts, and also to carry on re-educational work. The ULAG was a completely separate and independent part of the NKVD organization. They received a prisoner accompanied by a frayed document stating that he had been convicted on such-and-such an article. Beyond this they knew nothing. Their job was to build dams and railroads, and in the interest of high productivity, if for no other reason, they treated the prisoners as well as possible.

Arrived at the construction job, the prisoners received better food than they had had since their arrests and warm, sturdy clothes, and were told that from then on the thing that counted was their work. Until 1938, twenty, forty, or sixty per cent of their sentences were frequently commuted for good work.

After 1938, however, commutations of sentences became rare, probably because NKVD felt reluctant to release workers when so few new ones were coming in. In the camps, frequent meetings, newspapers, speeches were calculated to re-educate the prisoners in the spirit of liberty, freedom, and justice in the workers' fatherland under the new Stalinist constitution.

In Magnitogorsk in 1937 the activities of the NKVD were often characterized by great confusion. Prisoners were lost or their identity mistaken. The NKVD came around one night to arrest the former occupant of the apartment over ours who had left Magnitogorsk months before. There were cases where notices were sent to wives, informing them that their husbands had been arrested and requesting them to bring packages, when the husbands were living at home and working normally and continued to do so. These things bespoke the muscle-bound and inefficient organization of the NKVD apparatus.

Alexei Ivanovich Pushkov, the chief of the Magnitogorsk NKVD during 1937, was himself purged in 1939 for his excessive ardor in purging the people of Magnitogorsk.

VI

THE immediate effects of the purge were diverse and sometimes paradoxical. In cases where numbers of responsible workers and functionaries had been arrested at the same time, or within a few days of each other, production suffered heavily for a while. After Shevchenko's removal and arrest, for example, the coke and chemical output went down sharply for several weeks. During the first few days, chaos reigned in the plant. A foreman would come to work in the morning and say to his men, 'Now today we must do this and that.' The workers would sneer at him and say: 'Go on. You're a wrecker yourself. Tomorrow they'll come and arrest you. All you engineers and technicians are wreckers.'

Then things straightened out; a new chief was appointed and Syemichkin became assistant chief engineer. All through the plant young workers and foremen were pushed up a notch or two into the positions evacuated by those arrested. Often the new men were inexperienced, but, in some cases, within a few weeks they were working as well as their predecessors.

In some departments, as for instance on the blast furnaces, production suffered a prolonged setback after the beginning of the purge. Daily pig-iron production in the fall of 1936, for example, averaged around twelve hundred to thirteen hundred tons per furnace. By the end of 1937 it was in the neighborhood of eleven hundred tons per furnace, and in January, 1940, as nearly as could be judged from fragmentary reports, the average figure had fallen to below one thousand tons.

During the course of the purge hundreds of thousands of

bureaucrats shook in their boots. Officials and administrators who had formerly come to work at ten, gone home at four-thirty, and shrugged their shoulders at complaints, difficulties, and failures, began to stay at work from dawn till dark, to worry about the success or failure of their units, and to fight in a very real and earnest fashion for plan fulfillment, for economy, and for the well-being of their workers and employees, about whom they had previously lost not a wink of sleep.

On the other hand, the repeated nocturnal arrests, the fear and worry, and the terrorization of an organization which worked in secret, with the power to do what it wanted with anybody, and to whom there was no appeal, had their effects on a considerable section of the population, which read with a sneer and a groan Stalin's slogan, 'Life has become better; life has become more joyful.'

A maxim currently used by vigilant Communists and others was: 'In every backward department there is a wrecker.' The results of the application of such an affirmation are obvious. They played into the hands of the growing apparatus of the NKVD (whose local and national leaders at that time appear now to have been wreckers themselves). Many people reacted by shunning all responsibility. Another maxim became known: 'Seichas khorosho buit telegrafnim stolbom — Nowadays it is a good thing to be a telegraph pole.'

Still other people became exasperated and bitter. It is said that in Sverdlovsk one day several hundred women had come to the NKVD building with packages of food and clothing to be given to their arrested husbands. After standing for several hours awaiting the arrival of some functionary, they were told bluntly that no packages would be accepted that day. The worried women, some with babies in their arms, some who had left their jobs at the risk of being fired in order to give a little sugar and some clean clothes to their beloved ones, became incensed. Someone started a commotion. Someone was pushed against a window. Within five minutes every pane of glass on the first floor of the building was shattered. The authorities could find no leader to arrest. They couldn't run in five hundred women, the jails were already full.

Incidents of this kind, more or less serious, occurred in various parts of the Soviet Union, and reports of them in one form or another probably reached Stalin and the other leaders of the government. They were signals of warning that the purge, if carried too far, could have disastrous results, particularly in case of war. This was a major factor in determining the change in internal policy that took place in the end of 1938 and the beginning of 1939.

VII

ALL during the purge the people of the Soviet Union were told every day, in newspapers, over the radio, and in meetings, to cooperate with the NKVD and report any suspicious fact immediately.

The theater was likewise used as an instrument to make the population at large spy-conscious. In the height of the purge Masha and I took Joseph Barnes of the *New York Herald Tribune*, who was visiting Magnitogorsk, to see 'Ochnaya Stavka,' or 'The Confrontation,' one of the most effective of these purge propaganda plays. It is worth describing.

The first scene was in a large, richly furnished room. Beside the door, almost in the middle of the stage, was a rich suit of armor, with a lance extended in its hand. There were three gentlemen in the room, all in evening clothes. Two were sitting, one with his back to the audience. The third was standing near the table, holding a book in his hand.

'Here is all the material,' he said in a good deep voice. 'Be good enough to look it over. Now before we examine the graduates, perhaps you have some questions you would like to ask.'

'Yes,' said one of the seated gentlemen slowly. 'I have a question for the Herr Doctor Director.'

'Please, please,' said the standing gentleman, bowing slightly. 'I will answer any . . .'

'Why was it necessary to run the school first as an astronomical club, then as an automobile association, and later as something else? Why could you not have got a large place in the country with a high fence, and done your work under guard?'

The director rubbed his hands. 'You see, Herr Minister,' he said, 'in the preparation of first-class people it is necessary to watch their reactions under such circumstances as approximate those under which they will work later, when they graduate and go abroad. Here each student is gaining experience all the time, under our observation, because he has to mask as something which he is not . . .'

'I understand,' said the seated gentleman, raising his hand. 'Enough. I have nothing more to ask. Your expenses are reasonable considering the important work you do. If my colleague has no further questions we can proceed to examine some of your graduates.'

The gentleman with his back to the audience turned slightly, exposing a horse face, with long locks of black hair and a little black mustache. 'I have nothing to ask,' he said.

Most of the people in the audience were sitting on the edge of their seats. The tension in the theater was contagious. A young peasant-faced boy of eighteen sitting next to me clutched the handle of the seat with his big rough hands, and closed his mouth for a moment to swallow. He didn't know what kind of school it was, but there was something ominous about the fellow with his back to the audience — and all three of them were clearly 'burzhui.'

Masha had been the first of us to realize what it was all about. 'Spy school,' she said in my ear.

The acting was good. The actors controlled their voices well and did not hurry.

The director paced the floor for a moment, bowed stiffly to the seated gentlemen, and cleared his throat.

'The first student whom I will ask your permission to call is number forty-nine. You will find the material on page 136. He is prepared to work in Cameroon. By profession an archeologist, he speaks excellent French, and also several native dialects...' and the director launched into a long description. When he had finished, he pressed a button and a footman came into the room through the big doors.

'Number forty-nine,' said the director.

'What connections has he in the Fatherland?' asked the minister.

'Mother,' said the director. 'Unmarried — and he will not marry.'

At this point a stage hand in his shirt-sleeves with a cigarette hanging from his lips walked nonchalantly out on the stage from the extreme right. He suddenly saw the audience, realized where he was, and disappeared like a flash. No one in the audience paid the slightest attention to the incident.

The door opened and a man of thirty came in. He was dressed in excellent taste, was well-mannered and clean-spoken. He answered technical questions on archeological excavations in Africa which the minister put to him. Then the gentleman with his back to the audience asked in a deep hollow voice, with just a touch of impatience about it, 'Which do you prefer for blowing up railroad bridges, nitro-glycerine or ammonal?'

The graduating student bowed slightly. 'I prefer ammonal, or, in some cases, liquid oxygen.'

The examination was at an end. The student bowed and left. The seated gentleman congratulated the director on a promising pupil. The director described the next examinee.

'She is versed in all the niceties of Parisian life. She has already established contact with the sons of several of the French cabinet members, she knows the French diplomatic code by heart, and has a considerable training in pharmacy and in marksmanship.'

After a couple of questions, number ten was ushered in. She was a dazzling blonde, with a rangy voluptuous body and come-hither eyes. She answered several questions with ready wit. Finally the gentleman with his back to the audience asked in the same hollow voice as before:

'When hiring or otherwise recruiting an agent, how do you refer to yourself?'

The girl bowed and smiled. 'Always as the agent of a third power.'

The girl was escorted out, and the ministers congratulated the director again. The gentleman with his back to the audience was indifferent and sinister.

Next a terrorist and *agent provocateur* destined to work in Prague was examined. Then a butler who was going to work in the house of one of the leaders of the British government. Throughout the gentleman with his back to the audience never turned around, always spoke in the same hollow voice.

After the butler's exit the director cleared his throat and threw out his chest. 'And now, finally, I will introduce you to number one, the pride not only of this, but of many graduating classes. I am referring to Walter.'

Both ministers manifested great interest. Walter's fame seemed to have preceded him. The director gave a glowing description. 'Walter knows all codes, is as strong as a lion, and persevering as a bulldog. And we have prepared this master for the most important of all posts — for work in the country which is, perforce, our greatest enemy ...'

'For the Soviet Union?' asked the minister in astonishment. 'But there we have Keller, who for years has produced excellent results.'

'But Keller is getting old. He has long been asking for relief. We have decided to send Walter to take over his work. He knows Russian as well as his native tongue and is thoroughly acquainted with the political and economic theories prevalent in the Soviet Union. He knows the speeches of the Bolshevik leaders by heart and can qualify in Moscow as a teacher of the history of the Communist Party.'

At this point the gentleman with the black hair got up facing the director, his back still to the audience. He moved with nervous, almost pathological, energy. He shook his finger at the director. 'For the Soviet Union!' he said, in a voice distorted with rage — 'For the Soviet Union we must have the best that our great talent can produce. There must be no bungling! Do you understand? There must be no bungling!'

The director fell back a pace before this onslaught, then bowed and said in a steady voice: 'I stake my whole reputation on Walter. He will not bungle. He has received minute instructions as to the utilization of political opposition and minority groups in the Soviet Union who are anxious to strike back — he is even in contact with certain of these people. Everything has been done both in his training and in the arrangement of his contacts to ensure the success of his mission.'

The director rang the bell and the footman appeared.

'Number one,' said the director. The footman bowed and retired, shutting the door.

The black-haired minister turned and faced the audience, exposing a face made up as a take-off of Hitler. He then retired to one side of the stage, leaving the center free for the master spy, Walter. The director turned to the ministers.

'I neglected to tell you. His name on his Russian passport is Ivan Ivanovich Ivanov.'

The door opened and the curtain fell. The house lights blazed up and the audience relaxed as though each of them had been undergoing electric treatments and the switch had just been thrown off.

Then everyone burst into conversation, discussing the play and the acting.

The rest of the action took place in Moscow and on the Soviet side of the frontier. It showed the blue-capped NKVD investigator at work trying to find Ivan Ivanovich Ivanov. It showed how the old spy, Keller, who had worked in Moscow for a decade doing immeasurable damage, tried to escape and was caught, thanks to the vigilance of the Soviet public. It showed Ivanov disposing of a girl who, he feared, might betray him, by throwing her under the wheels of a train. It showed a humorous Jewish tailor hurrying to the investigator with information accidentally acquired, and a dozen other characters, whose voluntary help was indispensable to the investigator in catching the spies.

The fourth and last act was climactic. Here the 'Ochnaya Stavka,' or confrontation, took place. Ivan Ivanovich, caught red-handed and faced with all sorts of overwhelming evidence, had refused to admit his guilt. Keller, the old, cynical, hardened spy, caught under circumstances which made it impossible for him to deny his criminal activities, admitted them. He pleaded guilty. But he refused to give any information either as to his accomplices or his work. He even refused to state which country he served.

Keller and Walter-Ivanov were given a personal confrontation in the office of the investigator and in the presence of the entire cast (except the stuffed shirts from the first act). The investigator, using one against the other, broke them down. Ivanov pleaded for mercy, claiming to have seen the error of his ways, but asserting that he had been unable to stop his nefarious activities. Keller, defiant and bitter to the end, made a dramatic speech: 'The decisive battle is ahead of us. I will be shot, but you will go down in defeat. Your hateful people will be driven from your broad lands to make room for a more competent and more cultured race of men.'

The investigator hurled back the challenge. 'We will be the victors!' he shouted, and the entire cast stood in solidarity behind him.

The curtain fell amid wild applause and even wilder scrambling to be out and first in line at the coat room.

The workers of Magnitogorsk were greatly impressed by the play, as indeed were Joe Barnes and I. It demonstrated the necessity for the entire population to cooperate with the authorities in apprehending foreign spies. On the other hand, it failed to point out the danger and tragedy involved in over-enthusiastic purging.

'They may catch some spies now, but it will take a generation to live down the fear and suspicion being created,' Joe said as we left the theater.

VIII

AFTER the purge, the administrative personnel of the whole combinat was almost one hundred per cent young Soviet engineers. There were almost no prisoner specialists, and the foreigners had virtually disappeared. Yet by 1939 the work of certain departments had become better than ever before. This was the case with the railroads and with the coke and chemical plant. The key positions were held by men like Syemichkin, whose acquaintance we have already made.

Pavel Korobov succeeded Zavenyagin as director of the combinat when, in the beginning of 1937, the latter was appointed Assistant Commissar of Heavy Industry. (Zavenyagin was later dismissed from this post in disgrace, and then turned up as head of some Arctic Circle construction job — a definite demotion, but not as drastic as those suffered by Pyatokov, Mezhlauk, and other high functionaries of the Heavy Industry Commissariat.)

Korobov was a good example of the post-purge industrial leader. He was descended from a dynasty of blast-furnace workers, and was graduated from the university in the early thirties and then went to a metallurgical plant in the South. Within three years he had been pushed up to the post of manager of the blast-furnace department. He was sent to Magnitogorsk in that capacity in 1936, but before he had been working many months the vacancy of the post of chief engineer of the combinat, and then the directorship, gave him opportunities for further advancement. He became, at thirty, the director of a metallurgical combinat which turned out one-fourth of the iron ore produced in the whole Soviet Union, twelve per cent of the pig iron, and about ten per cent of the rolled steel; of a combinat which, furthermore, was working unsatisfactorily.

For the first few months the new director worked passively rather than actively. He avoided making sharp decisions where he was not sure of himself, and gave the department heads a fairly free hand. Production came up in several of the most difficult departments, such as the open hearth. And this was at a time when some of the best plants in the Union were not nearly fulfilling their plans, and where the most celebrated directors, like Gvakharia of Makeyevka, were being arrested and shot. Korobov studied continuously, read foreign technical journals, and worked tirelessly. He was well liked by most of those under him, although most of the older engineers had little respect for his technical training and capabilities.

Unfortunately, many foreigners left the Soviet Union during 1937 and 1938 for one reason or another, carrying away with them the impression that the purge ended everything, or at least ended something; an epoch, let us say. Everyone worth while had been arrested or shot, it seemed. This impression was basically incorrect. The purge caused many arrests, but the Soviet Union was large, and millions of Russians who had not been involved personally in the purge took it more or less as it came without allowing it permanently to influence their attitude toward the Soviet power. So that in the end of 1938 when the purge ended, when hundreds of arrested people were released with terse apologies for 'mistakes' of the investigators, when new arrests stopped or almost stopped, most of the workers in Magnitogorsk had an essentially cheerful and optimistic view of things.

And, indeed, according to most standards they had reason to be cheerful and optimistic. They were working and were sure of jobs and advancement as far ahead as they cared to see.

They enjoyed vacations and maternity vacations with pay, old age pensions, and other social legislation. They were studying, and had opportunities to apply what they learned to the benefit both of themselves and of society as soon as they graduated, or before. Their standard of living was rising. The cultural opportunities at their disposal grew daily more varied and extensive.

The purge had devastating effects on several millions of Soviet citizens, who were arrested and exiled. Most of these people were innocent, but some were guilty, and some, like Udkin, might have become excellent Nazi fifth-columnists.

Stalin considered the investment a good one.

PART EIGHT

PART EIGHT Socialist City

I

Our apartment was a pleasant refuge from the grimness and turbulence of the mill. After leaving the construction gang, my life was less chaotic and I spent more of it at home, playing with the baby, puttering about with electric appliances and radio sets, or thumping on my old three-decker Corona.

Masha was hard at work seven or eight hours a day, and Vera kept the flat in order and saw to it that there was always a kettle of shchi (cabbage soup) or borshch on the electric plate.

I began to have American visitors from Moscow. Tourists would stop in to see me and I would try to show them around. Professor George Counts and A. A. Heller came in 1936 and one day Bob Merriman blew in. Bob was very much interested in schools and hospitals, so I took my day off and we started out to see what we could. First we walked around the 'Socialist City,' or Sotsgorod.

The Socialist City, renamed the Kirov District, because it was not really a very good example of a Socialist city to put before the population, was composed of some fifty large apartment houses, three, four, and five stories high, containing seventy-five to two hundred rooms each. The houses were of brick and stone, stuccoed and painted various colors, which looked very well against the white background in winter. They were arranged in long rows, like military barracks, and were all of the same matchbox-on-edge shape. The metal roofs were painted red and blue. There were balconies in all the houses. Between the rows of houses there were wide streets, with sidewalks, along which many trees had been planted. In the center of the development there were two open squares, with fountains, benches, children's playground apparatus, flower gardens surrounded by neat, green iron fences, and what would be shade trees in ten years.

The sun shone brightly as we walked along, jostled by women with market baskets and by a few men in their day-off clothes.

Particularly in summer the Kirov District had definite charm; the fountains played, and innumerable little children, in bathing suits which left most of their sunburned bodies open to the fresh air, splashed and splattered about. The walks were crowded with workers of all ages taking the air. Benches were occupied by men and women, young and old, reading and talking. Singing societies, orchestras, as well as radios and phonographs, filled the air with music. I remember particularly a Ukrainian housewives' singing club, which used to practice evenings out-of-doors, surrounded and applauded by crowds of people, some of whom joined in the singing. Often workers would bring guitars and balalaikas into the street and sometimes one could have thought oneself in a small town in Italy. The traditional Russian habit of getting drunk *à la russe* on large quantities of vodka, which knock one out as though one had been hit on the head with a hammer, was less in evidence. Drunks were not allowed to career or lie around the streets, but were hauled in by the militia.

As we walked along I told Bob what I could about the Kirov District as a residential section. One tremendous shortcoming

was the fact that it was so crowded. In 1937 there were 3.34
square meters (35 square feet) of floor space per person on the
average in the district. This meant four to five people per room.
However, the Russians were used to crowding, and there was
much less complaint on this account than there would have been
in another country.

Disputes frequently arose as to who was to get a room or
apartment which had been vacated. Occasionally 'squatters'
would move into such apartments and refuse to leave or to admit those to whom the floor space had been assigned. Such
cases were the cause of much swearing, weeping, and gnashing
of teeth. The assignment of the living space was in itself a
complicated process. The buildings, instead of belonging to
the City Soviet, all belonged to the plant. The plant administration gave out a certain number of rooms and apartments
to each mill and department.

The rent varied with the salary, from approximately two to
ten roubles per month per square meter of floor space. We paid
about eighty roubles a month. All the houses in the Kirov
District were equipped with electricity, central heating, and
running water. Most cooking was done on coal stoves, although electricity, which cost only twelve kopeks a kilowatt
hour, was used more and more.

The furniture in the apartments was originally owned by
the plant, like the houses themselves. The tenant paid five per
cent of the assessed value of the furniture per year for its use.
As it deteriorated and disappeared, replacements were usually
made by the tenant himself, so that to an increasing degree the
worker owned his own furniture, which was simple, usually
wooden.

Whereas originally each apartment was equipped with a
bathtub, these had gradually disappeared or were used for other
things, for example, for storing coal. Most of the inhabitants

bathed in the community Russian bathhouses, of which there were many.

II

WE WENT to the big teachers' college where Masha had studied. I knew the director, and he talked to us for half an hour, giving Bob a lot of material on Magnitogorsk's schools. Bob was enthusiastic, and not without reason.

Almost everybody in Magnitogorsk studied or attended some educational institution, the director told us, and I translated. To begin at the beginning, a system of nurseries took children from a few weeks to three years old during the day or during the night, depending on the mothers' needs, or sometimes for twenty-four hours a day. These nurseries were run by the City Soviet and were heavily subsidized both by the Soviet and the plant. The parents paid from fifteen to fifty roubles a month per child. The buildings were in most cases light and clean, and the care was good. However, two serious shortcomings hindered the work of these institutions.

First, there were not enough of them. In order to permit every mother who so desired to put her child in a nursery it would have been necessary to multiply floor space, personnel, and equipment ten times. As this was impossible, it was very difficult to place one's child, particularly for those earning more than three hundred roubles per month. These 'highly paid' workers were expected to take care of their children themselves or hire a maid. The inadequacy of nursery capacity was greatly aggravated by the enormously high birth-rate in Magnito-gorsk (36 per 1000 in 1937).

Secondly, epidemics of common children's diseases, mumps, measles, diphtheria, and scarlet fever, spread rapidly among the children in the crowded nurseries and took quite a toll.

After the child reached the age of three to four, it was taken care of in kindergartens or playgrounds. The task of these organizations was less complicated and difficult than that of the nurseries. Their work was made easier by the wide steppe where the children of from four to seven could run and play with comparatively little supervision, while they absorbed fresh air and sunshine.

After the age of seven, the children started to go to the regular schools, and the parents were expected to take care of them outside school hours. In the few cases where the parents were unable to do this, the children lived in a 'children's home.'

During 1935 and 1936 the number of grade schools rose from thirty-four to forty-five; all the new ones being excellent, well-lighted, reinforced concrete buildings, well situated and well equipped. Not only were new schools built, old ones were enlarged, making it possible for about thirty thousand children to attend classes, most of them in one shift, instead of two or three as previously.

The ten-year middle school curriculum was something between that of the American high school and the French baccalaureate or English matriculation. The course of study included mathematics, up until the derivative, biology, general chemistry, general physics, one foreign language (no Latin), history (particular emphasis on Russian history, especially since the war, and very little attention to ancient, Renaissance, and American history), civics, astronomy, literature (again with overwhelming emphasis on Russian), economic geography, very elementary courses in music and art, political economy, and numerous courses and study circles in Leninism, the history and structure of the Communist Party, current events, and so forth. The students, much more enthusiastic about their studies than most students in America, learned a great deal, and finished their ten-year school with a very good foundation for a higher education, particularly in the sciences. No tuition was paid until 1940, after which time up to two hundred roubles a year was charged for schooling above the seventh grade.

Disciplinary and organizational matters in the schools were handled in a 'Prussian' manner. The child had very little choice as to what he studied and when. The Dalton Plan and other experimental, progressive, educational schemes, tried out in the years immediately following the Revolution, were abandoned. This was done because the Soviet Union needed engineers, chemists, accountants, teachers, and these professions required a thorough systematic knowledge of a given field. The various educational systems failed to give the child this necessary, thorough knowledge, but tended rather to develop his originality, his independence, his powers of critical thinking, which attributes in the Soviet Union made for potentially dangerous citizens, and were liabilities rather than assets from the standpoint of the 'dictatorship of the proletariat.'

So the Soviet educational system went back to an old, tried method, which produced results. Of course this did not entirely eliminate originality, independence, and critical thinking in the children. But it did facilitate the teaching of scientific subjects in a very thorough manner.

For those children who did not wish to go to the full middle school, but preferred to learn a trade, there existed two main trade schools, the FZD and the FZU factory schools. Both these institutions were well equipped and took students from thirteen years up who had finished the first six years of the regular primary school, trained them to be welders, machinists, electricians, and what not. After the age of fifteen the student spent half of his six-hour working day in a department of the mill in practical work, and the rest of the time in school in theoretical study. At eighteen the boy or girl was put on an equal basis with adults. One of these schools was run by the Board of Education and the other by the Personnel Department of the plant. The children were paid from thirty to eighty roubles a month. Both school buildings were equipped with machine shops, welding, forging and casting equipment, and woodworking machinery.

There were many national minority students in the FZU and FZD: Tartars, Kazakhs, Kirghizi, and so on. In order to accommodate these students, special sections at both these trade schools operated entirely in the native tongue, Russian being taught as a foreign language.

We visited some classes in the FZD school and saw a group of twelve- or fourteen-year nomads. Whereas any American boy of twelve can saw, plane, even make and repair simple electric motors, and the like, these sons and daughters of Tamerlane and Genghis Khan had never even seen a hammer. The only hammering they had ever done was driving a tent stake into the ground with a rock. They had to start at the very beginning.

Having finished the ten-year school or having done enough studying by himself to pass the examinations, the student, usually sixteen to eighteen years old, could enter a higher educational institution. Magnitogorsk offered a construction technicum, a metallurgical technicum, a mining and metallurgical institute (really a university), a medical college, a medical technicum, a pedagogical institute, a pedagogical technicum, special training schools for nurses, militiamen, and an aviation school and several military training courses organized by Osoaviakhim (the association for chemical and air defense).

The Construction and Metallurgical Technicums trained technicians whose knowledge in their respective fields was mainly practical. In the same way the Medical Technicum graduated a sort of midwife-intern who could deliver children, set broken arms, and listen through a stethoscope, but who had not nearly the theoretical training of a doctor. Admittance into all these technicums was open by competitive examinations to all those having finished eight years of the ten-year school. Until 1937 all technicums had day students who received stipends of about one hundred roubles per month and spent their entire time studying, and evening students who received no stipends. These evening students, however, tired out from work in the mill, could not do their studying satisfactorily. After 1936 the evening sections were abolished, as they were in the institutes a year later.

In the afternoon we trudged up the hill near the iron mine to the engineering school which I attended four or five evenings a week. The Mining and Metallurgical Institute was open to graduates of the ten-year school by competitive examination. There were about five hundred students. The course took five years. The library and equipment were fair. The staff was excellent, and the administration thoroughly incompetent.

About forty per cent of the students in this institute were women, about sixty per cent of the entire student body being Russian and the rest Tartars, Ukrainians, White Russians, and Jews. The average age in the evening groups was thirty-two or thirty-three, and for the full-time group twenty-five or twenty-six, though some of the students were as old as fifty.

The Pedagogical Technicum and Institute trained primary school and middle school teachers respectively. Entrance requirements and length of course were similar to those already mentioned for the Metallurgical and Construction Institutes and Technicums. After the drastic increase in teachers' pay in

1935, men, and particularly women, flocked to the Teachers' College or Pedagogical Institute as it was called, which had about six hundred students. Teachers worked a four-hour day, had a two-month vacation in summer, and earned from four hundred roubles a month up. These conditions of work looked very good indeed to the daughter or brother of a plant engineer of Magnitogorsk, who, when things were going badly, did not get a chance to take his clothes off for days at a time.

A great many of Magnitogorsk's students were grown men and women working their shifts in the mill by day. Schools for illiterate adults were organized by the trade unions from the very first days of Magnitogorsk's construction. In 1937 something over ten thousand adults attended these courses. The press complained, however, that this represented only half the actual number of illiterate adults in Magnitogorsk. These courses were usually taught by students in the regular schools who had the difficult task of teaching men, and particularly women, over forty to read and write, and sometimes even to count.

In attempting to supply the mill with the required skilled workers, excellent trade schools were organized all during the thirties. One of the best was that of the rolling mills, which I took Bob to see. This trade school first started functioning in one room in a barrack a month or two before the blooming mill went into operation. After that time it grew steadily. By January, 1936, it had nine hundred and fifty students, one hundred and twenty-five of whom went to school full time and received from one hundred to two hundred and fifty roubles monthly for doing so. The rest of the students went to school in the evenings.

The school prepared rollers, cranemen, electricians, mechanics, and heaters. The teachers were engineers from the mills, who received four to five roubles an hour for their instruction.

Only unskilled workers could enter the school, but a knowledge of reading and writing and the fundamentals of arithmetic were required. Workers who had already learned a trade were not supposed to expend the State's money by learning another one while thousands of peasants came to the industrial centers every year prepared for nothing but unskilled labor. The first course lasted six months. At the end of this time the students had learned enough elementary physics, chemistry, and mechanics, to understand their trades, and in addition they had received some practical training.

At the end of the six months the student was taken from his unskilled job and put to work at his new trade, receiving the fourth category. For the first few months one skilled worker was 'attached' to him, and received a few extra roubles a month to supervise the work of the newcomer, correct his mistakes, and help him generally.

After this, if the new mechanic or electrician desired still further to increase his qualifications, and he generally did, he went back to the trade school and took course No. 2, which lasted about eight months, and at the completion of which he got the fifth or sixth category. Each increase in category meant higher wages, which gave added stimulus to his desire to learn.

Beginning in the end of 1935 technical examinations were required of all workers, young and old. These examinations were carried out by the foremen, often with the aid of representatives of the administration, and included both practical and theoretical questions directly connected with the worker's job. After having passed this 'technical minimum' examination, every worker received a technical passport, certifying to his trade, category, and the mark received in the examination. Without this passport no skilled worker had the right to hold a job after the summer of 1936.

Having passed the examination for the eighth category, a

worker had nothing more to learn in the trade schools, and had to go to one of the technical high schools of the city or to the foremen's training course.

This complete system of trade schools did a great deal toward the liquidation of the traditional Russian illiteracy and technical incompetence.

Every night from six until twelve the street cars and buses of Magnitogorsk were crowded with adult students hurrying to and from schools with books and notebooks under their arms, discussing Leibniz, Hegel, or Lenin, doing problems on their knees, and acting like high-school children during examination week in a New York subway. These students, however, were not adolescents, and it was not examination time. They were just the run of the population of the Soviet Union making up for several centuries of lost time.

III

HAVING seen a number of schools, I took Bob to the hospital to get an impression of medicine in Magnitogorsk.

The Magnitogorsk Hospital was a collection of some twenty barracks, constructed in 1932, many of them without running water, steam heat, or sewerage facilities. In 1937 there were about fourteen hundred beds, distributed among the surgical, maternity, contagious diseases, internal therapy, infantile, and several other departments. The hospital was usually crowded, particularly in the surgical wards. The operating staff was good, but apart from this the hospital was understaffed, and the doctors and nurses usually lacked experience. The barracks were hot in summer and cold in winter, and often far from clean.

The hospital lay between the Metallurgical Institute and the street car line, and we of the Institute would stream through on our way to and from classes every evening. For two years a large barrel stood outside the maternity ward. On seeing it for the first time on my way to the Institute I looked into it curiously. After that I tried not to notice it when I passed. But one winter night I stumbled and fell over something on the ground. I picked myself up and went back to see what I had tripped over. Examination proved it to be an afterbirth which had spilled out of the barrel and frozen to the ground.

I spared Bob the barrel, but pointed out to him a sign over the door of the little barrack which served as a morgue: 'Corpses given out to relatives from three to five only.'

The food given to the patients in the hospital was often far from the best, the food allowance being, in 1936, about six roubles per day per patient.

The hospital, like all other sanitary facilities in the city, was free. It was necessary only to be sick to be admitted — if there was room. If there was not, the patient sometimes had to be sent home. An ambulance service organized on a fair scale in 1936 brought patients to the hospital, particularly accident cases from the mill. However, as late as 1937 an acquaintance of mine telephoned the hospital late at night and requested that an ambulance be sent for his sick wife. He was asked over the telephone, 'Is she still conscious?' and upon replying in the affirmative was told that there was no ambulance available.

Several departments of the Central Hospital were, for obvious reasons, situated in outlying parts of the town: The psychiatric ward with forty beds and sixty patients,[1] one doctor, and

[1] See *Magnitogorsk Worker* for October 29, 1937.

two nurses; the venereal diseases clinic and ward, and the tuberculosis department. The large typhus hospital, which existed in 1933 and which had a dire reputation in the city, decreased in size and was liquidated in 1936 when typhus was practically wiped out as the result of vaccination and generally improved nourishment and sanitary conditions.

The Board of Health ran eighteen clinics handling all kinds of work from dentistry to electro- and hydro-therapy. Some of these were much better equipped than the Central Hospital. The one in the Kirov District, for instance, was clean and well run, and had a small analytical laboratory, an X-ray laboratory, and first-class dental equipment.

In addition to the abovementioned units, the Board of Health ran first-aid stations in all the important departments of the plant, manned by trained nurses, and in some cases by doctors; and a large experimental hygienic laboratory which carried on research work in industrial hygiene and preventive medicine.

All the doctors and other employees of the hospitals and clinics received salaries from the Board of Health. Doctors earned from four hundred to several thousand roubles a month. Soviet doctors had a legal working day of four or five hours. If they worked more than this, they received overtime pay. In Magnitogorsk, due to the tremendous shortage of doctors, most of them worked one and a half to two, and sometimes even two and a half to three jobs, which meant up to fifteen hours. This was strictly illegal, but inasmuch as there were not enough doctors the Board of Health was permitted by the Medical Workers' Trade Union to allow its employees to work more than the legal working day.

In Magnitogorsk anyone who was sick received the best medical attention the community had to offer. The city spent about one quarter of its budget on medicine. The population of Magnitogorsk had learned to think of socialized medicine as natural, as a normal function of the State. To them it seemed incredible that in America there were many doctors who had no patients, while many sick men and women did not receive medical care.

IV

B<small>OB</small> and I got back at six o'clock just in time for dinner. I thought he would be ready to relax for a while, but he made me read the local paper to him for an hour after we had eaten. I translated part of the editorial entitled 'The Blast-Furnace Men Can and Must Fulfill the Plan.' It took the director of the department, Mikhailovich, to task severely:

> Unfortunately, however, Comrade Mikhailovich, and the other leaders of the blast furnace department attempt to explain everything on the basis of 'objective' factors. They complain unceasingly about the lack of good ore, bad transport, bad quality of coke, and make similar excuses. That this is nothing but childish excuse-finding is easily seen from the fact that while Comrade Mikhailovich and his pals complain continuously that there is not enough coke, during the month of February they managed to burn up twenty thousand tons more coke than they were supposed to have received for the month according to the plan....'

I read on to the end, through a few references to bad organization of the wages of the gas workers on the blast furnaces, and a very distinct warning to Mikhailovich that he had better get busy and have some concrete results to show by the first of May — or else...it might not be healthy for him.

There followed a column and a half of foreign news: A detailed account of the reorganization of the Spanish government: an abbreviated translation of the manifesto issued by the new Negrin government, calling for solidarity of all true Spaniards in executing in the course of the next few hours, or at most days, a purge of the Republican armies, to clean out all 'cowards, traitors, and wavering elements.' After this there was a verbatim translation of the manifesto of the polit-buro of the Spanish Communist Party, calling for the solid support of the whole Spanish nation to back up the United Front government and free Spanish territory from all traitors, interventionists, and renegades. Then a news report from Barcelona, full of confidence of a sure and almost immediate victory; then two items reporting victories of the Republican forces at two points on the front. I read a little notice at the bottom of the first page which interested both of us very much. It had to do with the construction of the new railroad from Magnitogorsk to Ufa which had been going on for the last five years, but never seemed to make any progress.

> Up until the present time the construction work on the Ufa-Magnitogorsk line which will cut the rail distance from our city to Moscow and the southern industrial districts by 500 kilometers, has practically stopped. The job was almost completely shut down. This year, however, work will be resumed. Railroad bridges over the Ural and Kizil Rivers will be built; and whole stretches of road already laid, will be ballasted. For this purpose the government has allocated 450,000 roubles, of which 50,000 will be spent on the cultural and communal needs of the workers on the construction job, and on the manganese ore mine site. The work will be carried on by the construction trust 'Magnito-stroi.'

On the next page I read a long article by a party section organizer, entitled 'Fulfill the Decisions of the District Plenum in a Bolshevik Manner.' It seemed that the district plenum had decided that a certain number of new party members be taken in in each section; however, the units were not on the job, and no new members were forthcoming. The writer of the article was beating his breast and explaining how he had failed to understand the decision about swelling the ranks of the party, but now understood and was setting to work. The article did not say that one of the main difficulties was that most of those desirous of entering the party could not get the necessary recommendations from old party members, because the latter were a diminishing tribe and more and more reticent about recommending people for anything.

On the other page was the report of the previous day's work at the mill.

Ore	14,280 tons	87.8% of plan
Coke	4,125 "	79.7% " "
Pig iron	4,700 "	79.8% " "
Steel	4,112 "	91.4% " "
All rolled products	2,481 "	68.3% " "
Blooming mill	4,518 "	103.8% " "
Mill 500	Shut down for repairs	
Mill 300 No. 1	312 tons	33.9% " "
Mill 300 No. 2	833 "	131.6% " "
Mill 300 No. 3	763 "	127.2% " "
Mill 250	573 "	95.5% " "
Agglomerating plant	14,820 "	87.8% " "

The third page was labeled 'Literary Page' in fancy large letters. There were some poems by schoolboys and pipefitters, and a long article by a local literary light, entitled 'The Beginner's First Poems.'

Bob left our apartment late that night, and I never saw him again. He was killed in Spain, where he fought as Major in the International Brigade. But, when packing in 1931, I found the newspaper I had translated to him and a carbon of his notes.

V

Late in 1937 I went to America on vacation. I had spent more than five years in Magnitogorsk working and studying. With the exception of several trips to Moscow and around the Urals for a week or two at a time, I had been on the job continuously. I wanted to get back and take a look at America. Masha would have come with me, but she was a Soviet citizen, and the authorities refused to give her a passport to go abroad.

After the usual delay I received a Soviet exit-re-entry visa, and set off for Moscow where I found to my delight that I could buy a ticket to New York for roubles, though I could not legally buy a single dollar or franc with the money I had earned in Magnitogorsk.

As I sped westward across Europe, cities and towns became progressively cleaner, stations and switching yards better kept, while the passengers getting in and out of the train were better and better dressed.

When I stepped out of the express in Paris, I was bowled over by the quantity of merchandise of all kinds on sale. At every step someone tried to sell me something. Stores were full of goods of all kinds begging to be bought. Apartments and hotel rooms stood empty waiting to be rented. In Russia one stood in line for minutes for bread or other groceries, hours for a good woolen suit, and days for a bicycle; in France and America a surplus of these things had been produced, and was interfering with the normal functioning of commerce and industry.

The Soviet Union was operating a deficit economy, while

the so-called capitalist countries were struggling with a surplus economy. I had known this for some time, but not until I walked out of the Gare du Nord into Paris after five years in the Soviet Union was the significance of the phrase brought home to me.

I went into a restaurant and bought the best châteaubriand in the house. While I was eating it, two able-bodied French working men, obviously unemployed, came around asking alms. In all Russia you could not have found a piece of meat cooked and served as well as that châteaubriand, but you could have traveled the Soviet Union from one end to another and not found two able-bodied men anxious to work and unable to find a job. On the other hand the two French chômeurs were better dressed than most Russian skilled workers.

Living standards in France and particularly in the United States were incomparably higher than those in the Soviet Union, and this fact hit me in the face every step I took during that trip in 1937. The dinners eaten by the coke-oven workers in Magnitogorsk consisted for the most part of a large plate of hot, but watery soup, and half a pound of black bread. The higher-paid workers ordered meat as well. The French workers ate much better dinners, often had bicycles, and usually two or three rooms per family. American standards were, of course, even higher. Russian families normally lived in one room; bicycles were a luxury, as were good leather shoes and good woolen clothes.

Still the divergence in the trends was very noticeable. In Russia during the five years I had spent there, material conditions had improved by at least a hundred per cent. In France they had stayed the same, perhaps had got worse. In America they may have improved slightly, though I doubt that there was much change. The Russian worker may not have had much, but he felt that he would have more the next year.

His children were going to school and sure of subsequent employment. He was secure against sickness, as were his children. Unemployment had been forgotten. He was, therefore, inclined to be essentially cheerful and optimistic, though harried by numerous current annoyances, absent in most countries.

I found my old friends in America worried about unemployment, increasing taxes, doctors' and dentists' bills; about putting their children through college; and perhaps more important about the general trend of American society and the validity of the sociological and economic principles upon which it was founded.

In talking with people in France and America I was impressed by the interest in the Soviet Union and the widespread misinformation about Russia and all things Russian. Everyone I met was opinionated. The Communists and their sympathizers held Russia up as a panacea. They would not even listen to any adverse criticism of the Soviet system, the Kremlin leaders, or 'Socialism' as worked out in the Soviet Union. Other people were steeped in Eugene Lyons' stories and would not concede the possibility that Russia had produced anything during recent years except chaos, suffering, and disorder. They dismissed the industrial and material successes of the Russians with an angry wave of the hand. Any economist or businessman should have been able to see that the tripling of pig-iron production within a decade was a serious achievement, and would necessarily have far-reaching effects on the balance of economic and therefore military power in Europe. Pig iron was pig iron, whether or not the blast furnace was constructed by prisoner specialists and disfranchised kulaks.

I had great difficulty in accustoming myself to American advertising after living in the Soviet Union. In Russia advertising was almost non-existent. The State advertised government bonds and savings banks in an effort to keep the people from buying scarce consumers' goods. With the exception of cosmetics almost no merchandise was advertised, either in the press, in subways, on billboards, or over the radio. Instead of being urged to buy and smoke a certain brand of cigarette, the Russian people were continuously exhorted to study Marx, Engels, Lenin, Stalin, to participate in civilian defense organizations, to increase production, lower costs, improve quality, and to be vigilant. They smoked whatever cigarettes they found in the store, and had enough money to buy.

I was struck at the time by the stupidity and uselessness of most of American advertising, and the comparative reasonableness and expedience of Russian political and economic advertising or propaganda. In later years I again left the Soviet Union and went to the 'capitalist world' on several occasions, and this impression was rather strengthened than weakened.

After a month in the States and two weeks in Moscow, I started back to Magnitogorsk. I was loaded down with merchandise of various kinds bought in America for Masha, the children, and our household. My many suitcases contained flashlights, eggbeaters, girdles, shoes, blankets, and countless other items. These were consigned to the baggage car and I traveled light. I likewise traveled 'hard' or third class, as I was nearly broke. For three days I bumped across Russia. Some of the passengers had mattresses. There were twenty for the car. First come, first served. I was one of the first when we left Moscow, and had one.

We arrived in Magnitogorsk finally and several hundred people staggered off the train and into the station, past the greasy buffet, the large, well-decorated newsstand, and out through the door on the other side. I was among the first. I knew the importance of being ahead of the crowd, and, not encumbered by much baggage, I could walk fast.

Fifty feet from the station was a wide road, over which there was obviously a good deal of traffic. On a telegraph pole was a sign 'Bus Stop.' Here a line formed.

Twenty minutes after the arrival of the train a bus pulled up and was assailed by ten or fifteen people who had not been in line, but just standing around. There was an immediate uproar. 'Hey, conductor, don't let the people out of line into the bus,' shouted those in the line. The undisciplined newly arrived said nothing, but shouldered their way toward the bus door. The conductor put her head out through the door and swore at the men blocking each other in their attempts to be first in the bus. 'Citizens!' she shouted with a village accent. 'What the hell is this? You'll break the bus, and no one will ride.'

I managed to squeeze in, and was jostled along the uneven road to the end of the streetcar line where the bus disgorged its load and went back to the station for another. The streetcar was less crowded and I rode in comfort as far as the Bazaar where several dozen men and women with bulging market bags got in. One woman had a burlap bag over her shoulder. The car had already started when a great rumpus began inside the bag. The woman became embarrassed and the passengers curious, until finally she opened it and two little pigs could be seen inside, fighting and squealing. The conductor rang the bell for the motorman to stop the car, and told the woman with the pigs to get off. There was some argument, but the crowd backed up the conductor who insisted that a streetcar was no place for suckling pigs.

VI

The next day, bathed and refreshed, I started out for the mill. I found that during my absence the purge had made astonishing headway. People were afraid of anyone and anything foreign. The general foreman of the coke plant told me evasively to go see Syemichkin.

Syemichkin looked haggard and harried. As I found out later he had been questioned by the NKVD several times, though he never was arrested.

'I'm sorry, Jack,' he said soberly. 'I have nothing against you. But we can't have foreigners here any more. Not only are you a foreigner, but you've just been abroad.'

I left the plant and went home to think it over. Masha told me that nearly all the foreigners had gone or were leaving; those with foreign passports back to their native countries, those who had taken on Soviet citizenship for Siberia under arrest.

I had a long talk with Kolya. 'Better leave,' he said. 'This is no place for foreigners now.'

Masha and I decided that night that we would go. The next day she applied for permission to go to America to live. It was nearly four years before the permission was granted. For three months I stayed in Magnitogorsk, living on Masha's money and waiting for her travel permit. I had no job and the doors of the Institute were therefore closed to me. I played chess with André until his arrest. I found my friends were uncomfortable when I came to see them, so I sat home most of the time pecking on the typewriter. Every night the arrest squads visited the Kirov District, staggering with fatigue, eyes bloodshot from lack of sleep.

VII

J OE BARNES came to Magnitogorsk for a few days, and I took him all over the town, though neither of us could get permission to go into the plant. The city was something worth seeing in 1938.

The mud huts and the wooden barracks had given way in part to reinforced concrete apartment houses. Well-lighted, paved streets, a city park, and even a local 'skyscraper' of nine stories had made their appearance. Though the city was still in a primitive state, and did not even approach the grandiose plans for the billion rouble model city which was to be constructed eventually on the other side of the lake, still it did boast fifty schools, three colleges, two large theaters, half a dozen small ones, seventeen libraries, twenty-two clubs, eighteen clinics, and many other communal and cultural institutions.

While the Kirov District was inhabited principally by foremen, brigadiers, and skilled workers, as well as a scattering of teachers, doctors, and various city employees, the high administrative technical and political personnel for the most part inhabited the quarters of the departed foreign specialists in Berezki. Here, in addition to the houses which had been built for the foreigners, and which were well made and equipped, Zavenyagin had constructed a dozen large houses for himself and his most valuable assistants. Designed by a young Russian

architect named Saprikin, these were copied almost exactly
from American architectural catalogues. The result was something very much approaching Mount Vernon, New York, or
Germantown, Pennsylvania, as Joe remarked. The houses were
situated on a hill. Each had a large garden, top soil for which
had in some cases been brought for miles in trucks. Zavenyagin's house was a palace in comparison with most Soviet habi-
tations. The three-story, fourteen-room, stuccoed brick house
contained a billiard room, a play room for Zavenyagin's two
little sons, a music room, a large study. A small deer park in
back of the house and a luxurious garden in front were surrounded by a high wall topped by a picket fence. A militiaman
was always on duty near the entrance.

The other houses, occupied by the chief engineer, the chiefs
of various departments, the head of the party, the head of the
NKVD, and also by two of the old prisoner specialists, Bogo-
lyubov from the mine, and Tikhomirov, the chief electrician,
were smaller than Zavenyagin's but still very comfortable, even
luxurious. All were fitted out with the best that the Khar-
kov furniture factory could supply. Zavenyagin's house was
furnished at a cost of 170,000 roubles, while the house itself cost
about 80,000 roubles. The others cost proportionally less.

An interesting point had arisen with regard to the rent to
be paid for these houses. Obviously, if calculated on the basis
of a twenty-year amortization, the rent for Zavenyagin's house
and furniture would be in the neighborhood of a thousand
roubles a month for amortization alone, plus at least as much
again for upkeep, garden, and so on. Zavenyagin's salary was
only just above two thousand roubles a month. The other
occupants were in a similar position. So it was conveniently
arranged that the cost of these houses was entered into the
books of the whole housing department of the plant administration, the amortization being shared by everybody who lived

in a plant-owned house. This, however, still left the inhabitants of these houses with a very substantial rent to pay because they had so much floor space. So it was arranged that their rent was to be paid by the plant as 'administrative expenses.' The automobiles at the disposal of department heads, chief engineers, and functionaries, which were used for hunting trips and for going to the theater, as well as for business, were likewise bought, kept up, and chauffeured out of administrative expense money.

Berezki boasted a very fine garden with a tennis court, which was converted into a skating rink in winter. Here the atmosphere of a summer evening was different from that in the Kirov District. There was a suspicion of the smugness of Park Avenue or of Chicago's Gold Coast, until the purge began to strike most frequently among those who thought they had 'arrived.'

Another part of the city I took Joe to see was 'Shanghai.' Here a collection of improvised mud huts huddled in a sort of ravine overlooking the railroad yards. The inhabitants were largely Bashkirs, Tartars, and Kirghizi, and had built their dwellings out of materials found or stolen over a period of years. The roofs were usually made of old scrap metal, sometimes covered by sod or by thatch. The same house was inhabited by the family, the chickens, the pigs, and the cow, if there was one. This manner of housing livestock was usual in the poorer sections of the Russian countryside. The dwellers in these 'zemlyanki' were laborers and semi-skilled workers and their families. Their possession of chickens and goats was witness of the fact that they 'were living well' by the standards of Russian peasantry. They had eggs and milk, while the fathers working in the mill supplied a cash income.

There remained a dozen sections of the town composed of temporary wooden structures, barracks, or frame houses. The best of these were equipped with central heat, running water, and sewerage, though most had none of these conveniences, and were similar to Barrack 17, where I lived in 1932 and 1933.

In 1938 Magnitogorsk's 220,000 inhabitants lived as follows, as closely as I could ascertain through a friend in the city planning commission:

	Per Cent
Berezki and the Central Hotel	2
Kirov District and other permanent apartment houses	15
Permanent individual houses	8
Barracks and other 'temporary' houses	50
Zemlyanki	25

The same friend told me that the city budget of Magnitogorsk reached twenty-three million roubles in 1937, thirty-one million in 1938. Of these sums, approximately fifty per cent went for the construction and operation of schools of all kinds and about thirty-five per cent for health and sanitation. The money came from taxes, paid mostly by the plant and other organizations, and by the more highly paid workers.

We trudged along the snowy streets to the very center of the town where a large park had been constructed in 1935 by the Metallurgical Workers' Trade Union. It contained a parachute jumping tower, two outdoor dancing floors, an outdoor and an indoor chess and checker club, a tennis court, basketball and volley ball courts, football fields, shooting galleries, two restaurants, and a very nice flower and shrub garden. Admission was fifty kopeks, and in summer the place was packed every evening.

Now it was empty and bleak, though we could still see the billboards advertising the Inter-Ural football (soccer) championship match which had been held in Magnitogorsk in September.

I showed Joe the ITK barracks where a mere two thousand

petty criminals lived while serving sentences up to five years for non-political offenses. Five years before the number of these prisoners in Magnitogorsk was ten or fifteen times as large.

Joe wanted to see a church, and I told him that Magnitogorsk was one of the few cities, perhaps the only one in the world, with a population of a quarter million, without a single church. The little village of Magnitnaya had had a small church which was made into a club room in 1934, then abandoned and submerged after the construction of the second dam. Its disappearance into the waters of the lake represented and was approximately coincident with the disappearance of religion as a social or political factor worthy of mention in Magnitogorsk. Occasionally one could see a peasant newly arrived from some obscure village cross himself in the old fashion; in the bathhouse one sometimes saw an oldish man with a little cross on a piece of string around his neck. These remnants of the tremendous influence previously exercised by the Greek Orthodox Church on the Russian people were not the object of persecution by the authorities. They were laughed and smiled at by the population as a whole, and a relentless campaign of atheist propaganda was carried on in the press and in the schools.

VIII

Joe was interested in the theater and cinema. Magnitogorsk had ten theaters with a total seating capacity of nine thousand, all attached to various clubs. So we went looking at clubs, of which the city boasted twenty-three.

The activities of these clubs were varied, and included dramatic circles, classes, sports circles, chess and checkers, art, and literary groups. The money for their upkeep came from the trade unions or cultural allocations from the plant administration. There were no club dues, and all parties, picnics, or functions were organized on a non-profit basis.

Social ballroom dancing in 1935 became a popular phase of the club activities and to a certain extent took the place of folk dancing. Music was generally furnished by an accordion.

We went to the movies in the cinema palace, the so-called 'Magnit,' which seated about a thousand. About twenty thousand people attended the cinema per month, which meant that the average Magnitogorsk adult went once every six weeks. The films shown were mostly Soviet, but certain foreign films, such as 'City Lights,' 'Sous les toits de Paris,' 'Modern Times,' and 'Peter,' were shown as well as an occasional Wild-West thriller, produced fifteen or twenty years ago.

There were two permanent professional theater groups in the city. The older one was known as TRAM (Young Workers' Theater). During the season of 1937–38, TRAM put on seventy performances of classics and thirty modern plays. The classics included Shakespeare, Schiller, and a great deal of N. A. Ostrovsky (the old playwright, not the contemporary novelist who died in 1937).

The TRAM theater group, organized in 1932, first lived and worked in a little wooden club house, belonging to the Railroad Workers' Union. In October, 1932 the city authorities gave TRAM a building, which they had barely equipped for producing their plays when it was ordered torn down because the materials were needed for other construction work. All through the summers of 1932 and 1933 the company traveled through the countryside, producing plays and short skits for the harvest workers. During the winter they produced plays in various clubs. The most popular actress and the one who took the lead in most of the contemporary plays was one Shura Kalgorodova, whose story is so interesting that it is worth telling.

Wanting to be an actress, fifteen-year-old Shura left her home and went to seek her fortune. Barefoot and undernourished, daughter of a landless peasant, she dreamed of the theater, of the glamor and fame of great stars who had risen from poverty. It was not long, however, before Shura had spent the few kopeks she had brought with her and faced hunger.

What was she to do? Go back home? Never! There was hardly enough bread to feed her little brothers and sisters properly, and besides, she wanted to be an actress. She dreamed of automobiles, and lights, and beautiful clothes, and in the village there were only rags, and mud, and lots of wood to cut for the local kulak at twenty kopeks a day. No, she would not go back. She pushed on to Moscow.

To keep from starving she became a thief, and then a bandit; a member of a real gang, working construction camps, trains, and bazaars. This was in 1928.

In the beginning of 1932 she came to Magnitogorsk with four others, three men and a woman. They came well-dressed, with money in their pockets, not to work, but to live by stealing and speculation. Shura was nineteen years old and very pretty. In the lining of her coat she carried a ten-inch dagger with a carved handle. And in the back of her head she still dreamed of being an actress. The first job she did in Magnitogorsk, a robbery of the apartment of one of the chief engineers of construction, she almost messed up by getting into a long conversation with the engineer about the theater in Leningrad, when she was only supposed to talk to him for five minutes or so until her pals got out of the apartment. This, however, was only the first of many difficult scenes with her fellow bandits.

In March, 1932, the Magnitogorsk Young Workers' TRAM Theater was organized. Shura announced that she was leaving the gang and going to the theater, whereupon the leader threatened her life. She went nevertheless.

Shura found it even easier than she expected. Showing immediate talent, she was given a place among those of the young workers who were freed from work and who became professional actors. She lived in the dormitory of the theater and set to work studying diction, grammar, and parts in several plays.

But the ties with the underworld were not easily broken. There were threats, and one night a short knife fight in which Shura got a cut on the hand. With the help of one of the young actors of the theater she managed to tie up the thief and turn him over to the militia.

Three months later the whole gang was arrested and Shura used as a witness in the trial. When the other four who came with her to Magnitogorsk had received two to five years, Shura felt that she had definitely outlived the four years of banditry which had been forced on her. She threw herself completely into her work in the theater.

I talked with Shura several times, and found her not only handsome and enthusiastic, but extremely intelligent. She was a rangy blonde with high cheekbones and a strong mouth and chin. She burned with ardor for the stage in general, and for her TRAM in particular.

During the days when the Young Workers' Theater was making itself known to the workers of Magnitogorsk, they did agitational skits on labor discipline, on cleanliness of the barracks, and fulfillment of the plan. Not having any real theater building, they put on many of these pieces in the mills, in Red Corners (small club rooms in barracks or houses), in clubs, and, when the weather permitted, out-of-doors in the manner of the

French Blue Blouse groups. The theater worked very closely with the Young Communist League of which most of the actors and actresses were members.

Since it was a young group, most of whom had only yesterday been workers at the bench, the ties with production were very strong. The theater dug out points of conflict between the workers and various organizations, and with their dramatization forced bureaucratic administrators to work better. For instance, the conflict between the workers of the blast furnaces and NARPIT (the Dining-Room Trust) was given such publicity by the theater and by the verses of one of the actors, Tolkachev, that the administration of NARPIT was changed, and the cold dinners which so irked the blast-furnace workers became a thing of the past.

At the same time the theater began to produce serious plays, 'Joy Street,' 'Girls of Our Country,' 'The Army of Peace,' and others. The work of the theater, however, was hindered by lack of a suitable building and competent direction.

In March, 1934, Shura and a half-dozen other young actors were sent to Moscow, where they gave a good account of themselves at the All Union Theater Olympiad, and then went to see Sergo Ordjonokidze, the Commissar of Heavy Industry, who decided all important questions dealing with Magnitogorsk. Sergo greeted the young artists cordially. 'I feel Magnitogorsk on me here,' he said, pointing simultaneously to his heart and his neck. And at the end of the conversation he said, 'Tell Zavenyagin that I am giving TRAM thirty thousand roubles and a truck, and I suggest that he do as much.'

On returning, the actors found that the administration of Magnitogorsk had already made its gift. This and the promise of a building raised the spirits of all the group to the heights. And a few months later the Maly Theater in Moscow took the Magnitogorsk Young Workers' Theater under its wing and sent a capable director and all kinds of scenery and properties.

By the end of 1935 the Young Workers' Theater was putting on plays by Ostrovsky and Gorky.

In 1936, with the completion of the new Metallurgists' Club, TRAM inherited the House of the Engineers and Technicians, whose theater seated fifteen hundred and had a big revolving stage. At the same time the Magnitogorsk Art Theater was organized with professionals, brought from Moscow and other big centers, and the two theaters entered into a sort of competition.

The newly organized Art Theater was fortunate in being made up of actors who had long stage experience, and in having more competent technical leadership, but TRAM had the boundless enthusiasm of young men and women like Shura Kalgorodov, who were finding themselves in an art of which they had dreamed for years, and also the advantage of strong ties with the life of Magnitogorsk.

An institution even more popular than the theater was the circus, which, for most of the workers with their agrarian or nomadic backgrounds, was more interesting than 'Macbeth' or 'The Enemies.' It was usually impossible to get seats for the circus except a long time in advance. The performance was of third-rate Barnum and Bailey quality. Occasional attempts to tie up the program with the construction of Socialism in one country or with plan fulfillment in the plant tended to be ludicrous.

IX

Aᴏ'ꜱ departure I was drafted into domestic service while Masha was in the maternity hospital and after she came home with our second daughter. Vera did the actual housework and I did the shopping. I would trudge off in the middle of the morning with a market bag and visit the main stores and the Bazaar. There was plenty of food, and as Masha received a four-month maternity vacation with full pay, we had money to buy all we needed.

The problem of supplying the workers with enough to eat and enough to wear had been difficult and sometimes impossible. For several years the cooperative stores had had nothing to sell except bread and occasionally a few other simple foods. During this period privately owned stores disappeared, and the only source of supply was the Bazaar — a big, open hillside and hilltop covering an area of three or four acres, where anybody could go and sell anything he had for as much as he could get while the police watched for stolen goods. During 1933 and 1934 the prices in the Bazaar had been prohibitive; bread, for example, cost up to ten roubles a kilogram, as compared to the store price of fifteen kopeks at the time.

After the visit of Ordjonokidze to Magnitogorsk in 1933, the plant administration and the local political leaders had begun to pay serious attention to the question of consumers' goods. Special State farms had been organized near Magnitogorsk to supply the city with potatoes, milk, cabbage, and meat. By 1936 the food question was solved. That is to say, there was enough food for everybody. The problem of distribution, however, remained.

Gradually stores and truck transport were organized and it became possible to buy the day's supply of food without standing in line for hours or paying someone else to do it. From 1935 to 1937 Magnitogorsk boasted five model 'Gastronom' food stores, which would have been considered clean, orderly, and well-stocked in any American city, though Magnitogorsk prices were considerably higher.

The following table will give an idea of food prices in Magnitogorsk in the winter of 1937–38. Prices are in roubles and kopeks. (One dollar equals five roubles and twenty-six kopeks by the nominal exchange rate. Average workers' wage in Magnitogorsk was something over three hundred roubles a month at that time.)

Milk, 2 roubles per liter (quart). Slight seasonal fluctuations.
Meat, from 3.50 to 10 roubles per kg. (1.60 to 4 per lb.) in the stores. From 5 to 20 roubles per kg. (2 to 8 per lb.) in the Bazaar.
Eggs, 1 rouble apiece (not always available).
Butter, 14 to 20 roubles per kg. (6 to 8 per lb.).
Sausage 7 to 20 roubles per kg. (3 to 8 per lb.).
Flour, 2 to 5 roubles per kg. (0.80 to 2 per lb.).
Rice, 5.50 per kg. (2.50 per lb.).
Other cereal grains, 3 to 5 roubles per kg. (1.30 to 2 per lb.).
Apples, 3.50 roubles per kg. (1.60 per lb.) Very bad, usually frozen, almost impossible to obtain, the demand was so great.
Potatoes, 0.50 roubles per kg. (0.20 per lb.).
Cabbage, 0.75 roubles per kg. (0.30 per lb.).
Turnips, carrots and beets, obtainable frequently at the same price as cabbage.
Cigarettes, 1 to 5 roubles for a package of 25.
Vodka, 12 roubles per liter.
Various wines, including champagne, from 6 to 20 roubles for a pint bottle.

During 1937, 212,500,000 roubles' worth of food and drygoods were sold by the various Magnitogorsk supply organizations. This represented only eighty-four per cent of the plan. The failure to fulfill the plan was due not to lack of buyers, but of things to sell.

The problem of drygoods, which was eclipsed by the food question until there was enough food, became exceedingly acute after 1936. The city was full of potential buyers, with steady incomes, their pockets full of money, who spent their free days every week hunting avidly for suits, furniture, sewing machines, materials, china, cutlery, shoes, radio sets, and the thousand and one other things which are furnished by light industry and distributed in the United States by Sears-Roebuck, Macy's, and Woolworth's.

Until twenty years ago the overwhelming majority of the Russian people lived in villages, and most of them never bought anything machine-made, except occasionally some nails, a plowshare, or a little yard goods. Each family made its own clothes, furniture, bedclothes, wooden bowls, and so forth, and each village had its own bootmaker.

Within the space of two decades, thirty-five million Russian peasants left the villages and became city dwellers, earning money, and demanding manufactured goods. The peasants still in the villages, collectivized or working on State farms, were also demanding manufactured goods. Soviet light industry, though growing, was completely unable to satisfy the overwhelming demand, particularly in view of the government's consistent policy of limiting imports to machinery and to pushing heavy industry and its products much more than light.

Quality of manufactured goods was generally low (shoes, suits, and materials were usually poor), though some things, the new short-wave radio sets, for example, were of comparatively high quality.

Prices of the manufactured goods were appallingly high. A good pair of shoes cost two hundred and twenty roubles in 1936 and three hundred in 1938. Good woolen suits were almost unobtainable, and when they did appear in the stores, if one was lucky enough to get one while they lasted, one had to pay from five hundred to fifteen hundred roubles (a month's wages for a skilled worker).

The years 1937 and 1938 saw the appearance of a number of
new manufactured articles, such as vacuum cleaners, eggbeaters, and the like; the queues for shoes and plain cotton or
woolen yard goods became shorter and the stores were cleaner,
the service better.

X

AFTER three months
of waiting, during which time I wrote an incredibly bad novel
and learned some Japanese, we decided something would have
to be done. Working in Magnitogorsk seemed out of the question. The authorities told us that Masha's application might
not be acted on for months.

We decided that I should go to Moscow and try to get a job
as translator or secretary to some foreign correspondent. It
meant breaking up the family temporarily, but there seemed to
be no alternative.

Being married to someone with a different colored passport
is always awkward, particularly so in times of crisis. In our
case it was nearly three years before we were able to make the
necessary arrangements to go to the United States all together,
and then it was mainly due to the help of the American Embassy in Moscow and of certain friends in Washington.

PART NINE

PART NINE Exeunt

I

I LEFT Magnitogorsk with considerable regret. I had put in five of the most active years of my life in its mills. My fingers had helped mold the blast furnaces, I had sweated in the heat of summer, frozen my nose and cheeks in the Arctic winter winds. I had watched millions of tons of iron and steel roll out of Magnitogorsk to Soviet machine-building and armament works.

When I left Magnitogorsk I was profoundly shocked by the fact that so many people I had known had been arrested. The whole thing seemed stupid, unreasonable, preposterous. The Stalinist constitution of 1936 had promised a democratic and free society. Instead the NKVD seemed to have run away with the show, the purge appeared to be consuming everything that had been created.

I mentioned this to Syemichkin when I went around to bid him good-bye. His attitude was much more sane and balanced than mine. 'If I am not mistaken,' he said, 'you in America tolerated chattel slavery for nearly a century after your great constitution of freedom went into force. Your elections were travesties of universal suffrage during the first decades after your revolution. Our Soviet constitution is a blueprint of the future. It is a picture of what we are building, and we will build it too. Now our elections are ludicrous, of course. Civil liberties are restricted. But we are not yet one generation old, and we are at war now. Do not forget it.'

Syemichkin was right, of course. Not only that, but many people in Magnitogorsk would have agreed with him. Very few of them had read American history, not many could have expressed their feelings as concisely as Syemichkin, but they felt that Russia was fighting a class war against the rest of the world, and at the same time laying the foundations for a new society farther along the road of human progress than anything in the West; a society which would guarantee its people not only personal freedom but absolute economic security; a society for which it was worth while to shed blood, sweat, and tears.

The millions of expropriated kulaks, the political exiles in Siberia were a lost tribe. They had been sacrificed on the altar of Revolution and Progress. They would die off in twenty or thirty years, and by that time, perhaps, Soviet society would be able to function without scrapping blocks of its population every decade. It was a cruel concept, but there it was, one item in a long list of expenditures for Magnitogorsk, for Stalin's Ural Stronghold, for survival.

One conclusion reached before I left Magnitogorsk I still believe to be sound. Westerners have no place in Russia. It is the Russian's country, and it is their Revolution. Men and women from Western Europe and America may occasionally succeed in understanding it, but it is almost impossible for them to fit into it.

I survived black bread, rotten salt fish, the cold, and hard work, which was unusual. I did not survive the purge. I think I understood it, its causes, its inevitability in Ubergangsperiod Russia, but I could not live with it. I probably could not have stuck it out, even had it tolerated me.

I went to Moscow and became an observer, which was, perhaps, all I had ever been really. Had it not been for Masha and the children I should have left Russia entirely. As it was I hung on for more than three years, until at long last we were able to go to America all together.

I left Magnitogorsk with the conviction that I had been a very minor actor in a world premier. I had participated in an enterprise carried out for the first time, and from which the rest of the world would learn much, both positively and negatively. Not only had I helped to build an industrial base which would prove of vital importance in the forthcoming war against Germany, I had participated in the collective effort of one hundred and seventy-odd million people building a society along collective lines, coordinated and synchronized by a general plan.

Blast furnaces were constructed in many countries. They were built by private enterprises for profit. The Magnitogorsk blast furnaces were built and operated collectively. No one made a profit on their construction and operation. They formed one part of a general plan.

It was an historic landmark.

The general plans of a decade and a half ago, along whose lines Magnitogorsk was projected, have already undergone fundamental changes and will certainly be further modified. The basic concept of the Ural-Kuznetsk Combinat was abandoned in the early thirties when new geological discoveries rendered it obsolete. Similarly, I believe, new discoveries and observations in other fields radically modified the Marxist-Leninist social precepts which underlay the theories of the proletarian revolution, of the construction of Socialism, as they were understood and applied by Lenin two decades ago, or by Stalin one decade ago. Such modifications will continue.

Socialism as it functioned in Magnitogorsk displayed numerous shortcomings, as did capitalism as operated in Gastonia, Dunkirk, or Coventry. But Socialism in Magnitogorsk did well enough so that I am convinced that many valuable lessons can be learned from a study of it.

PART TEN

Epilogue—What
Makes Russia Click

I

THE MAGNITOGORSK
I left in early 1938 was producing upward of five thousand tons
of steel daily and large quantities of many other useful products.
In spite of the purge, the town was still full of rough and earnest
young Russians — working, studying, making mistakes and
learning, reproducing to the tune of thirty-odd per thousand
every year. They were also writing poetry, going to see re-
markably good performances of 'Othello,' learning to play
violins and tennis. All this out in the middle of a steppe where,
ten years before, only a few hundred impoverished herders had
lived.

During the next three years, while I stumbled in and out of
Moscow, to Western Europe, the Balkans, the Near East, and
Japan, following the star of journalism, I managed to keep in
touch with Magnitogorsk. I arranged to see *The Magnitogorsk
Worker* and other local publications, and from time to time I
ran into old friends and acquaintances.

By and large, production increased from 1938 to 1941. By
late 1938 the immediate negative effects of the purge had nearly
disappeared. The industrial aggregates of Magnitogorsk were

producing close to capacity, and every furnace, every mill,
every worker, was being made to feel the pressure and tension
which spread through every phase of Soviet life after Munich.
'The capitalist attack on the Soviet Union, prepared for years,
is about to take place ...' boomed the Soviet press, the radio,
schoolteachers, stump speakers, and party, trade-union, and
Komsomol functionaries, at countless meetings.

Russia's defense budget nearly doubled every year. Immense
reserves of strategic materials, machines, fuels, foods, and spare
parts were stored away. The Red Army increased in size from
roughly two million in 1938 to six or seven million in the spring
of 1941. Railroad and factory construction work in the Urals, in
Central Asia, and in Siberia was pressed forward.

All these enterprises consumed the small but growing surplus
which the Magnitogorsk workers had begun to get back in the
form of bicycles, wrist watches, radio sets, and good sausage
and other manufactured food products from 1935 till 1938.

In 1939 the stores in Magnitogorsk had no cigarettes, vodka
was only occasionally available, shoes and suits had completely
disappeared. By 1940 bread cards were reintroduced in spite
of a law specifically forbidding them. Salt was not always
available. Teachers and other office workers did not receive
enough bread to live comfortably. They supplemented their
rations with bootleg bread bought at speculative prices.

While consumption was drastically reduced, extraordinary
measures were taken to increase the productive efforts of the
population. Speeches and propaganda were supplemented by
severe labor legislation. A series of decrees made it a crime to
come to work more than twenty minutes late. Offenders received up to six months at forced labor. It became illegal for a
worker or other employee to leave his job without the written
permission of his director, while on the other hand the commissariats were empowered to send any worker to any part of the

Soviet Union for as long as the interests of production demanded, whether or not he wanted to go. At the same time a decree made factory directors, departmental chiefs, and chief engineers responsible before a criminal court for non-fulfillment of plan, failure of produce to come up to specifications, or juggling of the books in an attempt to pass off to other factories or consumers articles of poor quality. The courts were busy with public trials in which responsible administrators, indicted under the above decrees, were given a fair chance to defend themselves, and received up to eight-year prison sentences when convicted. There was no talk or at least very little talk of Fascist spies, insidious murderers of great literary figures, and the like, as there had been in the purge. The defendants were accused of not producing as much as the country needed to defend itself.

In Magnitogorsk, however, these nation-wide phenomena were supplemented by some specifically Ural developments New factory buildings, not provided for by any of the plant projects, made their appearance. No one knew what they were for. Simultaneously every effort was made to increase the production of the power stations, in spite of the fact that, in Magnitogorsk at least, power supply was already more than adequate for the mills in operation.

Even in Magnitogorsk, thousands of miles from any frontier, preparations were made for blackouts. The red gas holders were painted black. Racks of gas masks appeared in all the shops and mills. The study of the machine gun became a required course in all high schools and higher educational institutions.

As war spread over Western Europe the workers of Magnitogorsk and hundreds of other Soviet cities produced more while consuming less. It was necessary to prepare to fight and defeat the enemy. Who, specifically, the enemy was to be, no one knew. But production was increased notwithstanding.

II

By 1942 the Ural industrial district became the stronghold of Soviet resistance. Its mines, mills, and shops, its fields and forests, are supplying the Red Army with the immense quantities of military materials of all kinds, spare parts, replacements, and other manufactured products necessary to keep Stalin's mechanized divisions in the field.

The Ural industrial region covers an area of some five hundred miles square almost in the center of the largest country in the world. Within this area Nature placed rich deposits of iron, coal, copper, aluminum, lead, asbestos, manganese, potash, gold, silver, platinum, zinc, and petroleum, as well as rich forests and hundreds of thousands of acres of arable land. Until 1930 these fabulous riches were practically undeveloped. During the decade from 1930 to 1940 some two hundred industrial aggregates of all kinds were constructed and put into operation in the Urals. This herculean task was accomplished thanks to the political sagacity of Joseph Stalin and his relentless perseverance in forcing through the realization of his construction program despite fantastic costs and fierce difficulties.

Several times during the late twenties animated discussions arose in Moscow's highest political circles: Should the country concentrate on light or heavy industry? Should new factories be situated in the old industrial districts of the Ukraine and around Leningrad or in the Urals and Siberia? Stalin's opinion on these questions was clear and well grounded.

'Russia must overtake and surpass the most advanced capitalist countries in industry and military achievement within ten

years or these capitalist countries will annihilate us,' said
Stalin in February, 1931. He further asserted that new industries must be concentrated in the Urals and Siberia thousands of
miles away from the nearest frontiers, out of reach of any enemy
bombers. Whole new industries must be created. Russia had
hitherto been dependent on other countries for almost its entire
supply of rubber, chemicals, machine tools, tractors, and many
other things. These commodities could and must be produced
in the Soviet Union in order to ensure the technical and military
independence of the country.

Bukharin and many other old Bolsheviks disagreed with
Stalin. They held that light industries should be built first; the
Soviet people should be furnished with consumers' goods before
they embarked on a total industrialization program. Step by
step, one after another these dissenting voices were silenced.
Stalin won. Russia embarked on the most gigantic industrialization plan the world had ever seen.

In 1932 fifty-six per cent of the Soviet Union's national income was invested in capital outlay. This was an extraordinary
achievement. In the United States in 1860–70, when we were
building our railroads and blast furnaces, the maximum recapi-
talization for any one year was in the neighborhood of twelve
per cent of the national income. Moreover, American industrialization was largely financed by European capital, while the
man power for the industrial construction work poured in from
China, Ireland, Poland, and other European countries. Soviet
industrialization was achieved almost without the aid of foreign
capital. While a few thousand foreign technicians assisted in
the work, the brunt of the immense task fell on the shoulders of
the Soviet peoples. Russia was industrialized with the sweat
and blood of the one hundred and sixty-odd million inhabitants
of the vast country.

In Magnitogorsk this process went on in microcosm. Steel

and equipment were brought in to the city, but often food, clothing, and other necessary supplies were forgotten or delayed. During the first year of my stay in the city butter was unheard of. Bread was issued in limited quantities according to a strict ration system. Meat was seldom obtainable. Thousands of gaunt workers shoveled and hammered with only black bread and occasionally some cabbage or potatoes to eat; died of typhus in winter, of malaria in summer. The construction work went on. In 1932 Magnitogorsk produced its first pig iron. Gradually conditions improved. Russian workers learned their jobs, became more efficient.

Today, after little more than a decade, Magnitogorsk stands one of the largest metallurgical plants in the world. It produces five thousand tons of pig iron, six to seven thousand tons of steel, more than ten thousand tons of iron ore every day, as well as millions of tons of chemical by-products, structural shapes, steel wire, rods, rails, plates, and strips annually. Furthermore, at the present moment, at least one armament factory previously situated near Leningrad has arrived in Magnitogorsk lock, stock, and barrel, complete with personnel, and is already going into production using Magnitogorsk steel.

Many plants in Stalin's Ural Stronghold I did not visit, but heard about from others. In the extreme northern end of the Ural industrial district is Usolye, an old salt mine, whose production is now being used for the manufacture of various chemical products. Near this lies the famous Berezniki chemical center where fertilizers and explosives are manufactured.

Just north of Berezniki are the rich potash deposits of Solikamsk. Here an estimated deposit of eighteen billion tons of rich cartalite and silvinite is being worked; production in 1940 was more than two million tons. A plant situated near the city produced metallic magnesium so necessary for the manufacture of incendiary bombs and shells.

A double-tracked railroad line connects these northern chemical centers with Kizel, a coal mining center which produced 3,600,000 tons in 1936. This coal is of inferior quality and can only be used in small proportions in the manufacture of coke. It is extremely useful, however, in the production of electric power. A local electric station of approximately one hundred thousand kilowatts supplies power for the Kizel–Sverdlovsk electric railroad.

South of Kizel an important ferrous alloy plant is situated at Chusovaya. Here iron is smelted with charcoal, thus guaranteeing high-grade steel for bearings and other working parts. A little more than a hundred miles west of Chusovaya the immense Perm aviation motor plant is situated. This vital factory was constructed in the early thirties and is thought to be the largest aviation motor plant in the Soviet Union. For years the district around Perm has been strictly guarded. No foreigners are allowed to look around it, while the Soviet workers in the plant are discouraged from traveling to centers where indiscreet remarks might give foreign observers indications as to the exact size and character of the Perm aviation motor plant. The Soviet Union guards well its military secrets.

A branch railroad running east from Chusovaya leads to the town of Krasnouralsk where a deposit of copper pyrite is being worked. A new copper smelter is in operation producing large quantities of high-quality pure copper — some of which, ironically, was exported to Germany during the two years of good relations and economic collaboration. Krasnouralsk also boasts a large sulphuric-acid plant.

About a hundred miles to the south is the immense railroad car plant at Nizhni Tagil. This plant has two large blast furnaces and an adequate open-hearth department for the production of iron steel necessary in the manufacture of some fifty thousand freight cars annually. Nearly forty thousand workers are employed in this enterprise.

The Urals are rich in non-ferrous metals. Chelyabinsk is a zinc-producing as well as a tractor and tank manufacturing center. Some nickel is produced at Kalilovo and also at Ufalei. Bauxite is mined and aluminum produced at a large modern plant at Kaminsk, while copper is turned out in quantities at Kyshtym. A few miles from Magnitogorsk an immense deposit of manganese was found and in 1934 mining was begun on a large scale. Today this manganese is used in blast furnaces all over the Soviet Union and exported as well. Copper and sulphur are produced from pyrites in Blyava.

One of the largest asbestos deposits in the world is located at Alpayevsk, where it is mined and shipped to the near-by town of Asbest to be processed.

The Ural industrial district is not entirely dependent on the Caucasian wells for oil. The largest single known petroleum deposit in the world is situated in and around Ishembayevo. A pipe line connects these oil fields with Ufa, where large cracking and refining units have been erected and put into operation. Here, in 1939, nearly three million tons of oil were produced. One difficulty with the Ufa petroleum is its sulphur content which runs up to three per cent and seriously complicates cracking and refining. In 1940 a high-octane gasoline plant was completed in Ufa for the manufacture of motor fuel for the Red air fleet. Its planned production was half a million tons annually and American engineers with whom I spoke, who had worked on the erection of the plant, told me that in their opinion it would produce nearly the planned amount of high-octane gasoline during the first year of production. Another high-octane gasoline plant was erected at Saratov on the Volga and is reported to have gone into operation early in 1941, though its capacity is not known.

Besides its oil industry, Ufa boasts one of the largest internal-combustion engine plants in the Soviet Union. Several times when passing through the town on the train, I saw the plant stretching mile after mile along the railroad. Its equipment is new and it is thought to produce tank and airplane motors.

The Ural industrial district is equipped with an immense electric power-producing network. The power plant in Magnitogorsk turns out more than one hundred thousand kilowatts annually, as does that in Sverdlovsk, while the plant in Nizhni Tagil is about half as powerful. Other plants are situated at Chelyabinsk, Berezniki, Perm, Zlatoust. Ural power production in 1934 was two billion killowatt hours, and is estimated to have been doubled by 1940. These power plants are connected together in one network so that if, for some reason, one unit is forced to shut down, the industrial plants in its neighborhood will be supplied by other Ural power stations.

The Urals are equipped with a good railroad network. The recent completion of the Ufa–Magnitogorsk and the Akmolinsk lines and of the short but important Chelyabinsk–Kaminsk railroad have relieved traffic from the older railroads and made it possible to keep freight moving at a rate of speed well above the average for the Soviet Union. One of the most difficult problems which the Bolsheviks had to overcome in the operation of the immense Ural industrial region was coal supply. Originally, most of the coking coal was brought from the Kuzbas coal region in Central Siberia, a distance of nearly two thousand miles. The Kuzbas district has estimated reserves of four hundred and fifty billion tons of good quality coal — five times the reserves in the Donbass in the Ukraine. Kuzbas production in 1938 was sixteen million tons and in 1940 was authoritatively asserted to have passed twenty-five million tons. The difficulty was in transportation. For years the government was forced to pay half the coal transportation bill for the Magnitogorsk coke plant in order to make it possible for it to compete with Siberian and Ukrainian plants whose source of coal supply lay in their front yard. The recent development of the Karaganda coal fields partly solved the problem. When I left Magnitogorsk in 1938, eighty-five per cent of the coal used came from Karaganda, a distance of only about six hundred miles southeast; about eight per cent from Kuzbas, and the rest from the local Ural mines. The Karaganda coal mines are now producing more than six million tons of coal a year and are thus able to supply most of the coking coal required in the Ural industrial district.

The industrial district created in the Urals during the thirties was formidable enough. However, during the last few months it has grown enormously. No figures are available regarding the quantities of factories and plants evacuated from Western Russia to the Urals and Siberia. It is known, however, that even before the outbreak of war, large electrical equipment plants were removed from White Belorussia on the German frontier and also from the Leningrad district to the Urals and Western Siberia. One such plant is reported to have been removed to Sverdlovsk during 1940 and to have been producing normally in March, 1941. Any plant except the largest smelting, steelmaking, and chemical works can be moved by railroad fairly quickly and with little damage.

As I have indicated, the Ural industrial district produces all the basic raw materials for the manufacture of tanks, trucks, artillery, airplanes, and sundry military equipment. Two things were lacking: machinery and labor power. These have now been sent to the Urals in large quantities. I have seen several of the large aviation plants near Moscow. The new Tsagi plant near Otdykh on the Kazan railroad is an immense affair running mile after mile along the railroad. It was constructed near Moscow rather than elsewhere principally because of the fact that many of the highly qualified engineers, technicians, and skilled workers lived in and near the capital and were loath to leave. Living conditions in Moscow have been consistently better than in outlying places like the Urals or Siberia and the workers preferred to stay where they were. Moscow aviation plants operated to a large extent on materials from the Donbass and the Urals. Now they are being removed with their workers and technicians closer to their source of raw materials. Since the summer of 1940 labor legislation has made it possible for the government to send workers wherever it seems necessary and keep them there indefinitely. Furthermore, now that Moscow and its environs are coming into the sphere of military operations, there is no difficulty in getting people to move. Russia's east-and-west railroads are jammed with trains bringing reserves and supplies to the front. The same freight cars are carrying machines and workers eastward. Thus, while no figures will be available for some time, it is my opinion that large portions of the industrial machinery formerly located in areas now occupied by the Germans, instead of being captured by them are already in operation a thousand or more miles east of the present front, in Stalin's Ural Stronghold.

Even if Moscow is lost, the Red armies will be able to go on fighting for months, even years, basing themselves on the stronghold of the Urals supplemented by factories and skilled workers evacuated from the western parts of the Soviet Union. All this sums up one basic reason why the Soviet Union has not suffered decisively as a result of Hitler's attack.

The second basic reason is the Soviet people.

III

In 1940 I saw Sy-
emichkin for a few minutes in Moscow. He was on his way to
the Ukraine for a vacation, his first in three years. Things
looked good in the mills in Magnitogorsk, he told me, and rather
grim in people's homes. People worked eight hours instead of
seven, and everyone put in overtime as well. Stores were empty.

I mentioned the Soviet-German pact. Syemichkin shrugged
his shoulders. 'Stalin did it,' he said. 'Yemu Vidnyei — He
knows what he is doing.' He did not say this for effect. He felt
that way. He was a Soviet engineer, and had become a very
good technician and administrator. He knew his business. He
made mistakes sometimes, but by and large he knew how to run
a coke by-products plant. Stalin had worked his way to the top
of the complicated Soviet State apparatus. He had done well
in steering the Soviet Ship of State through the stormy seas of
recent European politics. He might make mistakes sometimes,
but by and large he knew his business.

This typified the attitude of the Soviet people.

I went to a workers' meeting in a large Moscow factory in
1940. I saw workers get up and criticize the plant director,
make suggestions as to how to increase production, improve
quality, and lower costs. They were exercising their rights of
freedom of speech as Soviet citizens. Then the question of the
new Soviet-German trade pact came up. The workers unani-
mously passed a previously prepared resolution approving the
Soviet foreign policy. There was no discussion. The Soviet
workers had learned what was their business and what was not.

Many Soviet workers had become competent technicians.

They made planes which flew well, and their pilots operated them with great skill. I know, I flew in them on several occasions. The Soviet railroad system carried more freight and more passengers per mile of track and per unit of rolling stock than any other railroad system in the world including the American.

The purge liquidated many workers and technicians, but Russia was a very large country. Most of the population stayed in their shops and factories, worked and produced. They were a little worried, perhaps, but they continued to turn out tanks, to read *Pravda*, and to practice air-raid alarms on their free days.

Life was hard for the Russian people in 1940 and 1941, and, of course, much harder after the German attack, but the Russian people were used to hard lives. They had never been softened by easy living. The papers told them every day that they were the luckiest people in the world, and they believed it. They had work and bread.

Millions of Syemichkins and Kolyas had been preparing for war for a decade, industrially, personally, and ideologically.

IV

Here, then, lies the answer to the question so many people in America have been asking themselves since June 22, 1941: 'How are the Russians able to do so well? What makes Russia click?'

Russia has always had masses of men and incalculable natural resources. During the last ten years the Russian people shed blood, sweat, and tears to create something else, a modern industrial base outside the reach of an invader — Stalin's Ural Stronghold — and a modern mechanized army. In the process millions of Russians and Ukrainians, Tartars and Jews, became competent technicians and efficient soldiers.

At the same time the population was taught by a painful and expensive process to work efficiently, to obey orders, to mind their own business, and to take it on the chin when necessary with a minimum of complaint.

These are the things that it takes to fight a modern war.

THE END

Appendix

1

A FURTHER immigration of Kirghizi two centuries later was instrumental in bringing many hands to the construction work in Magnitogorsk. This was caused by the Kirghi uprising in 1916 and the subsequent migrations.

In 1916 the Czarist armies were losing heavily. They needed men and horses. The Russian governors and officials in Kirghizia were ordered to recruit both from the wild Kirghiz herders. They followed orders, but met with such resistance from the Kirghizi that they had to call in armed forces.

At the appearance of the Russian soldiers the Kirghizi united and attacked the Russians and their institutions all over the country. Most of the Russians gathered in the Kirghizi capital, Pishpeck (now called Frunze after the Red general). Here they barricaded themselves and awaited the arrival of a considerable military force from Russia. The soldiers routed the Kirghiz herdsmen who were unorganized and without leadership and drove them off into the mountains. The nomads fought bravely, but were beaten in every open encounter. They retreated farther and farther into the mountains. As they went they killed their herds for food. After several months, they ceased organized resistance and emigrated in large numbers. Of some 800,000 Kirghizi, roughly 200,000 emigrated to western China, where they lived for several years. Some came back to their own country in 1923 and 1924 when Soviet power was consolidated in all the Central Asiatic territory, while many of them (about 100,000) remain in China to this day. Many of the Kirghizi, however, went north instead of east and settled or wandered in Kazakhstan, Bashkiria, and farther north.

2

In an extraordinary speech made in Moscow on February 4, 1931, to the conference of factory managers, Stalin said in part:

' ... To slacken the tempo [of Soviet industrialization] means to fall behind. And the backward are always beaten. No, we do not want this. Incidentally the history of old Russia is the history of defeat due to backwardness. She was beaten by the Mongol khans. She was beaten by the Turkish beys. She was beaten by the Swedish barons. She was beaten by the Japanese barons ... because she was backward.... We are fifty to one hundred years behind advanced countries. We must cover this distance in ten years. Either we do this or they will crush us. ... '

3

The 1928 project envisaged the following plant details:

A coke plant consisting of three batteries, sixty-three ovens per battery — production of 656,000 tons a year; a blast-furnace department consisting of four furnaces, volume of 788.5 cubic meters (23,250 cubic feet) each, and efficiency coefficient of 1.31, making yearly production of 656,000 tons; two steel manufacturing departments; open-hearth department consisting of four hearths, 100 tons capacity each, with a total yearly production of 325,000 tons of steel; and a bessemer department of two twenty-ton converters, with a capacity of approximately 327,000 tons a year.

According to this project the plant was to have been completed in five years; that is, by the first of January, 1934. However, some people among the construction and projecting engineers held that it would take seven years to do the work.

The corrected projected budget was as follows: In millions of roubles per year to be spent on construction: First year, 5; second year, 26; third year, 32; fourth year, 35; fifth year, 32; sixth year, 25; seventh year, 22.

Millions of roubles actually spent: 1929, 8.2; 1930, 46; 1931, 170.3; 1932, 201; 1933, 181.

No figures were ever published as to actual expenditures on construction during later years. However, it is generally known that the allocations decreased drastically after 1935. From 1936 until 1939 almost nothing was done at all on plant construction. In 1939 and 1940 several million roubles were spent on the construction of the second open-hearth department where five hearths were in operation early in 1941.

4

The newest furnaces in the United States are 1000 cubic meter volume; therefore it was decided that the Magnitogorsk furnaces should have a volume of in the neighborhood of 1100 cubic meters instead of 788 cubic meters. It was likewise decided that the other units of the plant should also exceed in size the best achievements of Germany and the United States as a prerequisite to 'equaling and surpassing' the achievements of the capitalist world in the field of technique.

5

The total amount of metallurgical iron ore was 227,900,000 tons. The ore is concentrated in two small mountains in a total area of not more than two square miles. Qualitatively the ore varies greatly and can be divided into the following groups:

1. Blast-furnace ore — iron content 56 per cent or more, and sulphur content less than 0.2 per cent.

2. Mixed ore — with iron content of 30 to 56 per cent, sulphur to 0.18 per cent. This ore requires working over before it can be used in blast furnaces.

3. High sulphur content ore likewise requiring working over.

4. Poor ore — iron content 30 per cent and lower.

The ore in groups 1 and 2 was found to lie very shallow and to be completely accessible to open cut mining. The quantity of group 1 ore was found to be in the neighborhood of 80,000,000 tons.

6

An iron mine producing 7.5 million tons of blast furnace ore per year; two crushing plants, capacity of 10,000 tons a day; a washing and sorting unit; two agglomeration plants.

Eight batteries of 69 coke ovens each; average coking period 13 hours, capacity of ovens, 14 tons; total daily production, 8000 tons.

Eight blast furnaces, volume 1186 cubic meters (36,660 cubic feet) each; daily production 1000 tons each.

Three open-hearth departments consisting of 12 hearths each, capacity 150 tons per hearth; three mixers, 1300-ton capacity each.

A rolling-mill department comprising three blooming mills, three 630-millimeter and one 450-millimeter mill, two cross-country 500-millimeter mills, two 350- millimeter strip mills, four small merchant mills, two heavy-wire mills, one rail mill: Total, 18 mills.

A power house, capacity, 248,000 kilowatts.

Two fire-brick plants producing 188,000 tons of assorted fire-bricks of all kinds per annum.

A well-equipped machine shop, forge shop, boiler-making and repairing shop, iron, steel, and copper foundries, roller foundry and turning shop, and ingot-mold shop to do repair work and take care of all current replacements of the giant mill.

Magnitogorsk was to comprise all these according to the 1934 project.

7

Construction of the budget projected in 1934 provided for the following expenses (in millions of roubles):

Preparatory work	113.1
Blast furnaces	128.4
Open hearths	155.1
Rolling mills	276.2
Auxiliary shops	26.9
Fire-brick factories	8.1
Ore mine	108.2
Power plant lines and substations	185.1
Transport (internal)	167.6
Water supply and drainage	67.1
Coke and by-products plants	152.0
General plant buildings	35.3
Miscellaneous plant expenses	5.1
Training of skilled workers	94.9
The city	1,000.0
Total	2,523.1

Unfortunately, expenses in gold for foreign equipment were reckoned in these figures according to the nominal rouble value in gold, which gives no real idea of what it cost the Soviet Union to buy and install foreign equipment for Magnitogorsk. Of the above-cited sum of nearly 2.5 billion roubles, some 700 million represent expenses in gold for imported equipment.

8

TABLE OF UNITS OF INDUSTRIAL EQUIPMENT PROVIDED FOR BY

	Project 1928	Project 1934	In operation 1938	In operation 1941
No. of blast furnaces......	4	8	4	4
No. of coke batteries......	3	8	4	4
No. of open hearths.......	4	34	12	16
No. of rolling mills........	5	18	10	12

TABLE OF PRODUCTION IN THOUSANDS OF TONS PER YEAR

	Capacity Projected in 1928	in 1934	1932	Actual Production 1933	1936	1937	1938
Ore...................	1125	7500	1343	2080	5414	6575	....
Pig iron..............	656	2750	361	572	1557	1530	1535
Steel ingots...........	337	3050	....	87.4	1163	1403	1490
Rolled steel...........	574	2485	....	57.9	959	....	1200
Coke................	656	2750	380	675	1977	1920	1515

9

The coefficient of utilization of excavators and cement mixers in comparison with American norms:

Mechanism	U.S.A.	U.S.S.R. average	1930	1931	Magnitogorsk 1932	1933 (by quarters) 1st	2nd	3rd
Excavators........	100	40	30	38	11	15	23	40
Cement mixers....	100	35	..	28	20	13	29	34

The fall in efficiency in 1932, due to administrative difficulties and to the commencement of the exodus of value paid foreign specialists, is clearly visible.

10

The following table shows the increase of population in Magnitogorsk:

Village of Magnitnaya Original Population			Magnitogorsk Wage Workers		
	1929	1930	1931	1932	1933
250	1157	8239	22,565	32,372	25,022

To give an idea of where these workers came from, the following table for the years 1932–33 shows the arrivals broken up into groups according to derivation:

Origin	1932		1933	
	Absolute	Per Cent	Absolute	Per Cent
Total from all origins............	62,216	100	52,954	100
Came of their own free will.......	43,913	70.6	39,938	75.2
Recruited......................	18,303	29.4	13,016	24.8

Disfranchized kulaks and ITK prisoners are not counted in the above figures.

11

The absolute figures of losses of labor time according to the reason for the loss are given in the following table:

Years	Total	Rest	Stalling	Poor Organization	Accidental	Materials	Absenteeism
1932.............	41.2	16.3	1.9	5.2	1.1	8.0	8.7
1933 (10 months).	42.5	12.2	6.5	6.3	3.1	8.5	6.0
1933 (November)..	38.1	11.7	8.0	4.4	3.0	6.0	5.0

This table is taken from a report of a construction director to his chief, printed in a private edition of a book entitled *Magnitostroi 1934*, page 84.

12

The following table shows the materials actually received in Magnitogorsk in percentage of plan:

Name of material	1931	1932	1933
Cement................	83.6	47.2	48.6
Lumber (unmilled)......	78.8	65.5	48.5
Lumber (milled)........	110.0	45.0	39.0
Ties (railroad)..........	69.0	24.0	0.0
Rails..................	74.0	34.0	39.0

13

The following table shows the material balance in the storehouses of Magnitogorsk on the first of January for the years 1931–1934:

January 1, 1931.......	27,750,000 roubles worth	
January 1, 1932......	41,180,000	" "
January 1, 1933......	60,500,000	" "
January 1, 1934.......	36,800,000	" "

14

The following table shows the percentage of planned equipment received and erected:

Department	According to plan to have been erected by January 1, 1934 (In thousands of roubles)	Erected by January 1, 1934	Fulfillment of plan in per cent
Blast furnace...........	24,306	10,508	43
Open hearth...........	39,792	5,961	15
Rolling mill............	125,578	12,673	10
Iron mine.............	45,690	6,425	14
Power supply..........	115,562	33,563	29
Auxiliary..............	15,141	2,134	14

15

The amounts by which the construction organizations overexpended their budgets is indicated by the following table, given in percentages:

1929–30	1931	1932	1933	Average
11	25	41.5	13.7	25.5

Thus, during five years the builders spent 25 per cent more money than the budget allowed them, while building, as we have seen above, approximately half of what the plan provided for.

16

ORE PRODUCTION FROM THE MAGNITOGORSK IRON MINE
(in millions of metric tons)

	1931	1932	1933	1936	1937	1938	1940
Rough ore................	0.5	2.17	3.8	....	....	....	....
Blast-furnace ore..........	0.2	1.34	2.0	5.4	6.5	6.3 *	6.9 *

* Estimated.

17

Year	1932	1933	1934	1935	1936	1937	1938
Thousands of tons.......	326	588	1150	1252	1500	1530	1535
Coefficient *.............	1.77	1.74	1.22	1.13	1.03	1.00	....
Tons per worker.........	468	628	1030	1163	....	2004	....

* The coefficient of use of blast-furnace volume is calculated by dividing the number of cubic meters of furnace volume by the number of tons per day.

These figures are taken from an article by Klishevich, then chief engineer of the combinat, in the *Magnitogorsk Worker* for February 2, 1936, entitled 'Make All Magnitogorsk Stakhanovite,' and from an article by Surnin, an engineer, in the *Magnitogorsk Worker* for November 3, 1937.

18

The monthly project capacity of the mill as calculated by the German manufacturers was 26,660 tons.

MONTHLY PRODUCTION FOR 1935
(in tons of produce, not counting scrap)

Jan.	Feb.	March	April	May	June	July	Aug.	Sept.	Oct.
15569	15332	18711	17354	20129	18667	30338	28565	27006	39005

19

The question arose occasionally as to whether it was worth while to pay the workers such big premiums for production above plan, which was sold at the same price as any other. The following table shows a breakdown of the cost of production of steel rails for Mill 500 for October. The units are roubles per ton of finished metal:

Cost of basic raw material (steel billets)......................	109.26
Cost of scrap and of stub ends.............................	2.40
Wages..	7.00
Bricks, gas, light, water, power, spare parts, transport, etc. (all fixed costs)...	5.89
Amortization...	3.43
Administrative costs..	3.00
Total cost of one ton of goods production	130.98

The amortization on the mill, which amounted to about 120,000 roubles a month was calculated on a ten-year basis for most of the equipment, and twenty years for the building.

Amortization, administrative costs, light, spare parts, etc., are all fixed charges and amount to nearly twice the salary item, so that the administration could afford to pay double and triple wages for increased production because of the savings in these fixed charges.

20

The following table of average monthly wages, average productivity in tons, plan fulfillment, and technicians' salaries gives an idea of how the mastering of the mill in the summer and fall of 1935 made itself felt:

Month	April	May	June	July	Aug.	Sept.	Oct.
Plan fulfillment in percentage.	78	85	75	120	100	91	132
Production in tons...........	17534	20128	18667	30038	28565	27006	39005
Average wages of workers.....	231	272	241	289	305	308	407
Average wages of technicians..	534	922	923	1195	1438	1056	1527
Productivity per worker (in tons).....................	28	33	31	47	46	42	59

The plan fulfillment did not rise steadily because the plan was being steadily pushed up.

21

Table of production of the various units of the Magnitogorsk plant in thousands of tons per year by years:

	1932	1933	1934	1935	1936	1937	1938
Iron ore.......	1340	2000			5400	6575	
Pig iron.......	320	588	1150	1252	1500	1530	1535
Steel ingots....		87	436	815	1163	1403	1490
Rolled steel....		58			959		1200
Coke..........	330	843	1590	1733	1977	1920	1515

As no complete table of yearly production was published, so far as the author knows, the above table was compiled from various sources, as follows: All the 1936 figures were taken from the large Soviet calendar for 1938, page 71. All the 1938 figures were taken from the *Magnitogorsk Worker* of January 3, 1939, from an article by Engineer Perlman. All figures up till 1934 were taken from *Magnitostroi*, page 103. The 1937 open-hearth figures were taken from the *Magnitogorsk Worker* of January 1, 1938. Other 1937 figures were taken from the *Magnitogorsk Worker* of January 1, 1938 from an article by Korobov. The coke and blast-furnace figures for all years were taken from the *Magnitogorsk Worker* of February 2, 1938. Other figures were taken by subtraction from the *Magnitogorsk Worker*, which, on every anniversary of the construction of Magnitogorsk, published figures of the total production of plant for all the years it had been in operation.

The figures of project capacity follow (thousands of tons per year):

	Project of 1928	Project of 1934
Ore................	1125	7500
Pig iron...........	656	2750
Steel ingots........	337	3050
Rolled steel........	574	2485
Coke..............	656	2750

These figures were taken from *Magnitostroi*, pages 4, 5, and 6.

22

Inasmuch, however, as the absolute rise in production was often due to the operation of new industrial units, I will cite the example of productivity and costs of production, which gives a more characteristic picture of the results of the Stakhanov movement.

CHART OF THE PRODUCTIVITY OF LABOR IN THE MAGNITOGORSK PLANT

Figures represent tons of produce per average worker per year. The two years taken are 1935 and 1937, which can be more or less pointed out to be the beginning and the end of the effects of the Stakhanov movement.

	1935	1937
Iron ore...........................	2017	3361
Coke..............................	1324	1684
Pig iron..........................	1163	2004
Steel.............................	574	894
Finished rolled steel................	294	511

It would, of course, be incorrect to say that all this increase was immediately due to the Stakhanov movement. Some was due to the mastering of new equipment, which should have taken place in any case. At the same time the Stakhanov movement had a great deal to do with it.

23

The following table gives an idea of the new norms in relation to the old norms, to the original production capacities, to the newly fixed production capacities, and to the records in each case. All figures indicate tons per shift.

Unit	Project Capacity According to Original Project	New Capacity Laid Down by Conference in Moscow in March 1936	Record Shift	Old Norm	New Norm
Blast furnaces, per furnace........	333	436	544	383	400
Open hearth........	90	191	167	93	117
Blooming mill.......	1000	1400	1500	800	1200
Mill 500............	320	1000	1000	366	600
Mill 300............	280	500	600	260	365
Mill 250............	120	250	215	70	140

The working norms were increased by a third to a half, but these new norms did not nearly equal the ultimate capacities of the different mills as worked out by the Iron and Steel Industry Conference in Moscow.

24

	1933	1934	1935	1936	1937	1938
Production in thousands of tons per year...........	87	436	815	1163	1403	1490
Average tons of steel per m^2 of hearth per melting....	3.37	3.73	4.19	—	5.49	—
Productivity of labor per worker (tons per worker per year)..............	334.8	478.0	604.8	720.0	894.0	—

Addendum

Dispatches from Moscow, 1938

This addendum consists of three dispatches sent from the U.S. Embassy in Moscow to the State Department, containing information given by John Scott to an embassy official in early 1938. Embassy officials regularly debriefed American citizens living and working in the USSR. The texts of these numerous interviews were later declassified and deposited in the National Archives. They comprise fourteen reels of microfilm. The three reproduced below are from decimal files 861.5048/107, 861.651/17, and 861.5017/804 respectively.

S.K.

PENAL LABOR

January 28, 1938

Types of Penal Labor

In discussing the forced labor colony at Magnitogorsk it should be borne in mind that the following four categories of prisoners or ex-prisoners may be clearly distinguished:

1. A colony of so-called "kulaks" which is composed of peasants who opposed in one way or another the collectivization of individual farms during the years from 1930 to 1934 and who are undergoing what is termed by the Soviet authorities as "dekulakization."

2. Ordinary criminals who compose the ITK, that is, the Corrective Labor Colony (Ispravitelno-Trudovaya Koloniya).

3. Specialists who are for the most part engineers trained prior to the

revolution and who have been condemned to forced labor for political reasons.

4. Foreign-born refugees, the majority of whom have fled to the Soviet Union for one reason or another in search of "Utopia."

I *The Formation of the Kulak Colony*

The peasants began to arrive at Magnitogorsk at the end of 1931. They came in large numbers during all of 1932. The majority of them were from Kazan and its surrounding districts. They were a motley crowd, about half of whom were Russians, the rest being Ukrainians, Tartars, Bashkirs, and Kirgizes.

These peasants were shipped like cattle to Magnitogorsk at the point of bayonets in closed box cars in which a small window had been cut. Twelve days were frequently passed in making the trip, during which the peasants were occasionally fed black bread and forced to perform their natural functions through a hole in the floor of the car.

Most of these so-called "kulaks," who were generally peasants with a certain amount of property, had been arrested by the GPU soon after the poorest peasants of the village with little or no property had voted for collectivization. The process often met with considerable resistance on the part of the better-off peasants which resulted in the property of the "dekulakized" peasants, including everything except the clothing on their backs, being confiscated. The entire family of these peasants were usually sent to Magnitogorsk.

I have talked with many of these peasants and I have come to the definite conclusion that although certain criteria were resorted to in theory by the village Soviets in liquidating individual peasants, such as the extent of resistance to collectivization and the number of hired laborers employed, in actual practice they were judged largely on the basis of the amount of property they had which would be of use to the new collective farm. Personal grudges and dislikes also caused many peasants to lose their property. The poorer and less scrupulous elements of the villages frequently denounced the peasants who were better off, a practice which was not discouraged by the local Party leaders charged with establishing the best possible collective farms.

The arrival of the kulaks in Magnitogorsk. When these peasants arrived in Magnitogorsk they were taken under guard to an outlying part of the city. There they were told to make their own houses and given tents to live in. Since there was no lumber or other materials with which to construct better shelters, they lived through the winter of 1932−33 in these tents. By the end of 1933 this tent colony was composed of about 35,000 persons. Ten percent or more of the colony died of exposure and malnutrition during this winter. Practically no children under ten lived through the winter of 1932−33. The temperature was often forty below zero.

The nature of the work performed by the kulaks. From the first day the entire group, except children under twelve or fourteen, were put to work. At that time excavations were being made and they worked at this. A few became carpenters, pipe-fitters, and so forth. The entire colony was guarded by armed forces at this time and the peasants went to and from work under convoy.

By the next winter barracks of a sort had gradually been constructed. These shelters, which afforded at least a roof over their heads, were terribly crowded, two or three families being forced to live in one small room. There was much sickness.

The famine of the winter of 1932−33. At the beginning of 1933 there was a bad food shortage in Magnitogorsk. Although the kulaks possessed bread cards, they were unable to obtain enough food for themselves and their families. All garbage dumps were watched constantly by women and children, who carried bags in which to place the decayed foods which they could find. There was actual starvation. By the spring there were embryonic strikes and passive resistance among groups of these peasants. News of this trouble finally reached certain higher authorities and ended in the arrest of two scapegoats, the chief of the labor colony and his assistant, both officers of the GPU, who received long sentences.

The number of kulak prisoners. The four or five thousand workers who died during the winter of 1932−33 were replaced by newcomers who were mostly runaway peasants from other colonies. The total population of the Magnitogorsk colony, about thirty or forty thousand, thus remained about constant. The colony played an important role in the establishment of the plant because it performed practically all the heavy construction work.

Attitude toward the Soviet power. Among this group of prisoners no Soviet propaganda was carried on. They were treated as class enemies and were made to feel that they would never be considered otherwise. Many of these peasants were terribly embittered because they had been deprived of everything and had been forced to work under a system which, in many cases, had killed off members of their families. The only case of sabotage that I have actually seen with my own eyes in the Soviet Union was motivated by the blind rage of one of these miserable men. I once saw an old peasant throw a crowbar into a large generator and then give himself up to the armed guards laughing gleefully.

Most of the group, however, worked doggedly. They learned their jobs and some managed to increase their wages and thus improve somewhat their living conditions. The average wage was about 80 rubles a month. A certain number succeeded in becoming skilled workmen or even foremen, earning from two to three hundred rubles a month. It should be kept in mind in this connection that the so-called "kulak class" was generally composed of the more intelligent, thrifty, and industrious elements of the villages who had worked hard, saved money, and acquired not only some property but skill in certain trades. Their diligence made itself felt even under the harsh conditions of Magnitogorsk. The rise of some of these men was heroic.

Liberation. In the beginning of 1935 a few, perhaps several hundred, of these peasants were reinstated as citizens, received their passports, and were given permission to leave. By this time many of them had laid out gardens and bought cows and small stock which they kept in the small yards around their miserable barracks. Life began to reach a level not far below that which many were accustomed to in the villages. Because of this, a certain number of the liberated peasants remained at Magnitogorsk.

At the present time this colony at Magnitogorsk numbers about 30,000 persons. They still live in wretched wooden barracks but, as I have already said, many of them live comparatively well since they have little gardens, cows, and chickens. There are no longer any armed guards. There are three schools for their children. All of them have been officially reinstated as citizens; all had the right to vote in the last elections on December 12, 1937, but only about a quarter have obtained passports. Consequently, the majority of them cannot leave Magnitogorsk.

The present mentality of the kulak group. The majority of these former peasants still work on construction jobs but a few have responsible positions. I consider that most of them are bitter over their fate but realize that any agitation or action would only lead to arrest and a worse life. They live on and work, hoping vaguely that some day their fate will be better.

The children. The children of the peasants are an interesting group. My wife worked for one year teaching in one of the schools which I have mentioned. This school has better pupils than any of the forty-odd schools in the rest of the city. The kulak children feel that they belong to a persecuted group and like such groups it includes a large number of children who study and work hard in an attempt to better themselves and prove that they are as good as, if not better than, the children of the non-kulak groups. They are not convinced by the political propaganda carried on in the school since they feel a bond with their parents who have lost everything.

Potential enemies. In the event of a war, invasion or internal breakdown, serious trouble would probably arise from the kulaks. If no such crisis should occur within the next ten years, I believe that the group will gradually be absorbed by the community since the old members will soon die off and the youth will lose to a great extent their feeling of inferiority and bitterness.

As an example of what is happening within this group I shall cite the case of my maid. Her father was a well-to-do peasant who did not choose to become a collective farmer. This family was "dekulakized" in 1932 and sent to Magnitogorsk. During the first winter, the mother and two young children died. The father worked as a laborer. At the present time the son is a mechanic who earns about three hundred rubles a month, and the sister, our maid, goes to school every other morning to learn reading and writing. She is bitterly hostile but, except for an occasional slip, holds her tongue.

The effect of the purging process on the peasant colony. The great purging process which had been going on during the last two years has hardly touched this colony. There were perhaps fifty arrests, which is nothing in comparison with what took place among other groups of the population at Magnitogorsk and elsewhere.

The reason for this is that these peasants were never trusted with administrative or political positions which were affected by the purge more than any other category of worker. The GPU had already investigated these people, knew their backgrounds and did not begin to make investigations of their lives as it did in the case of all other workers, particularly those holding responsible administrative and technical positions.

II *The Corrective Labor Colony*

The ITK (Ispravitelno-Trudovaya Koloniya), which means the Corrective Labor Colony, is administered by the People's Commissariat for

Internal Affairs. It receives non-political prisoners from all parts of the country and puts them to work on construction. There are five such colonies in Magnitogorsk, containing from about fifteen to eighteen thousand prisoners.

Types of prisoners. Ninety percent of this group is composed of "drunk and disorderly conduct" cases, but there are a number of professional thieves, prostitutes, embezzlers, and so forth. Their terms vary from six months to five years. There is one small group consisting of orthodox clergy. Most of these priests have been charged with burning grain or some such semi-criminal, semi-political offense. They still wear long hair and go to work in their old dome-shaped hats and ragged clothes. Many apparently never wash.

Propaganda. The majority of the ITK prisoners are under thirty years of age and are illiterate or semi-literate. The administration carries on propaganda work in a vigorous manner within this group. Dramatic clubs, orchestras, trade schools, brigade competition, and so forth, are resorted to in the endeavor to kindle in these people some social consciousness. Ten percent of their wages go toward the expenses incurred by the administration. They study trades and have to read and write. A few of them learn to value human labor. Armed guards for this group were unknown until 1936 when, because of increasing run-aways, they began to be used. At the present time these convicts work under armed convoy and are confined to their own barracks at night.

Kind of work performed. With respect to the type of work which these prisoners perform it should be pointed out that the practice is to force them to work at common labor such as digging ditches during the first three months. After this period they may do any work for which they are qualified. A few obtain responsible positions. For instance, the chief electrician of the blast furnace construction in 1933 and 1934 was an ITK man. He was serving five years for embezzlement. His salary was seven hundred rubles a month and he had a horse and wagon to drive around in.

When they start work these men are supplied canvas overalls, canvas shoes or overshoes and gloves, and are told to pitch in and work hard. They are well fed in the Russian style with plenty of black bread, cabbage, potatoes and a little meat. During their first three months many of them learn a real lesson in labor.

Attitude toward the Soviet authorities. In general the ITK man and woman are not against the Soviet power to the extent that the kulaks are. They are criminal elements who are receiving at least as good a break as they would get under some other form of government. Most of them either consciously or unconsciously realize this and would hesitate to take any action directed against the Soviet authorities. In a crisis, however, they would in all probability create disorder by running away. Magnitogorsk is not a pleasant place in which to live and most of them undoubtedly would prefer to go to their former homes.

III *Specialists under Sentence*

In 1932 between 20 and 30 specialists were sent to Magnitogorsk by the GPU. All of them had been charged with wrecking and most had been involved in the so-called "Industrial Party Trial of 1930."

The majority of this group were real specialists, who had been trained in the best schools of Tsarist Russia or abroad and many of them had occupied high industrial posts before and during the war.

On reaching Magnitogorsk they were assigned the best apartments available, given automobiles and special contracts under the terms of which some earned as much as 3,000 rubles a month. They were also given highly responsible positions and instructed to work hard in order to prove that they really intended to become good Soviet citizens. The reactions of this group to their position were somewhat different. I shall give you the following examples:

The case of Georgy Ivanovich Bulgakov. Bulgakov was educated in Germany before the war. He became an organic and industrial chemist. He met the revolution with enthusiasm and soon occupied one of the highest positions in the Soviet chemical industry. Until 1930 he was a member of the Collegium of the Chemical Industry of the Soviet Union. In that year he was arrested as a member of the Industrial Party and sentenced to ten years imprisonment. During the entire investigation, which lasted about a year, Bulgakov never admitted any guilt.

In 1932 he came to Magnitogorsk under sentence. Under his contract he received 2,500 rubles a month and a car in return for his services as chief engineer of the chemical plant which was then under construction.

The attitude of Bulgakov toward the authorities was known to be openly hostile. He was not as conscientious about his work as he might have been. Every free day Bulgakov went hunting and he took no part in the social and cultural activities of the city. He was looked upon with a certain amount of suspicion.

In 1936 there was a bad explosion in the chemical plant. Bulgakov was indicted for criminal negligence because there had been no emergency instructions in the machine house where the explosion took place. He pleaded not guilty but was convicted. He received six months, although he was serving a ten-year sentence at the time.

After this conviction he became even more bitter and hostile toward the Government. He expressed hatred to me several times of the Government and particularly the GPU.

In 1937 there was a general purge of the whole technical personnel of the chemical as well as other parts of the metallurgical plant which swept up Bulgakov. His wife was given a bed in one of the barracks and 50,000 rubles belonging to her were confiscated along with all of his and her clothing. Six months later she learned that he had received another ten-year sentence after pleading not guilty. Several weeks following his conviction she was arrested on the charge of criminal complicity for not having reported the facts of his criminal activities (Article 58−12 of the Criminal Code) and sent to join her husband in Kamchatka.

Bulgakov was a highly competent chemist and the author of several works on the subject of benzol fractioning and tar distillation. I know that he was firmly convinced that he had never committed any crime against the Soviet Government and he never admitted anything. Many foreign observers have the idea that all such specialists plead guilty to charges of wrecking, sabotage, and so forth. This is incorrect. One simply seldom hears about those who do not plead guilty.

The case of Ilya Gavrilovich Tikhomirov. Tikhomirov was the chief engineer of a large Belgian firm in the south of Russia before the war. He had also received a ten-year sentence at the "Industrial Trial" and was sent to Magnitogorsk in 1931. He was made chief electrician of the entire plant, which included such important units as a power station with a 98,000 kw. capacity and a large blowing station. His salary is 3,000 rubles a month. He has held this position ever since. Tikhomirov is an excellent administrator and thoroughly competent. He worked hard. In 1936 when a number of other engineers were arrested he was given a Soviet passport and completely reinstated as a citizen. He could probably leave Magnitogorsk but he prefers to stay there. He pleaded guilty at his trial and in all likelihood has given information to the GPU at Magnitogorsk. In this way he bought his freedom.

It would be incorrect, however, to assume on the basis of the foregoing that Tikhomirov is essentially pro-Soviet. He is as hostile as ever and is very bitter over the irony of fate that he has gained freedom by admitting falsely to guilt. He has sworn to me that he never committed any crime but that he thought it best to say at the trial that he had done so.

Other cases of specialists. Of the original twenty or thirty specialists who were sent to Magnitogorsk about ten have received new sentences and have been exiled somewhere in the Far East. Five or six have received orders for distinguished work and are holding high positions. The rest are like Tikhomirov, working along and being trusted more or less. Many of them are still definitely hostile and are undoubtedly potentially active enemies of the present Government. At present they are terrorized but in the event of some crisis they might become dangerous to the dictatorship. The Soviet authorities realize this and I am convinced that as soon as these specialists can be replaced they will be taken out of responsible work.

Most of these men are deeply conscious of the fact that they are Russians and believe that the present regime, whatever they may hold against it, is building a strong Russia which should be supported and protected. It is possible that because of this feeling they might support the present Soviet Government if it should be attacked from the outside. They would, for instance, be much more likely to give their whole-hearted support to Stalin than to Trotski, since they are totally out of sympathy with the theory of the World Revolution and the building of a classless society.

IV *The Refugees*

During 1932 and 1933 several groups of foreigners were sent to Magnitogorsk. These people had run across the Soviet border to what they thought would be the "Fatherland of the Working Class." They expected to find jobs and the good things of life. There were approximately 2,000 Poles, mostly Jews; 200 Finns, mostly ex-smugglers; 50 Bulgarians; 30 Germans; and a few Rumanians and Turks.

These refugees were arrested as soon as they crossed the border. They were shipped to Magnitogorsk and placed under the surveillance of the GPU.

The Finns. Although they were given somewhat better food supplies than the average run of Russian workers, conditions were so much worse, particularly in 1933, than they had ever dreamed of finding that trouble broke out. The Finns went on a strike in 1935 and the whole group was arrested and disappeared. They have never been seen again in Magnitogorsk.

The Poles. The Poles, mostly Jews, were wise enough not to resort to a strike. They worked at the labor which they were given and some of them soon became supply agents, nurses, German teachers, doctors, designers, and so forth. In 1935 and the early part of 1936 it looked as if they would become the most prosperous people in Magnitogorsk.

The turn came in 1936. Several of this group were arrested. The others were already completely disillusioned by conditions in the Soviet Union after these arrests. Many attempted to escape. A number of them endeavored to procure the assistance of the Polish Consul in Moscow by writing and having friends see him. When the authorities heard of this they were arrested. I believe that two Poles did succeed in escaping with the aid of the Polish Consul. By the end of 1937 almost the entire group had been liquidated. The total number of arrests of Polish refugees during 1936 and 1937 was around 1,200. Apparently no difference was made between those who had acquired Soviet citizenship and those who were still expatriates and living under the direct surveillance of the GPU. All were arrested.

In my opinion this group was composed for the most part of unreliable and slippery persons. Certainly from the viewpoint of the authorities their removal was beneficiary. As I say, they were an unstable lot and could not be depended upon to stick at a job until it was finished.

The Germans and Bulgarians. The German and Bulgarian refugees also lived under the surveillance of the GPU. They were tremendously dissatisfied with the Soviet Union and most of them tried to run away. All the Bulgarians, with the exception of a barber who is still there, have been convicted of espionage or of trying to escape.

Several of the Germans, one of whom worked in a garage, stole a car and started out in 1936 for Germany. They were caught sixty miles from Magnitogorsk and given five years each. Some of these Germans were openly pro-Hitler. They would gather in their rooms and listen to the speeches of the German leaders over the radio.

The colony at the present time. At the present time the forced labor groups include about 25,000 so-called "ex-kulaks" who still have no right to leave the city but who are not under military guard; about fifteen or twenty thousand ITK men who are there under guard. The total population of Magnitogorsk is approximately 145,000. Consequently, over 30 percent of the population work under various conditions of forced labor.

WRECKING ACTIVITIES

February 8, 1938

Wrecking as defined by the Soviet authorities and as understood by myself.

In reply to your question whether I have good reason to believe that actual wrecking activities have been resorted to in the Soviet Union by certain discontented elements such as the ex-kulaks, counter-revolutionists, anti-Stalinists in general, and so forth, I think it best to begin by stating first, that I have knowledge of certain cases of wrecking on the part of individuals, some of which I consider, judging by American standards, to be real, some of a doubtful nature, and others purely imaginary; and secondly, by emphasizing the fact that in discussing wrecking in the Soviet Union it should be clearly borne in mind that, leaving aside the question of the activities of the secret police in practice, the Soviet Criminal Code defines wrecking in so general a manner as to make it possible to include therein activities which an American would consider naturally as bad workmanship, slovenliness, unintentional negligence, and so forth. The Soviet authorities apparently make no distinction between actions of an intentional and unintentional nature, or between those which are remunerated and those for which no recompense is received. The fact is that all actions which the Soviet authorities consider detrimental to the national economy constitute wrecking. In giving you the following account of so-called wrecking I shall endeavor, therefore, to separate those cases which I consider to be actual wrecking or sabotage, that is, those which, according to the general acceptance of the word in most countries, may be regarded clearly as intentional or malicious destruction of property, and those which are of a doubtful nature or purely fictitious.

I *Real Wrecking*

The case of a foreman of a blast-furnace blowing station. I knew the foreman of a blast-furnace blowing station in Magnitogorsk who openly boasted to me several times that he intended "to wreck the works" some day. His parents, both of whom were of bourgeois families, had been killed during the Revolution as enemies of the State. He had saved himself as a young man by losing his identity in the masses and by gaining skill as a metallurgical worker. According to Soviet standards he had even become well to do by engaging on the side in petty speculation of various sorts. He felt, however, that his life had been ruined by the Revolution and he naturally blamed the Soviet authorities for his fate. He drank rather heavily and he usually made threats against the Soviet authorities when under the influence of liquor.

One day a wrench was found in the smashed blades of one of the Teison blowers, which are a kind of wind turbine of a very intricate and delicate make and which are essential to blast furnaces. This machinery must have cost the Soviet Government twenty or thirty thousand gold rubles. It was completely ruined. A few days afterwards the foreman was arrested. He confessed and according to what I heard from some of the workers in his shop, received a sentence of imprisonment for eight years.

Ground glass in turbines. Another case with which I am personally familiar involved certain ex-kulaks who were working as forced laborers at Magnitogorsk. As you know, these ex-kulaks are used mostly on construction work. The turbines of the second half of the Magnitogorsk power plant are still under construction. These turbines are large, some having a fifty thousand kilowatt capacity; and others twenty-four thousand kilowatt. The concrete and foundation work, laying of floors, and so forth, was being done by ex-kulaks. As on most Soviet construction jobs, equipment was being installed prior to the completion of the foundations and buildings. Because of this the ex-kulaks were on the job when certain turbines had been installed. One morning the mechanics found the main bearing of one of the turbines stuffed with ground glass. Investigations were immediately made and a pail of glass was found near a shack where the ex-kulaks reported for work in the morning. The electric welders had been using it in solution for electrode coating. It was apparent that one of the ex-kulaks had taken a pocketful and put it in the bearing. Some peasant had struck back at the Soviet power in revenge for the collectivization, that is, confiscation of his property. As I have already told you, most of these peasants are terribly embittered and some of them become so wrought up by hatred of the Soviet authorities that they resort to deliberate wrecking. I have already told you about the peasant whom I saw throw a crowbar maliciously into a generator at Magnitogorsk.* After such incidents the ex-kulaks were taken off construction work or watched extremely closely by GPU guards when equipment was being installed.

*Reference is made to Embassy's dispatch of January 28, 1938.

The embezzling director. The director of the construction enterprise in charge of building new houses for the workers of the plant was dissatisfied with his salary of one thousand rubles a month and his two-room apartment. So he built a home for himself. He moved in after a year. It was a five-room house and he was able to furnish it with silk curtains, a grand piano, rugs, and so forth. Then he began riding around the city in an automobile at a time—it was the beginning of 1937—when there were few private cars in the city. In the meantime the annual construction plan of his enterprise had been fulfilled by about sixty percent. He was questioned at meetings and in the papers as to why his work was being carried out so badly. He answered that there was no building material, insufficient labor forces, and so forth. An investigation followed. It was found that he had been embezzling state funds, selling building materials to neighboring state farms at speculative prices. It was also discovered that he had a group of followers in his organization who were paid a rake-off to keep the "racket" going. There was an open trial of these men which lasted several days. It became the one topic of conversation in Magnitogorsk. The charges made by the prosecutor were not stealing or bribing, but wrecking. It was alleged that the director had sabotaged the construction of workers' living quarters. He was convicted after a full confession and shot.

What is wrecking? The above cases should probably in all fairness be called wrecking. Certainly the first two cases, in my opinion, can be thus classified. Among the hundreds of men and women, however, whom I have known and who have been arrested, perhaps ten percent might come under this category. You will note that these cases concern individuals who for personal reasons hated the Soviet dictatorship, but who were not acting as members of any counter-revolutionary organization. By far the largest number of cases which have come to my attention might be termed doubtful, since it is difficult to come to any definite conclusion as to guilt because the GPU never publishes the results of its investigations.

II *Doubtful Cases of Wrecking*

Swastikas on the Kremlin. At the end of 1936, the local newspaper, the *Magnitogorsk Worker*, published a picture in one of its issues of the Kremlin at Moscow. If one looked at it closely with a magnifying glass the glass stars on the towers of the Kremlin had the appearance of swastikas. The issue was confiscated early in the morning but many people had already bought a copy. The editor of the paper was immediately arrested and his staff combed by the GPU. Several Polish immigrants working in the photograph department were arrested.

The situation became complicated. The entire population began to talk about the affair and one by one everyone saw the swastikas in somebody's carefully concealed copy. People then began to ask each other what was back of it. Some maintained that it was the work of the GPU which was merely justifying its existence. Others held that it was just an accident, a chance photographic trick resulting from a blur. A few swore that it was the work of the Gestapo. The Poles were not released and your guess is as good as mine as to whether there was wrecking or counter-revolutionary activity.

The case of Zavenyagin. At the end of 1936 it was apparent that a spontaneous combustion was taking place in the large supply of reserve coal of the Magnitogorsk plant. Zavenyagin, the director, who was also an alternate member of the Central Committee of the Party, decided to use the coal in the reserve stocks. No new coal was ordered for some time since Zavenyagin apparently considered it financially advantageous not to have idle capital on his books in the form of a large coal reserve. He probably planned to renew his stocks as soon as the supply became low. Nature played a trick on him. Just when practically all the coal was used up and a few trainloads of new coal were on the way from Kuznets there was a blizzard. The road was tied up for a week. Since only scanty supplies were obtainable and since it requires about seven thousand tons a day for normal operations at Magnitogorsk, the plant had to shut down for a number of days. The drifts were finally cleared and the plant resumed operations.

Although this incident cost the plant millions of rubles no mention was made of wrecking. Zavenyagin himself was busy at this time purging the plant of wreckers, and his mistake was passed off as an unfortunate break.

Later Zavenyagin was appointed First Assistant Commissar of Heavy Industry and left Magnitogorsk. He was also elected to the Supreme Soviet and spoken of as a coming man. Suddenly he disappeared.

It was rumored at Magnitogorsk plant that the coal incident was one of the principal causes of his departure from the Soviet scene. I knew Zavenyagin and I can inform you of certain other factors which probably had more to do with his downfall.

Zavenyagin is or was the son of a poor Jewish peddler. Precise, clever, and at heart a kind and human sort of person, he rose largely through sheer ability. An outstanding student at the Mining Institute at Moscow, Zavenyagin soon drew the attention of the Soviet authorities by his ability and was given responsible positions in metallurgical plants in the south. He was a devout and pious Communist until power turned his head at Magnitogorsk. When he came to the plant in 1933, in order to put things in order, he was about thirty years of age. By that time he was already an alternate member of the Central Committee of the All-Union Communist Party and a rising star on the Bolshevik horizon.

Power apparently turned his head at Magnitogorsk. He became bureaucratic and somewhat tyrannical. He really liked people and wanted to be liked, but certain persons took advantage of his friendship and position. Finally he made himself inaccessible. The purge for which he was partly responsible deprived the plant of some of his best engineers. The plant showed no marked improvement under his control.

In my opinion, however, his end was approaching when he shocked the few conscientious and pious Communists at Magnitogorsk and aroused the envy of others by building unnecessarily commodious and comfortable houses for himself and a certain number of followers, including the local head of the GPU. His house, the best, had fourteen rooms. When furnished, it cost about 300,000 rubles. Such action would not have been so much noticed and commented on if it had not been in Magnitogorsk where the workers live in crude wooden barracks and the engineers and technicians in rather dilapidated apartments; where there is only open sewage and, worst of all, where the hospital is still in unheated barracks partly without floors.

Soon after Pyatakov was arrested and shot in January 1937, Zavenyagin was appointed Assistant Commissar of Heavy Industry, first under Mezlauk until the latter's disappearance and then under Kaganovich. He seemed to please the Politbureau. His star continued to rise. As I have already stated, he was the son of a poor peddler and was almost entirely educated under the Soviet regime which is an ideal background for any ambitious youth in the Soviet Union. I consider him to be a typical "vydvizhenets" (person promoted from the ranks by the authorities, generally on the basis of a certain amount of merit), examples of whose rise have been particularly numerous during the last eighteen months. He is typical particularly of that type of "vydvizhenets" who in my opinion cannot last long under the Stalinist regime. Zavenyagin was too young and ambitious. He also knew too much and was too intelligent and sane to be a Stalinist fanatic.

He has probably been arrested and exiled. He may make a comeback working under conditions of forced labor with the GPU on one of their big projects. The dictatorship needs such men. Was his fall caused by wrecking? If one considers his history, even from the Soviet point of view, as I have related it, I think that one should classify it as a doubtful case.

Forced production, resulting in disaster. In 1935 there was a big explosion of blast furnace No. 2 at Magnitogorsk. The bricks in the tapping hole had become too worn and iron had entered into the cooling places. It ate through the cast iron cooling plates and several cubic meters of water came in contact with several hundred tons of molten iron in the furnace. The explosion blew the roof off the cast house and injured several people seriously. The cost of repairs came to about a million rubles and the blast furnace was shut down an entire month.

At this time the blast-furnace workers were being driven hard to increase production. Brigades were competing with one another. The foreman, the superintendent, and nearly everyone knew that the tapping hole of No. 2 was in bad condition, but nobody would take the responsibility for shutting down for current repairs. The director himself was being pushed by Moscow to maintain the pace. The result was that nothing was done about the tapping hold until after the explosion. Then the director of the blast furnace department was arrested and, according to plant rumor, given ten years. These rumors are hard to check since the only people who generally find out about the fate of those arrested are parents or relatives and even they often wait years before they ascertain the fate of their kin.

The commission of technical experts which investigated the explosion came to the conclusion that it was due to "barbarous exploitation, indifference to plant equipment and wrecking activities."

Errors in the building of gas tanks. At Magnitogorsk engineers tell the story of the two gas tanks which were bought in Germany and installed by Germans at a total cost of about two and a half million gold rubles. When the money had been paid, the equipment delivered and checked, and the erection about eighty percent complete, some curious individual asked whether the tanks would stand the extremely cold temperature of Magnitogorsk. When the German engineers were asked about this, they replied that the tanks were made to work at not less than fifteen degrees below zero (Fahrenheit). During the winter in Magnitogorsk it often falls to as low as thirty or forty degrees below zero.

It appears that the tanks were impractical because, if used, the high humidity of the gas would have collected and frozen against the walls, and the thick layer of gas thus formed would have broken the tank with its weight. The tanks stood unfinished for a year while the GPU investigated.

The investigation. The investigations of the GPU were never published. The story goes, however, among engineers at Magnitogorsk that even the GPU with all its talents for rooting out sabotage could find no evidence of wrongdoing. The Germans had received the order, performed all the work, and been paid. The various Soviet organizations had done their part. There had been nobody at the time that the order was given whose job it was to check up on whether the tanks would properly function under Magnitogorsk weather conditions. The only person or organization against which the GPU could bring an indictment was apparently Soviet administration in general. The case has apparently been dropped, although it is possible that some scapegoat may be found.

The case of Comrade Shevchenko. Shevchenko, the former director of the coke plant at Magnitogorsk, had the misfortune of once having served under the White General Deniken in the Ukraine. When the general was defeated by the Reds, Shevchenko, who was the son of a bartender, managed to shed his past and become a trade-union official. He was energetic and decisive, as well as a roughneck, which fast made him so much more useful as a trade-union official. He joined the Party and rose finally to be manager of construction of coke batteries in Magnitogorsk in 1932.

The wooden structure built over the coke oven for the purpose of equalizing the temperature during brick-laying caught fire and burned. The firemen, instead of letting it burn, turned their hose on the hot brick and thereby ruined one million two hundred thousand gold rubles of imported German firebrick. Shevchenko was on the spot at the time and he and another man were jailed. Then the director of construction, Maryasin, stepped in and presumably by pulling strings in Moscow, succeeded in getting both of them out of trouble.

The incident was more or less forgotten. The case, of course, remained in the files of the local GPU. Shevchenko was promoted to be manager of production in the coke and chemical plant. He was more ardent than ever at Party meetings and he even publicly stated that he received the Order of Lenin because of his good standing in the Party. He continued to be energetic and worked harder than most managers.

Then his friend Maryasin was arrested as a leading Trotskiist in the pay of the Japanese secret service. How much truth there was in the charge against Maryasin I am not sure, but I do know that henceforth Shevchenko looked like a man haunted by fear. To make matters worse, a workman from the Ukraine came to the plant and began to tell stories about Shevchenko's past under General Deniken. Then "connections" were found between Maryasin and Shevchenko. The latter was taken off the job. A month later he was deprived of his Order of Lenin and arrested.

There is, of course, a faint possibility that Maryasin did have some kind of a counter-revolutionary or espionage organization in Magnitogorsk and he obtained assistance by blackmailing persons who were trying to hide their past. It is possible that he learned about Shevchenko's service with General Deniken as well as his petty grafting. The whole story was extremely hazy and the nature of the activities of the organization, if any existed, is not known. Shevchenko got ten years. Was he a wrecker? I give this case as a typical doubtful case which may have some basis of truth.

The shutdown of the electric station. On the 7th of November last year a scandal took place at Magnitogorsk. On the twentieth anniversary of the Revolution the electric station was shut down for many hours. The plant had to take power from Chelyabinsk and Zlatoust, which do not have enough for themselves. It was bad business and the GPU got busy. The shift engineer was arrested and an investigation began.

What had happened was this. As is well known to scientists, water under certain conditions freezes so that it forms a special kind of ice which is called by the Russians "bottom ice" since it does not float. This sometimes hinders pumps from working. Last summer the outlet of warm dirty water from the chemical plant was led off to a distant part of the lake so that it would not warm up the incoming water, part of which was used for purposes of cooling. This change was made with everyone's knowledge and had the desired results. The incoming water was colder and everyone was happier. On November 6, 1937, there was a heavy frost and the intake for water for the power station became obstructed with this heavy ice. Since a power station requires a great deal of water, the shift engineer was forced to shut off the engines. As far as I know, the GPU has never released this engineer.

The Polish spy. There was a young Polish Communist refugee in Magnitogorsk who became a student at the Institute. He was an easy-going happy-go-lucky type who preferred girls to books. In the summer of 1936 he was expelled from the Institute as well as the Young Communist League. Later he was arrested. The charges were that he had worked as a Polish Secret Service agent by seducing many of the girl students, thereby preventing them from studying.

I knew him well and although the charge of being something of a Don Juan has an element of truth in it, the accusation that his amorous activities were designed for the purpose of sabotaging the studies of his sweethearts is too ridiculous to be believed. Most of the students did not take this charge seriously but none of them dared to say so at the meetings.

III *The "New People"*

In connection with the rise and fall of such men as Zavenyagin, it is my opinion that a study would be worthwhile of the types of new men who are being promoted by the Kremlin. Some of these men will turn out to be Zavenyagins, others may rise and survive. It may interest you to know something about certain of these "vydvizhenets."

Pavel Ivanovich Korobov. Korobov is in his early thirties. He belongs to a remarkable family, a dynasty of metal-workers. His father has been a blast-furnace worker for forty-five years. Several brothers are also metal-workers. The entire family has been decorated with the Order of Lenin and was recently received by Stalin in the Kremlin.

Korobov is a graduate of Moscow University. Upon graduation he was sent to work in metallurgical plants in the south. After three years he became director of a blast furnace department. In 1936 he came to Magnitogorsk in that capacity. When the big purge began that year the chief engineer and director disappeared. Korobov became first chief engineer and then the director of the entire plant. At thirty he was in charge of an enterprise which turns out about ten percent of the rolled metal and approximately twelve percent of the pig iron of the Soviet Union. During the purge which has been carried on since he has taken charge and over which he has had little influence, Korobov has had to be a careful worker. He has apparently not been very sure of himself. However, by the time I left the plant he had succeeded in raising production in certain shops, including the openhearth departments, at a time when the output of most other plants was declining and when celebrated metallurgists such as Gvakharia at Makeyevka were being arrested.

Korobov studies and works hard. His reading includes foreign technical journals. He is liked and respected by those under him. The older engineers, however, laugh at his technical abilities and training. Secretly he wants to be a writer and is very fond of literature. As a man he is sensitive and sincere. As a communist he is pious and devout.

The rise of Korobov has placed him in a position where he is beginning to see things that never entered his head before. I have talked with him several times and I sense that his study of foreign journals, as well as his widened experience, is causing him to wonder if the Soviet system will ever catch up with advanced foreign countries like the United States. He is also beginning to have a close view of the shady as well as the heroic side of Soviet life; sees the careerism, toasts, decorations, arrests, pull, petty graft, intrigue, and so forth.

Director Korobov has so far gotten along fairly well but mostly because of his reputation. Experience and responsibility are teaching him quickly, and if he is lucky and hangs on another ten years he may develop into a good administrator. He is approaching the critical state, however, and his questioning of certain aspects of Soviet life may lead him to such a critical attitude that he may eventually fall a victim to the Stalinist purging process.

Sergei Vassilyevich Saltikov. The history of Saltikov is also typical of a new class of men who are rising as a result of the purge. This man is half Tartar, the son of a nomad. In 1930 he was taken by the scruff of the neck and sent to the Mining Institute in Moscow. Until then his education had not equaled that of a fourth grade pupil in the United States. At that time the Institute was open to such men although I understand that the scholastic standards have now been raised to a certain extent. By 1934 Saltikov had received his diploma but little knowledge of engineering. However, he had joined the Party and had learned how to talk well at meetings.

At Magnitogorsk he became the managing foreman of the benzol shop of the chemical department. He received a room about nineteen cubic meters and married a pretty Russian girl. Life seemed good to Saltikov; he attended all Party meetings, paid his dues regularly, and said everything a good Stalinist should say.

Then came the big purge which swept away almost the entire technical staff of the chemical plant. Saltikov found himself head of the whole department. By that time he had two years experience, but still little knowledge of chemistry. However, he tried hard to make up for his lack of training and the plant continued to work along more or less normally. Having risen from nomad to be head of a department, enjoying good living conditions judged from his standards, and possessing authority, Saltikov now represents the contented type of "new man." He does not know or care about what goes on in the world outside, never reads any classical literature and is satisfied that the Soviet system is the best in the world since it has given him a chance to rise.

If no explosions or accidents occur and his work progresses more or less normally, Saltikov will probably not be arrested or get in trouble. It is extremely doubtful that he will ever think impious thoughts, at least not for many years to come. He has not yet and may never reach what I call the dangerous period for good Stalinists.

Atyasov. Atyasov is twenty-six years of age and secretary of the factory committee (*zavkom*) of the coke plant at Magnitogorsk. He was pushed into this job from the cabin of a loading crane where he had become a Stakhanovite workman. The purge had wiped out the old labor union officials and someone had to replace them. As you probably know the factory committee is a labor union organization under the direct control of the management.

Atyasov's idea of labor union work was hazy but he probably knew enough to realize vaguely that the factory committee exists for the purpose of aiding the administration to cut costs, improve quality, maintain labor discipline and so forth. He probably also knew or was tipped off by someone that there are certain laws and regulations relating to working conditions which should be abided by, but when violated too flagrantly might result in public criticism, a lot of talk with no after effects and eventual silence on the subject.

The father of Atyasov was a poor peasant with the result that the son received no formal education. His handwriting is childish and he adds with great difficulty. I have seen his office and it is such a mess that Saltikov can never find anything. But he is delighted with his job and he goes to the Secretary of the Shop Party Committee for help. He has not reached the questioning stage and perhaps never will. No questions, qualms, or heretical thoughts plague him; he is as faithful as a dog. Unless he falls in with bad company or has the misfortune to be made a scapegoat for some accident, he will undoubtedly rise fairly high in the Stalinish hierarchy.

Conclusion. Young men and women without education and training are being given more responsibility than ever in the Soviet Union. The lack of training is not so bad for many of them because they learn by experience and things muddle along somehow. But many of these young people have ambitions, hopes, illusions, and even ideals which may easily be shattered. The last year has been a terrifying experience for them because they have seen not only many of the old and honored Bolsheviks disappear but many of the rising stars like Zavenyagin. Some of the new men will live more or less normal lives and never be troubled but others will enter the questioning stage that I have talked about. They will begin to question, pick holes in the Kremlin's fabric of propaganda because of the enormous gap between the facts and the propaganda. The arrests of leaders, the activities of the GPU, the paradoxes and inconsistencies, these things are sure to react badly on many of them.

The future of the Soviet Union does not look bright to me. Unless the Party is restored to at least some of its former position as a leading force in the country and permitted to propagate certain basic socialist principles, there will be no cement to prevent demoralization and breakdown, no ideology to act as a religion or faith for youth. I have just read in the *Pravda* of January 27, 1938, that 100,000 new men have been promoted to positions of responsibility. How many will lose their heads, because of authority and power, how many will become critical, talk and be arrested? How many Saltikovs and Korobovs will join the broken men such as Zavenyagin in Siberia? Many will without doubt. This process has gone on in the past but will probably proceed at a much faster pace for the next few years at least. Life is cruel in the Soviet Union and the regime knows no pity.

IMPRESSIONS

March 10, 1938

I have just spent two weeks traveling in the Urals, where I visited Sverdlovsk, Magnitogorsk, and Chelyabinsk. I shall sum up for you my impressions in general, which are based largely on a comparison with my experience in the Ural region, particularly in Magnitogorsk, from 1932 to the end of 1937.

First of all, I may say on the one hand that there are more foodstuffs, better food, lower prices, and more passable service in general in the three cities previously mentioned than in Moscow. Secondly, all these things are somewhat better than a year ago.

On the other hand, I gained the clear impression that political arrests are more widespread, and that local officials are more frightened and "jittery" than they were a year ago, and more so at the present time.

Material conditions. Butter was for sale in Sverdlovsk, Chelyabinsk, and Magnitogorsk. It was, however, being rationed. One could not purchase in quantities ordinarily desired. Sometimes it was the 15.5- or 13.5-ruble high-grade butter. Most of it, however, was the inferior grade which sold for from 5 to 8 or 9 rubles per kilo.

There was a fairly large assortment of cereals, flour and other products. Milk was obtainable daily in the shops and from private traders on the street. The store price was 1.50 per liter; private traders were asking from 1.80 to 2.00 rubles.

Manufactured articles were available in much larger quantities than a year ago and usually the assortment was larger than in Moscow. The choice of shoes for men, women, and children was particularly large. Prices thereof varied from twenty rubles for small children's shoes, men's and women's canvas shoes, and rubber-soled shoes, to 200 rubles for the best women's evening slippers. Comparatively good leather shoes for men were purchasable at about 150 rubles. For 60 rubles, a worker may purchase inferior leather shoes with leather soles.

Part wool overcoats for men and women were being sold for about 400 rubles, or well over a month's average industrial salary. In respect of textile goods, I found that Magnitogorsk was less well supplied than either Sverdlovsk or Chelyabinsk. In all three places, however, suits are difficult to find and piece goods are practically unavailable.

In this connection I should point out that at Chelyabinsk I saw about fifty people waiting for woolen material and another line of people of a similar length in the same store waiting for men's undershirts. I also saw a long line of women in Sverdlovsk waiting for stockings.

With regard to such goods as electric articles, small tools, and so forth, I am sure that the Ural cities are better stocked than Moscow. Soviet-made typewriters are on sale for 9,500 rubles, electric vacuum cleaners for 400 rubles, as well as many sorts of electric equipment within the reach of the better-paid workers and technicians. There was likewise a good selection of pottery, chinaware, and kitchen utensils at fairly reasonable prices.

Rooms are much easier to find than in Moscow and rent is somewhat lower. Wages are about the same as in Moscow.

I drew the conclusion from my trip that the population is enjoying a slowly improving standard of living and that many material comforts are coming within the reach of the average better-paid worker. This is, in my opinion, what the average Soviet citizen is interested in more than anything else.

Nowhere on the whole trip did I see signs of hunger or of a food shortage. On all trains and at all railway stations, there were buffets well stocked with rolls, bread, sausage, cheese, and sometimes butter. Certain prices were lower than in Moscow. For instance, oranges sold for 1.25 rubles and cheese at 12 rubles a kilo.

Thus those who are at liberty appear to be working and enjoying the good things of life more than they were able to during the last few years. But many are not at liberty and that leads to the negative side of my impressions.

The terrorism. The purge is more widespread and deep rooted than in the capital. I saw no signs indicating that its momentum may be slackening.

Local officials are frightened half out of their wits. For instance, in Chelyabinsk I went to the City Committee of the Party, to the editor of a local paper, to police headquarters, and talked to scores of people. No one would tell me even what the population of the city is. I had credentials from the People's Commissariat for Foreign Affairs. They were completely disregarded. The bureaucracy is afraid to say *anything* to a *foreigner.*

It was impossible to get near any of the large mills and plants. I was soon informed that at that time there were no excursions.

I found out that the main reason why the officials are so frightened is because they are for the most part new men who have replaced those who have been arrested or shot. In Magnitogorsk, where I formerly worked, and still have friends, I ascertained that the entire Party organization has been cleaned out three times during the past three years. Each time something happened to one of the heads of the Party committee, he dragged with him practically the entire apparatus. The first of these Party leaders to fall in Magnitogorsk was Lominadze, an old Bolshevik oppositionist, who shot himself a few days after the murder of Kirov. The second was Khitarov, an old Bolshevik, who was arrested in Chelyabinsk. The third was Bermen, who was arrested about three months ago. One of his brothers is still, I believe, Chief of the Administration of Penal Camps of the People's Commissariat for Internal Affairs (GPU) in White Russia. Another is still People's Commissar of Communications of the Soviet Union. It is no wonder that most local officials have a good case of the "jitters." Those with whom we talked would not say hardly a word until they called up someone and carried on a short whispered conversation.

One phase of the purge which is not, I believe, quite so much in evidence in Moscow is the arrest of the wives and families of the victims. In all three cities, according to casual conversations which I had with friends, there are apparently no cases of arrests where the wives and families have not also been arrested and convicted of the crimes enumerated in Article 59 of the Criminal Code of the RSFSR. The wives are usually indicted for not having informed the authorities of the criminal activities of their husbands. They receive sentences varying from six months to ten years. The children, with the exception of babies feeding from their mother's breasts, are taken away. It is understood that the mothers will never see them again since the State is charged with their upbringing on the theory that traitors, spies, and such people are not fit to raise children in the country of Socialism.

When one gets away from the circle of the middle and petty official and talks with the more or less average Soviet citizen in the trains, at home, and so forth, the terror appears to be somewhat less than might be expected. Several people with whom I spoke on the train and some of my friends expressed themselves quite freely. The general tenor of their conversation did not exactly follow the line of an editorial in the *Pravda*.

The rank and file of the workers, with the exception, of course, of a great many foreign-born workers, do not appear to have been affected by the purge. Only a small percentage of workers from the bench, so far as I have been able to ascertain, have been arrested. In most cases the victims are officials of all grades, engineers, business managers, and so forth.

The workers are often quite gleeful about the arrest of some "big bird," as they are termed by the laborers, whom they have not liked for one reason or another. The workers are also very free in their criticism at meetings as well as out of official gatherings. I have heard them use the strongest language in describing the bureaucracy and inefficiency of individuals and organizations.

The industrial situation. I may briefly describe the industrial situation in the Urals in the following manner. The coal shortage is still being seriously felt. One way of coping with the situation is to economize power since all the Ural power-plants utilize coal. In Magnitogorsk the electric current for the residences is turned off from 9 in the morning until 5 in the evening, and from 2 to 5 in the morning. In early February in that part of the Urals it is dark from 5 in the afternoon until about 8 in the morning. This system prevents people from using irons, electric stoves, and so forth in the day time. It also prevents the old Russian practice of burning lights all night in order to keep the bedbugs from coming out.

Production at the Magnitogorsk metallurgical plant is up. Pig iron is about 4,500 metric tons a day and steel somewhat more. At Chelyabinsk, however, the tractor plant is turning out only about forty units a day. A few years ago this plant was producing 50,000 tractors a year. This drop has been caused primarily by the transfer to Diesel motors and probably in part by the turning over of parts of the plant's equipment to "Stankostroi," a large Chelyabinsk plant which, according to local sources of a trustworthy nature, manufactures tanks for the Red Army.

The large Ural Heavy Machine-Building Factory in Sverdlovsk has become entirely inaccessible. It is a large and well-built plant. I went through it in 1932 and again in 1934. The foundries are equipped with the best American, English, and German machinery, and the plant might be compared favorably with the General Electric Works at Schenectady. According to local sources of information, submarines are being made by it and transmitted in pieces to the north and Far East.

The railroads appeared to me to be in good condition. I saw a great deal of freight movement, much of it going east. I saw prison trains in two places going east. They were guarded by regular soldiers with bayoneted rifles. The windows of the boxcars were so small and so high that it was impossible to see even the heads of the prisoners.

The trains are running faster than in the past. The run from Moscow to Magnitogorsk, for instance, took four-and-a-half days in 1932, three-and-a-half in 1934, and now only two-and-a-half days. The roadbeds are better, being equipped in many cases with hard ballast instead of the sand which was formerly used on all Central-Russian roads.

The passenger trains were as usual crowded and every station had a line of people waiting to get tickets. There were many peasants with their families carrying all their worldly belongings in rough burlap bags. They were on their way east, where the Government will assist them in getting settled on the land.

As far as I could ascertain there were nowhere any indications of widespread popular unrest. I believe that the popular feeling in the Urals is that the present regime has given them, and is giving them, more goods and comforts than they have had before. It is possible that as long as the Soviet regime is able to keep the people at work and give them enough purchasing power to buy the things essential to their low standards it will endure. It is undoubtedly true that a small minority believes that the revolution has been betrayed and that more democracy and freedom should be permitted but the interests of the average workers are for the most part limited to primitive creature comforts and desires. To date people in the Urals are working, eating, and buying essentials and will not in my opinion make trouble. I believe that the economic battle is gradually being won.